PENGUIN  CLASSICS

A Complete Annotated Listing

CONTENTS

PENGUIN CLASSICS   3
(ARRANGED ALPHABETICALLY BY AUTHOR)

SUBJECT CATEGORIES   221

READERS GUIDES   246

NOBEL PRIZE WINNERS   248

NEW TITLES FOR 2003   249

TITLE INDEX   256

Penguin Classics Readers Guides are available online at www.penguinclassics.com/guides

Great Books Foundation Discussion Guides for Penguin Classics titles are available online at www.penguinclassics.com/guides and www.greatbooks.org

Tables of contents for Penguin Classics titles are available online at www.penguinclassics.com/toc

* Indicates a new edition of a Penguin Classic that has undergone substantial revisions and/or has additional and enhanced apparatus

PUBLISHER'S NOTE

For more than half a century Penguin has been the leading publisher of classics in the English-speaking world. Since the publication of the first Penguin Classic in 1946—E. V. Rieu's translation of *The Odyssey*—we have honored our founder Allen Lane's original mission: to make the great books of all time available at a reasonable cost. To this end, Penguin is dedicated to making sure that these books speak to contemporary readers by embracing excellence in scholarship, translation, and book design.

Over the next two years, our entire Classics backlist will be repackaged with a striking new look—a process that has already begun. In addition, the Twentieth-Century and Penguin Nature Classics, as well as the Portable Library series are now part of Penguin Classics. All of these changes are reflected in this catalog, which provides complete, annotated descriptions of all books currently in our Classics series, as well as those in the Pelican Shakespeare series.

From Renaissance philosophy to the poetry of revolutionary Russia, from the spiritual writings of India to the travel narratives of the early American colonists, from *The Complete Pelican Shakespeare* to *The Portable Sixties Reader*, there are classics here to educate, provoke, entertain, and enlighten readers of all interests and inclinations. We hope this catalog will inspire you to pick up that book you've always been meaning to read, or the one you may not have heard of before.

To receive more information about Penguin Classics or to sign up for a newsletter, please visit our Classics Web site at www.penguinclassics.com.

EDWIN A. ABBOTT
1838 – 1926, British

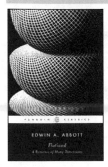

Flatland
A Romance of Many Dimensions
Introduction by Alan Lightman

Abbott's delightful mathematical fantasy about life in a two-dimensional world brilliantly satirizes Victorian British society.
128 pp.   **0-14-043531-X**   **$8.95**

PETER ABÉLARD
1079 – c. 1144, French

HÉLOÏSE
c. 1098 – 1164, French

The Letters of Abélard and Héloïse
Translated with an Introduction by Betty Radice

This collection of writings offers insight into the minds of two prominent Christian medieval figures—the French scholastic philosopher Peter Abélard and his beloved Héloïse, who became a learned abbess—and their celebrated but tragic love affair.
312 pp.   **0-14-044297-9**   **$13.00**
See The Portable Medieval Reader.

HENRY ADAMS
1838 – 1918, American

The Education of Henry Adams
Edited with an Introduction and Notes by Jean Gooder

In this memoir Adams examines his own life as it reflects the progress of the United States from the Civil War period to the nation's ascendancy as a world power. A remarkable synthesis of history, art, politics, and philosophy, *The Education of Henry Adams* remains a provocative and stimulating interpretation of the birth of the twentieth century.
624 pp.   **0-14-044557-9**   **$12.95**

Esther
Edited with an Introduction and Notes by Lisa MacFarlane

Originally published in 1884 under a female pseudonym and set in Old New York, *Esther* is a memorable love story and an insightful portrait of a confident age encountering the tensions between science, art, and religion.
256 pp.   **0-14-044754-7**   **$9.95**

Mont-Saint-Michel and Chartres
Introduction by Raymond Carney

A philosophical and historical meditation on the human condition, Adams's journey into the medieval consciousness synthesizes literature, art, politics, science, and psychology.
448 pp.   **0-14-039054-5**   **$16.00**

JANE ADDAMS
1860 – 1935, American

Twenty Years at Hull-House
Introduction by Ruth Sidel

Addams's account of the famed settlement house she founded and of the principles of social justice that inspired her, tells in lucid, unsentimental prose the real stories of the people fictionalized in the novels of Theodore Dreiser and Upton Sinclair.

320 pp. **0-14-118099-4** **$12.95**

ADOMNÁN OF IONA
c. 628 – 704, Irish

Life of St. Columba
Translated with an Introduction by Richard Sharpe

This biography, written one hundred years after the death of St. Columba (597) and drawing on both oral and written materials, presents a richly detailed portrait of religious life in the sixth century.

432 pp. **0-14-044462-9** **$15.00**

AESCHYLUS
525 – 456 B.C., Greek

The Oresteia
Agamemnon/The Libation Bearers/ The Eumenides
Translated by Robert Fagles with an Introduction, Notes, and Glossary by Robert Fagles and W. B. Stanford

The Oresteia—the only trilogy in Greek drama that survives from antiquity— takes on new depth and power in Fagles's acclaimed modern translation.

336 pp. **0-14-044333-9** **$9.95**

The Oresteian Trilogy
Translated with an Introduction by Philip Vellacott

Justice, vengeance, and the forces of fate provide the themes for *Agamemnon, The Choephori,* and *The Eumenides.* Vellacott's verse translation is presented with a short introduction to Greek mythology and the historical context of the trilogy.

208 pp. **0-14-044067-4** **$9.95**

Prometheus Bound and Other Plays
Translated with an Introduction by Philip Vellacott

Prometheus Bound, The Suppliants, Seven Against Thebes, and *The Persians,* presented here in verse translation, demonstrate that reason, not violence, is the proper principle of civilized life.

160 pp. **0-14-044112-3** **$9.95**
See The Portable Greek Reader.

AESOP
c. 6th cent. B.C., Greek

The Complete Fables
Translated by Olivia and Robert Temple with an Introduction by Robert Temple

This definitive and fully annotated modern edition is the first translation ever to make available the complete corpus of 358 fables attributed to Aesop. Revealing a rawer, racier, very adult aesthetic, this version includes 100 fables not previously published in English.

288 pp. **0-14-044649-4** **$10.00**
See The Portable Greek Reader.

ANNA AKHMATOVA
1889 – 1966, Russian

Selected Poems
Translated with an Introduction and Notes by D. M. Thomas

Akhmatova's poems bear witness to the terrors of Stalinism, the loss of all whom she loved, and the blessings of memory. These outstanding translations by novelist D. M. Thomas do honor to the works of one of the greatest poets in modern history.

160 pp.   0-14-018617-4 $12.95

See The Portable Twentieth-Century Russian Reader.

HENRI ALAIN-FOURNIER
1886 – 1914, French

Le Grand Meaulnes
Translated by Frank Davison

The only novel by Alain-Fournier follows a young man killed in action in World War I, and is a masterly exploration of the transition from boyhood to manhood.

208 pp.   0-14-018282-9 $14.00

LEON BATTISTA ALBERTI
1404 – 1472, Italian

On Painting
Translated by Cecil Grayson with an Introduction and Notes by Martin Kemp

The first book devoted to the intellectual rationale for painting, Alberti's discussion of the process of vision, painting techniques, and the moral and artistic prerequisites of the artist remains a classic of art theory.

112 pp.   0-14-043331-7 $13.00

See The Portable Renaissance Reader.

LOUISA MAY ALCOTT
1832 – 1888, American

The Portable Louisa May Alcott
Edited by Elizabeth Lennox Keyser

Alcott's vast body of work is celebrated in this wide-ranging collection that includes samples from her novels, novellas, children's stories, sensationalist fiction, gothic tales, memoirs, letters, and journals.

704 pp.   0-14-027574-6 $16.95

AESOP

Aesop was probably a prisoner of war, sold into slavery in the early sixth century B.C. on the Greek island of Samos, who represented his masters in court and relied on animal stories to put across his key points. However, the Aesop known to the ancient Greeks and Romans was quite different from the one generally known to modern English speakers. As was the custom with translations of ancient texts from the eighteenth century through the early twentieth century, editions of Aesop's fables were very selective and expunged of material deemed offensive to Victorian decorum. Far from being the author of edifying children's stories, the real Aesop was a man who cloaked a rather grim yet pragmatic vision of human life in the tales of nature.

The Inheritance

Edited with an Introduction by
Joel Myerson and Daniel Shealy

Alcott's first novel, written in 1849, when she was seventeen, is the captivating tale of a young orphan girl whose inheritance is a secret locked in a long-lost letter. Inspired by the sentimental novels and Gothic romances of her day, *The Inheritance* illuminates Alcott's early influences and foreshadows her mature style.

208 pp.   0-14-043666-9 $12.00

Penguin Readers Guide Available

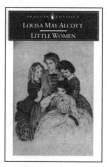

Little Women

Edited with an Introduction by
Elaine Showalter and Notes by
Siobhan Kilfeather and Vinca Showalter

Alcott's beloved story of the March girls — Meg, Jo, Beth, and Amy—is a classic American feminist novel, reflecting the tension between cultural obligation and artistic and personal freedom.

544 pp.   0-14-039069-3 $7.95

Work
A Story of Experience

Edited with an Introduction by
Joy S. Kasson

A story about a nineteenth-century woman's search for a meaningful life through work outside the family sphere, *Work* is at once Alcott's exploration of her personal challenges and a social critique of America.

384 pp.   0-14-039091-X $13.00

ALFRED THE GREAT
849 – 899, Anglo-Saxon

ASSER
d. c. 908, Anglo-Saxon

Alfred the Great

Translated with an Introduction and Notes
by Simon Keynes and Michael Lapidge

This comprehensive collection includes Asser's *Life of Alfred*, extracts from *The Anglo-Saxon Chronicle*, and Alfred's own writings, laws, and will.

368 pp.   0-14-044409-2 $13.95

HORATIO ALGER, JR.
1832 – 1899, American

Ragged Dick and Struggling Upward

Edited with an Introduction by Carl Bode

Alger's characteristic theme of youths achieving the American dream through hard work, resistance to temptation, and goodwill is presented in these two tales that reflect nineteenth-century life.

304 pp.   0-14-039033-2 $9.95

KINGSLEY AMIS
1922 – 1995, British

Lucky Jim

Introduction by David Lodge

Originally published in 1954, this hilarious story of Jim Dixon's adjustment to teaching in the stultifying world of the university was the first modern British novel to plumb the comic possibilities of academic life.

256 pp.   0-14-018630-1 $14.00

AMMIANUS MARCELLINUS
c. 330 – 395, Roman

The Later Roman Empire
(A.D. 354–378)

Selected and Translated by Walter Hamilton
with an Introduction and Notes by
Andrew Wallace Hadrill

Considered to be the last great Roman

historian, Ammianus Marcellinus continues the histories of Tacitus, describing the reigns of the emperors Constantius, Julian, Jovian, Valentinian, and Valens.

512 pp.   0-14-044406-8 $15.95

MULK RAJ ANAND
b. 1905, Indian

Untouchable
Preface by E. M. Forster

Anand, hailed as his country's Charles Dickens, presents a portrait of India's untouchables written with an urgency and fury that has made this his richest and most controversial novel.

160 pp.   0-14-018395-7 $13.00

SHERWOOD ANDERSON
1876 – 1941, American

"Sherwood Anderson was the father of all my works—and those of Hemingway, Fitzgerald, etc. We were influenced by him. He showed us the way."

—WILLIAM FAULKNER

Winesburg, Ohio
Introduction by Malcolm Cowley

Anderson's 1919 volume of interconnected stories about an ordinary small town whose citizens struggle with extraordinary dreams and grotesque disappointments has become an emblematic saga of American loneliness.

256 pp.   0-14-018655-7 $8.95

ANNA COMNENA
1083 – c. 1148, Byzantine

The Alexiad of Anna Comnena
Translated with an Introduction by E. R. A. Sewter

A Byzantine emperor's daughter vividly records the turbulence that marked the rule of her father, Alexius I (1081–1118).

560 pp.   0-14-044215-4 $15.00

See The Portable Medieval Reader.

ANSELM OF AOSTA
c. 1033 – 1109, English (b. Italy)

The Prayers and Meditations of St. Anselm
Translated with an Introduction by Sr. Benedicta Ward and a Foreword by R. W. Southern

Combining personal ardor and scrupulous theology, *Prayers and Meditations* offers an intimate view of this Archbishop of Canterbury, most noted for his acceptance of rational inquiry into the mysteries of faith.

288 pp.   0-14-044278-2 $14.00

MARY ANTIN
1881 – 1949, American (b. Russia)

The Promised Land
Introduction and Notes by Werner Sollors

Interweaving introspection with political commentaries, biography with history, *The Promised Land* (1912) brings to life the transformation of a Russian Jewish immigrant into an American citizen. Antin not only describes her own personal journey but illuminates the lives of thousands.

400 pp.   0-14-018985-8 $10.95

APOLLONIUS OF RHODES
c. 3rd cent. B.C., Greek

The Voyage of the Argo
The Argonautica
Translated with an Introduction by E. V. Rieu

Apollonius used the manner and matter of epics but wrote from a personal viewpoint, as a critical observer, in his *Argonautica*, the fullest surviving account of Jason's voyage in quest of the Golden Fleece.

224 pp.   0-14-044085-2 $12.95

APPIAN
c. 2nd cent. A.D., Greek

The Civil Wars
Translated with an Introduction by John Carter

Covering the period from 133 to 35 B.C., this exploration of the decline of the Roman state details the struggles of Marius against Sulla, Caesar against Pompeius, and Antonius and Octavian against Caesar's assassins, Brutus and Cassius.

480 pp.   0-14-044509-9 $15.00

APULEIUS
c. A.D. 125 – 180, North African

The Golden Ass
Translated with an Introduction and Notes by E. J. Kenney

Lucius, a young man who believes witchcraft can transform him into a bird, instead becomes a donkey. Anticipating the modern novel, Apuleius combines satire and buffoonery with deep moral seriousness, and magic and fantasy with sincere religious feeling.

304 pp.   6 maps   0-14-043590-5 $12.00

See The Portable Roman Reader.

THOMAS AQUINAS
1225 – 1274, Italian

Aquinas: Selected Writings
Edited and Translated with an Introduction by Ralph McInerny

Though he was controversial in his day, Aquinas would significantly influence Catholic tradition and dogma. Arranged chronologically, this volume includes sermons, commentaries, responses to criticism, and important extracts from one of Christianity's supreme masterpieces, the *Summa Theologica*.

880 pp.   0-14-043632-4 $14.95

See The Portable Medieval Reader.

The Portable Hannah Arendt

Edited by Peter Baehr

This collection includes substantial excerpts from Arendt's greatest works, including *The Origins of Totalitarianism*, *The Human Condition*, and *Eichmann in Jerusalem*.

480 pp.   **0-14-026974-6**   **$16.95**

Between Past and Future

Arendt's penetrating analysis of the complex crises of meaning in modern society and political philosophy is presented with her impassioned exercises for guiding readers toward the reinvigoration of the concepts of justice, reason, responsibility, virtue, and glory.

320 pp.   **0-14-018650-6**   **$13.95**

Eichmann in Jerusalem
A Report on the Banality of Evil

Arendt's internationally famous and controversial report on the trial of Nazi leader Adolph Eichmann deals with the problem of the human being within a modern totalitarian system. This posthumously revised edition contains a postscript by Arendt and further factual material revealed after the trial.

320 pp.   **0-14-018765-0**   **$13.95**

Great Books Foundation Readers Guide Available

On Revolution

This pioneering analysis of the principles that underlie all revolutions discusses three classic revolutions—the American, the French, and the Russian—and shows how both the theory and practice of revolution have developed.

352 pp.   **0-14-018421-X**   **$15.00**

HANNAH ARENDT

Born in Hanover, Germany, in 1906, Hannah Arendt moved with her family to Königsberg when she was three years old. Her mother interested her in contemporary politics, in particular the Spartacist faction of the Social Democratic Party and its leaders, Rosa Luxemburg and Karl Liebknecht. Arendt studied philosophy at the University of Hamburg with Martin Heidegger in 1924 and with Karl Jaspers from 1925 until 1929. She married Gunther Stern in 1929 in Paris, returning in 1933 to avoid the Nazis and living there until 1940. After escaping to New York, Arendt served as one of the premier members of the faculty of the New School for Social Research and also as a Visiting Fellow of the Committee on Social Thought at the University of Chicago. She originated the concept of the "banality of evil" in *Eichmann in Jerusalem*, her account of Adolf Eichmann's war-crimes trial, and wrote extensively on political and Jewish issues. She died in 1975.

Orlando Furioso

Translated with an Introduction by Barbara Reynolds

A dazzling kaleidoscope of adventures, ogres, monsters, barbaric splendor, and romance, this epic poem stands as one of the greatest works of the Italian Renaissance.

Part I: 832 pp. 0-14-044311-8 **$16.95**
Part II: 800 pp. 0-14-044310-X **$16.95**

See The Portable Renaissance Reader.

The Frogs and Other Plays

Translated with an Introduction by David Barrett

The Wasps, The Poet and the Women (Thesmophoriazusae), and *The Frogs* use parody and low comedy to convey the spirit of Athens during the long, tragic war against Sparta.

224 pp. 0-14-044152-2 **$11.00**

The Knights/The Peace/The Birds/ The Assembly Women/Wealth

Translated with Introductions by David Barrett and Alan H. Sommerstein

Representing Aristophanes's sharply satirical comedy, this collection is prefaced by an introduction to the history and literary style of the author.

336 pp. 0-14-044332-0 **$10.95**

Lysistrata and Other Plays

Translated with an Introduction by Alan H. Sommerstein

Lysistrata, The Acharnians, and *The Clouds* comedically reflect Aristophanes's longing for the return of peace and honest living in Athens.

256 pp. 0-14-044287-1 **$7.95**

See The Portable Greek Reader.

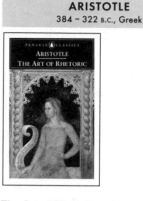

The Art of Rhetoric

Translated with an Introduction and Notes by Hugh Lawson-Tancred

With this book, Aristotle established the methods of informal reasoning, providing the first aesthetic evaluation of prose style and detailed observations of character and emotions.

304 pp. 0-14-044510-2 **$13.95**

The Athenian Constitution

Translated with an Introduction and Notes by P. J. Rhodes

This is the single most important extant source for the study of the institutions of classical Athens. "Clearly and accurately translated....Lucid introduction and notes, and excellent analytical summaries, introduce each chapter." —S. M. Burstein, California State University, Los Angeles

208 pp. 0-14-044431-9 **$11.00**

De Anima (On the Soul)

*Translated with an Introduction and Notes
by Hugh Lawson-Tancred*

Considering the nature of life, Aristotle
surveys and rejects the ideas of Plato
and the Presocratics, developing his
philosophy of the soul and mind, and
introducing the central concepts of
form and matter to explain perception,
thought, and motivation.

256 pp.   0-14-044471-8 $14.00

Ethics

*Translated by J. A. K. Thomson with an
Introduction and Bibliography by
Jonathan Barnes and Revised with
Appendices and Notes by Hugh Tredennick*

In a work that had tremendous impact on
Western moral philosophy, Aristotle treats
ethics as a practical rather than a theoretical
science, and introduces psychology into
the study of human behavior.

384 pp.   0-14-044055-0 $10.95

The Metaphysics

*Translated with an Introduction by
Hugh Lawson-Tancred*

One of the cornerstones of Western
speculative thought, *The Metaphysics* is
Aristotle's first mature statement of his own
understanding of reality. An extraordinary
synthesis of the natural and rational
aspects of the world that probes some of
philosophy's deepest questions, it is now
available in a highly readable translation.

528 pp.   0-14-044619-2 $11.95

Poetics

*Translated with an Introduction and Notes
by Malcolm Heath*

In one of the most perceptive and influential
works of criticism in Western literary history,
Aristotle examines the literature of his time,
describing the origins of poetry as an
imitative art and drawing attention to the
distinctions between comedy and tragedy.

144 pp.   0-14-044636-2 $10.95

The Politics

*Translated with an Introduction by
T. A. Sinclair and Revised and
Re-Presented by Trevor J. Saunders*

The search for the ideal state and the best
possible constitution is the basis for the last
great work of Greek political thought.

512 pp.   0-14-044421-1 $12.95

See Classical Literary Criticism *and*
The Portable Greek Reader.

ARRIAN
2nd cent. A.D., Greek

The Campaigns of Alexander

*Translated by Aubrey de Sélincourt and
Revised with a New Introduction and Notes
by J. R. Hamilton*

Written four hundred years after Alexander's
death, this is the most reliable account of the
conqueror's life, character, and achievements.

432 pp.   0-14-044253-7 $15.00

ASSER

See Alfred the Great.

FARID UD-DIN ATTAR
c. 1142 – c. 1220, Persian

The Conference of the Birds

*Translated with an Introduction by
Afkham Darbandi and Dick Davis*

Consisting of a group of stories bound
together by a pilgrimage, this great twelfth-
century poem is an allegorical rendering
of the *Way of the Sufi*, the secretive and
paradoxical form of Islamic mysticism.

240 pp.   0-14-044434-3 $14.00

JOHN AUBREY
1626 – 1697, British

Brief Lives

Selected and Edited with an Introduction, Glossary, and Notes by John Buchanan-Brown and a Foreword by Michael Hunter

Vividly evoking Elizabethan and Stuart England, Aubrey's deft prose portrays a host of both well-known and forgotten but fascinating statesmen, poets, philosophers, and scientists. *Brief Lives'* mixture of entertainment and erudition revolutionized the art of English biography. This edition also includes "An Apparatus for the Lives of Our English Mathematical Writers" and "The Life of Thomas Hobbes of Malmesbury."

528 pp.   **0-14-043589-1**   **$15.00**

SAINT AUGUSTINE
354 – 430, North African

City of God

Edited by David Knowles and Translated by Henry Bettenson with an Introduction by John O'Meara

Augustine examines the inefficacy of the Roman gods and of human civilization in general. Blending Platonism with Christianity, he created the first Christian theology of history—planning a city based not on the Roman pantheon but on Christian love.

1,152 pp.   **0-14-044426-2**   **$15.95**

Confessions

Translated with an Introduction by R. S. Pine-Coffin

This autobiography is both an explanation of Augustine's own conversion to Christianity and an attempt to convince the reader that it is the one true faith.

352 pp.   **0-14-044114-X**   **$8.95**

JANE AUSTEN
1775 – 1817, British

Emma

Edited with an Introduction and Notes by Fiona Stafford

Considered by most critics to be Austen's most technically brilliant achievement, *Emma* sparkles with ironic insights into self-deception, self-discovery, and the interplay of love and power.

448 pp.   **0-14-143958-0**   **$7.95**

Lady Susan/The Watsons/Sanditon

Edited with an Introduction by Margaret Drabble

These three works—one novel unpublished in her lifetime and two unfinished fragments —limn an intriguing picture of Jane Austen's development as a great artist.

224 pp.   **0-14-043102-0**   **$9.00**

Mansfield Park

Edited with an Introduction and Notes by Kathryn Sutherland

Mansfield Park is Jane Austen's most sustained examination of family life, and while it echoes and extends the themes of *Pride and Prejudice*, it is more serious in both tone and intent.

480 pp.   **0-14-143980-7**   **$6.95**

Northanger Abbey

Edited with an Introduction by Marilyn Butler

Catherine Morland is invited to Northanger

Abbey, where she believes she has discovered all the trappings of the Gothic novels she so loves reading—and must learn to distinguish literature from life.

288 pp.   0-14-143979-3 $6.95

Persuasion

Edited with an Introduction by
Gillian Beer

Anne Elliot, the heroine of Austen's last and most mature novel, overcomes social obstacles, her father's selfishness, and a seven-year misunderstanding in order to win the love of and marry the man she desires.

272 pp.   0-14-143968-8 $5.95

Pride and Prejudice

Edited with an Introduction and Notes by
Vivien Jones

Few have failed to be charmed by the witty and independent spirit of Elizabeth Bennet. Her early determination to dislike Mr. Darcy is a prejudice only matched by the folly of his arrogant pride. Their first impressions give way to true feelings in a comedy profoundly concerned with happiness and how it might be achieved.

384 pp.   0-14-143951-3 $8.00
(Available January 2003)
Penguin Readers Guide Available

Sense and Sensibility

Edited with an Introduction by
Ros Ballaster

In her first novel, Austen is already mistress of gentle irony and keen observation,

sparing no one in this lively study of the constraints placed on gentry-women in the eighteenth century.

368 pp.   0-14-143966-1 $6.95
Penguin Readers Guide Available

MARY AUSTIN
1868 – 1934, American

The Land of Little Rain

With an Introduction by
Terry Tempest Williams

Mary Austin calls it the Country of Lost Borders—the desert and foothill lands between Death Valley and the High Sierras. In this collection of essays, Austin breathes life into the landscape, describing in loving and knowing detail its savage beauty, opening our eyes to a wider world.

128 pp.   0-14-024919-2 $12.00

ISAAC BABEL
1894 – 1941, Russian

Collected Stories

Edited and Translated with an
Introduction and Notes by David McDuff

These stories, including Babel's masterpiece, "Red Cavalry," illuminate the author's life-long struggle both to remain faithful to his Russian Jewish roots and to be free of them, a duality of vision that infuses his work with a powerful energy.

400 pp.   0-14-018462-7 $14.00

The Essays

Edited with an Introduction by
John Pitcher

Including the fifty-eight essays of the
1625 edition, this collection comprises
reflections on the successful conduct of
life and management of men, as well as
reworkings of many of the ideas of Bacon's
philosophical and scientific writings.

288 pp.   0-14-043216-7 $14.00

See The Portable Renaissance Reader *and*
The Portable Enlightenment Reader.

HONORÉ DE BALZAC
1799 – 1850, French

The Black Sheep

Translated with an Introduction by
Donald Adamson

Two brothers—one a dashing, handsome
ex-soldier, the other a sensitive artist—
struggle to recover the family inheritance
in a novel that explores the devastation
that poverty can bring.

344 pp.   0-14-044237-5 $13.95

Cousin Bette

Translated with an Introduction by
Marion Ayton Crawford

Vividly bringing to life the rift between
the old world and the new, *Cousin Bette* is
an incisive study of vengeance, and the
culmination of *The Human Comedy*.

448 pp.   0-14-044160-3 $10.95

Penguin Readers Guide Available

Cousin Pons

Translated with an Introduction by
Herbert J. Hunt

The companion novel to *Cousin Bette*,
Cousin Pons offers a diametrically opposite
view of the nature of family relationships,
focusing on a mild, harmless old man.

336 pp.   0-14-044205-7 $14.00

HONORÉ DE BALZAC

The son of a civil servant, Honoré de Balzac was born in 1799 in Tours, France. After
attending boarding school in Vendôme, he gravitated to Paris where he worked as a
legal clerk and a hack writer, using various pseudonyms, often in collaboration with
other writers. Balzac turned exclusively to fiction at the age of thirty and went on to
write a large number of novels and short stories set amid turbulent nineteenth-century
France. He entitled his collective works *The Human Comedy*. Along with Victor Hugo
and Dumas *père* and *fils*, Balzac was one of the pillars of French romantic literature.
He died in 1850, shortly after his marriage to the Polish countess Evelina Hanska,
his lover of eighteen years.

Eugénie Grandet

Translated with an Introduction by
Marion Ayton Crawford

The love of money and the passionate pursuit
of it, a major theme in *The Human Comedy*,
is brilliantly depicted in the story of Grandet
and his obsession with achieving power.

256 pp.   0-14-044050-X $12.00

A Harlot High and Low

Translated with an Introduction by
Rayner Heppenstall

Finance, fashionable society, and the
intrigues of the underworld and the police
system form the heart of this powerful
novel, which introduces the satanic genius
Vautrin, one of the greatest villains in
world literature.

560 pp.   0-14-044232-4 $15.00

History of the Thirteen

Translated with an Introduction by
Herbert J. Hunt

This trilogy of stories—"Ferragus: Chief of
the Companions of Duty," "The Duchesse
De Langeais," and "The Girl with the Golden
Eyes"—purporting to be the history of a
secret society, laid the foundation for
Balzac's *Scenes of Parisian Life* and is a
stunning evocation of all ranks of society.

392 pp.   0-14-044301-0 $13.95

Lost Illusion

Translated with an Introduction by
Herbert J. Hunt

This novel of a young man who is bored
with provincial life and tries to make
his way in Parisian society is part of
The Human Comedy.

384 pp.   0-14-044251-0 $15.00

Old Goriot

Translated with an Introduction by
Marion Ayton Crawford

The intersecting lives of a group of people
living in a working-class boardinghouse in
nineteenth-century Paris form the background of this indictment of the cruelty of
city society.

304 pp.   0-14-044017-8 $10.95

Selected Short Stories

Selected and Translated with an
Introduction by Sylvia Raphael

This collection includes "El Verdugo,"
"Domestic Peace," "A Study in Feminine
Psychology," "An Incident in the Reign of
Terror," "The Conscript," "The Red Inn,"
"The Purse," "La Grande Bretèche," "A
Tragedy by the Sea," "The Atheist's Mass,"
"Facino Cane," and "Pierre Grassou."

272 pp.   0-14-044325-8 $12.95

The Wild Ass's Skin

Translated with an Introduction by
Herbert J. Hunt

Balzac is concerned with the choice
between ruthless self-gratification and
asceticism, and dissipation and restraint, in
a novel that is powerful in its symbolism
and realistic depiction of decadence.

288 pp.   0-14-044330-4 $13.00

MATSUO BASHŌ
1644 – 1694, Japanese

The Narrow Road to the Deep North and Other Travel Sketches
Translated with an Introduction by Nobuyuki Yuasa

Bashō's haiku are a series of superb pictures in which whole landscapes and seasons are evoked by description of the crucial details.

176 pp.   **0-14-044185-9**   **$11.95**

On Love and Barley
Haiku of Bashō
Translated with an Introduction by Lucien Stryk

These 253 selections reveal Bashō's mastery of the genre.

96 pp.   **0-14-044459-9**   **$9.95**

CHARLES BAUDELAIRE
1821 – 1867, French

Baudelaire in English
Edited by Carol Clark and Robert Sykes

This superb anthology brings together the translations of Baudelaire's poetry and prose poems that best reveal the different facets of his personality: the haughtily defiant artist, the tormented bohemian, the savage yet tender lover, and the celebrant of strange, haunted cityscapes.

336 pp.   **0-14-044644-3**   **$14.95**

Selected Poems
Translated with an Introduction by Carol Clark

In both his life and his poetry, Baudelaire pushed the accepted limits of his time. His dissolute bohemian life was as shocking to his nineteenth-century readers as was his poetry. Writing in classical style but with brutal honesty, Baudelaire laid bare human suffering, aspirations, and perversions.

256 pp.   **0-14-044624-9**   **$12.95**

See The Penguin Book of French Poetry: 1820–1950.

L. FRANK BAUM
1856 – 1919, American

The Wonderful World of Oz
The Wizard of Oz/The Emerald City of Oz/Glinda of Oz
Edited with an Introduction and Notes by Jack Zipes

This fully annotated volume collects three of Baum's fourteen Oz novels in which he developed his utopian vision and which garnered an immense and loyal following. Also included is a selection of the original illustrations by W. W. Denslow and John R. Neill.

368 pp.   **0-14-118085-4**   **$13.95**

PIERRE-AUGUSTIN CARON DE BEAUMARCHAIS
1732 – 1799, French

The Barber of Seville and The Marriage of Figaro
Translated with an Introduction by John Wood

Known to us almost exclusively through the operas of Rossini and Mozart, these two plays, written with a delightfully light touch, marked high points in eighteenth-century comedy.

224 pp.   0-14-044133-6 $11.00

See The Portable Enlightenment Reader.

BEDE
c. 673 – 735, Anglo-Saxon

Ecclesiastical History of the English People
Edited with a New Introduction and Notes by D. H. Farmer and Translated by Leo Sherley-Price

Opening with a background sketch of Roman Britain's geography and history, Bede recounts the development of the Anglo-Saxon government and religion during the formative years of the British people.

400 pp.   0-14-044565-X $12.95

BEDE
c. 673 – 735, Anglo-Saxon

BRENDAN
d. 575, Irish

EDDIUS STEPHANUS
c. 8th cent., Anglo-Saxon

The Age of Bede
Edited with an Introduction by D. H. Farmer and Translated by J. F. Webb and D. H. Farmer

Four of the finest medieval hagiographies provide valuable insight into the religious life and thought of the period. This collection includes *The Voyage of St. Brendan*, Bede's *Life of Cuthbert*, *Lives of the Abbots of Wearmouth and Jarrow*, and Eddius Stephanus's *Life of Wilfrid*.

256 pp.   0-14-044727-X $12.00

APHRA BEHN
1640 – 1689, English

Oroonoko, The Rover, and Other Works
Edited with an Introduction by Janet Todd

This rich collection of works by Aphra Behn—poet, playwright, novelist, feminist, activist, and spy—reveals the talents of the first professional woman writer in English.

400 pp.   0-14-043338-4 $11.00

EDWARD BELLAMY
1850 – 1898, American

Looking Backward
2000–1887
Edited with an Introduction by Cecelia Tichi

When first published in 1888, *Looking Backward* initiated a national political- and social-reform movement. This profoundly utopian tale addresses the anguish and hope of its age, as well as having lasting value as an American cultural landmark.

240 pp.   0-14-039018-9 $11.95

The Adventures of Augie March

Ranging from the depths of poverty to the heights of success (and back), this is the sprawling chronicle of a modern-day Columbus in search of reality and fulfillment.

544 pp.   0-14-018941-6 $13.95

Penguin Readers Guide Available

"[Bellow's] body of work is more capacious of imagination and language than anyone else's....If there's a candidate for the Great American Novel, I think this is it."—SALMAN RUSHDIE

Dangling Man

Expecting to be inducted into the army, Joseph has given up his job and carefully prepared for his departure to the battle front. When a series of mix-ups delays his induction, he finds himself facing a year of idleness. *Dangling Man* is his journal, a wonderful account of his restless wanderings through Chicago's streets and his musings on the past.

208 pp.   0-14-018935-1 $12.95

The Dean's December

Switching back and forth between two cities and scenes of humanity struggling within them, *The Dean's December* represents Bellow's "most spirited resistance to the forces of our time" (Malcolm Bradbury).

320 pp.   0-14-018913-0 $13.95

Henderson the Rain King

Bellow evokes all the rich color and exotic customs of a highly imaginative Africa in this comic novel about a middle-aged American millionaire who, seeking a new, more rewarding life, descends upon an African tribe. Henderson's awesome feats of strength and his unbridled passion for life win him the admiration of the tribe—but it is his gift for making rain that turns him from mere hero into messiah.

352 pp.   0-14-018942-4 $13.95

Herzog

Introduction by Philip Roth

Hailed by the *New York Times* as a "masterpiece," *Herzog* is a multifaceted portrait of a modern-day hero. As his life disintegrates around him, Herzog writes unsent letters to friends, enemies, colleagues, and famous people, revealing his wry perceptions of the world and the innermost secrets of his heart.

352 pp.   0-14-243729-8 $14.00
(Available March 2003)

Penguin Readers Guide Available

SAUL BELLOW

Saul Bellow was born in Canada of Jewish immigrant parents and reared and educated in Chicago. A winner of numerous prizes, including the Pulitzer Prize (1975), the Nobel Prize in Literature (1976), and three National Book Awards, Bellow often delineates the experiences of the conflicted Jewish American intellectual who struggles to deal with spiritual and humanistic dilemmas in a world that has shed its traditional values and ethics. He has been praised for his vision, his ear for detail, his humor, and the masterful artistry of his prose.

Him with His Foot in His Mouth

This dazzling collection of short fiction describes a series of self-awakenings— a suburban divorcée deciding among lovers, a celebrity drawn into his cousin's life of crime, a father remembering bygone Chicago, an artist, and an academic awaiting extradition for some unnamed offense.

304 pp.   0-14-118023-4   **$14.95**

Humboldt's Gift

Introduction by Martin Amis

For many years, the great poet Von Humboldt Fleisher and Charlie Citrine, a young man inflamed with a love for literature, were the best of friends. At the time of his death, however, Humboldt is a failure, and Charlie's life has reached a low point. And then Humboldt acts from beyond the grave.

496 pp.   0-14-018944-0   **$14.95**

Mosby's Memoirs and Other Stories

In six darkly comic tales, Saul Bellow presents the human experience in all its preposterousness, poignancy, and pathos. The stories include "Leaving the Yellow House," "The Old System," "Looking for Mr. Green," "The Gonzaga Manuscripts," and "A Father-to-Be."

192 pp.   0-14-018945-9   **$11.95**

Mr. Sammler's Planet

Introduction by Stanley Crouch

As the country anticipates the first moon shot and visions of Utopia vie with predictions of imminent apocalypse, Sammler, a Holocaust survivor, recalls the horrors of the past while enmeshed in the madness of the present, and finds himself intrigued by the possibilities of the future.

352 pp.   0-14-018936-X   **$13.95**

Seize the Day

Introduction by Cynthia Ozick

Deftly interweaving humor and pathos, Bellow evokes in the climactic events of one day the full drama of a man's search to affirm his own worth and humanity.

144 pp.   0-14-018937-8   **$12.00**

Great Books Foundation Readers Guide Available

To Jerusalem and Back
A Personal Account

In this "impassioned and thoughtful book" (*The New York Times*), Bellow records the opinions, passions, and dreams of Israelis of varying viewpoints and adds his own thoughts on being Jewish in the twentieth century.

192 pp.   0-14-118075-7   **$13.95**

The Victim

Leventhal is a man uncertain of himself, who believes a down-at-the-heels stranger's accusation enough to find he has become... a victim.

288 pp.   0-14-018938-6   **$14.00**

STEPHEN VINCENT BENÉT
1898 – 1943, American

The Devil and Daniel Webster and Other Writings
Edited with an Introduction and Notes by Townsend Ludington

Through a versatile array of masterly short stories, the two-time Pulitzer Prize–winner explored such subjects as American society, history, politics, and the supernatural. Sensitively selected and thoughtfully arranged, this vibrant anthology reintroduces readers to an American master.

400 pp.   0-14-043740-1 $13.95

ARNOLD BENNETT
1867 – 1931, British

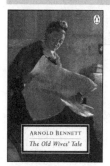

The Old Wives' Tale
Introduction and Notes by John Wain

First published in 1908 and mirroring the achievements of the French realists, this perceptive novel of British provincial life details the affairs of two suffering sisters.

624 pp.   0-14-018255-1 $11.95

JEREMY BENTHAM

See John Stuart Mill.

GEORGE BERKELEY
1685 – 1753, Irish

Principles of Human Knowledge and Three Dialogues Between Hylas and Philonius
Edited with an Introduction by Roger Woolhouse

These two masterpieces of empirical thought, whether viewed as extreme skepticism or enlightened common sense, are a major influence on modern philosophy.

224 pp.   0-14-043293-0 $11.95

BÉROUL
c. 12th cent., French

The Romance of Tristan
Translated with an Introduction by Alan S. Fredrick

This edition contains perhaps the earliest and most elemental version of the tragic legend of Tristan and Yseult in a distinguished prose translation. Alan S. Fredrick summarizes missing episodes and includes a translation of "The Tale of Tristan's Madness."

176 pp.   0-14-044230-8 $10.95

AMBROSE BIERCE
1842 – c.1914, American

Tales of Soldiers and Civilians and Other Stories
Edited with an Introduction and Notes by Tom Quirk

This collection gathers three dozen of Bierce's finest tales of war and the supernatural, including "An Occurrence at Owl Creek Bridge" and "The Damned Thing."

256 pp.   0-14-043756-8 $12.95

ALGERNON BLACKWOOD
1869 – 1951, British

Ancient Sorceries and Other Weird Stories

Edited with an Introduction and Notes by S. T. Joshi

By turns bizarre, unsettling, and sublime, Blackwood's writings all tread the nebulous borderland between fantasy, awe, wonder, and horror. Includes "The Willows," "The Wendigo," and "The Man Whom the Trees Loved."

384 pp.　　**0-14-218015-7**　　　**$12.00**

> **"The one absolute and unquestioned master of weird atmosphere."**
>
> —H. P. LOVECRAFT

WILLIAM BLAKE
1757 – 1827, British

The Portable Blake

Edited by Alfred Kazin

This essential collection of Blake's most important works contains *Songs of Innocence, Songs of Experience*, selections from his Prophetic Books, the cream of his prose, and the complete drawings for *The Book of Job*.

734 pp.　　**0-14-015026-9**　　　**$17.00**

> **"One of the most prophetic and gifted rebels in the history of Western man."**
>
> —ALFRED KAZIN

The Complete Poems

Edited by Alicia Ostriker

This edition contains all of Blake's poetry, with more than 150 pages of explanatory notes, including plot outlines of the more difficult poems, a chronology of Blake's life, a supplementary reading list, and a dictionary of proper names.

1,072 pp.　　**0-14-042215-3**　　　**$18.00**

See English Romantic Verse *and* The Portable Romantic Poets.

WILLIAM BLIGH
1754 – 1817, British

EDWARD CHRISTIAN
1758 – 1823, British

The *Bounty* Mutiny

Edited with an Introduction by R. D. Madison

For the first time, all of the relevant texts and documents related to the famous mutiny, including the full text of Bligh's *Narrative of the Mutiny*, the minutes of the court proceedings, and a rich selection of subsequent *Bounty* narratives.

224 pp.　　**0-14-043916-1**　　　**$13.00**

GIOVANNI BOCCACCIO
1313 – 1375, Italian

The Decameron
Translated with an Introduction and Notes by G. H. McWilliam

Read as a social document of medieval times, as an earthly counterpart of Dante's *Divine Comedy*, or even as an early manifestation of the dawning spirit of the Renaissance, *The Decameron* is a masterpiece of imaginative narrative whose background is the Florentine plague of 1348.

992 pp.   **0-14-044930-2**   **$13.95**

See The Portable Renaissance Reader *and* The Portable Medieval Reader.

ANCIUS BOETHIUS
c. 480 – 524, Roman

The Consolation of Philosophy
Translated with an Introduction by V. E. Watts

This influential book mingles verse and prose in a sacred dialogue reflecting the doctrines of Plato, Aristotle, the Stoics, and the Neoplatonists.

192 pp.   **0-14-044208-1**   **$13.95**

HEINRICH T. BÖLL
1917 – 1985, German
Nobel Prize winner

Billiards at Half-Past Nine
Translated by Leila Vennewitz

Böll's vehement opposition to Fascism and war informs this extraordinary exploration of the legacy of Nazi Germany.

288 pp.   **0-14-018724-3**   **$13.95**

The Clown
Translated by Leila Vennewitz

Through the eyes of a despairing artist Böll draws a revealing portrait of German society under Hitler and in the postwar years.

272 pp.   **0-14-018726-X**   **$13.95**

The Lost Honor of Katherina Blum
Translated by Leila Vennewitz

In this masterful journey through a labyrinth of threats, untruths, and violence, a young woman's association with a hunted man makes her the target of an unscrupulous journalist, and she sees only one way out.

160 pp.   **0-14-018728-6**   **$12.95**

TADEUSZ BOROWSKI
1922 – 1951, Polish (b. Ukraine)

This Way for the Gas, Ladies and Gentlemen
Selected and Translated by Barbara Vedder with an Introduction by Jan Kott, Introduction Translated by Michael Kandel

Published in Poland after World War II, this collection of concentration camp stories stands as cruel testimony to the depths of inhumanity of which human beings are capable.

192 pp.   **0-14-018624-7**   **$12.95**

JAMES BOSWELL
1740 – 1795, Scottish

The Life of Samuel Johnson
Edited and Abridged with an Introduction and Notes by Christopher Hibbert

This seminal biography, completed in 1791, is based on Boswell's conversations with Johnson, documents and letters, and anecdotes from friends, all shaped by Boswell's incomparable wit and originality.

384 pp.   **0-14-043116-0**   **$13.00**

See Samuel Johnson.

MARY ELIZABETH BRADDON
1837 – 1915, British

Lady Audley's Secret

Edited by Jenny Bourne Taylor with an Introduction by Jenny Bourne Taylor with Russell Crofts

Lady Audley's Secret epitomized the scandalous and irresistible "sensation" fiction of the period and established Braddon as the doyenne of the genre.

512 pp.   0-14-043584-0 $10.95

BRENDAN
d. 575, Irish

See Bede.

JEAN-ANTHELME BRILLAT-SAVARIN
1755 – 1826, French

The Physiology of Taste

Translated with an Introduction by Anne Drayton

First published in 1825, this book is a brilliant treatise on the pleasures of eating and the rich arts of food, wine, and philosophy, written by a famed French gastronome. Recipes are included.

384 pp.   0-14-044614-1 $13.95

VERA BRITTAIN
1896 – 1970, British

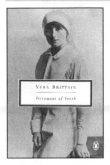

Testament of Youth

Brittain's pacifist and feminist memoir of the First World War, in which she served as a nurse in London, Malta, and in France at the front, is a classic account of an entire generation marked by fatal idealism and changed by war.

672 pp.   0-14-018844-4 $16.95

ANNE BRONTË
1820 – 1849, British

Agnes Grey

Edited with an Introduction and Notes by Angeline Goreau

A young governess experiences disillusionment and discovers love in this elegant novel, which George Moore found the "most perfect prose narrative in English literature."

272 pp.   0-14-043210-8 $8.95

The Tenant of Wildfell Hall

Edited with an Introduction by Stevie Davies

A passionate portrait of a woman's struggle for independence, *The Tenant of Wildfell Hall* is the story of Helen Graham, who flees a disastrous marriage, assumes a false identity, and attempts to make a life for herself and her child in a desolate mansion on the English moors, emerging as a woman of unusual strength and resolve.

576 pp.   0-14-043474-7 $7.95

CHARLOTTE BRONTË
1816 – 1855, British

Jane Eyre

Edited with an Introduction and Notes by Michael Mason

First published in 1847, *Jane Eyre* embodies many of the melodramatic conventions of the Gothic novels of the period. Charlotte Brontë, however, transcends melodrama to create an atypical romantic heroine of independence, intelligence, and integrity.

576 pp.   **0-14-243720-4**   **$7.95**
(Available February 2003)

Great Books Foundation Readers Guide Available

The Professor

Edited with an Introduction by Heather Glen

Published posthumously in 1857, Brontë's first novel is a subtle portrayal of a self-made man and his use of power in an individualistic society that worships property and propriety.

320 pp.   **0-14-043311-2**   **$8.95**

Shirley

Edited by Andrew and Judith Hook

Brontë grapples with the social and political issues of the mid–nineteenth century in a sweeping novel that explores the possibilities of reconciling romantic love and the demands of social convention.

624 pp.   **0-14-043095-4**   **$7.95**

Villette

Edited by Mark Lilly with an Introduction by Tony Tanner

An autobiographical novel, *Villette* is a moving portrait of the tensions between inner and outer experience and of the anguish of unrequited love.

624 pp.   **0-14-043118-7**   **$10.95**

EMILY BRONTË
1818 – 1848, British

*Wuthering Heights

Edited with an Introduction and Notes by Pauline Nestor and a Preface by Lucasta Miller

The story of the passionate love between Catherine Earnshaw and the wild Heathcliff, told with wholly original emotional and imaginative power, has the depth and simplicity of an ancient tragedy.

400 pp.   **0-14-143955-6**   **$7.00**
(Available January 2003)

Penguin Readers Guide Available

CHARLES BROCKDEN BROWN
1771 – 1810, American

Edgar Huntly
Or, Memoirs of a Sleep-Walker
Edited with an Introduction by Norman S. Grabo

One of the first American Gothic novels, *Edgar Huntly* (1787) mirrors the social and political temperaments of the post-revolutionary United States.

288 pp.   0-14-039062-6   **$12.95**

Wieland and Memoirs of Carwin the Biloquist
Edited with an Introduction and Notes by Jay Fliegelman

A terrifying account of the fallibility of the human mind and, by extension, of democracy itself, *Wieland* brilliantly reflects the psychological, social, and political concerns of the early American republic. In the fragmentary sequel, *Memoirs*, Brown explores Carwin's bizarre history as a manipulated disciple of the charismatic utopian Ludloe.

416 pp.   0-14-039079-0   **$10.95**

WILLIAM HILL BROWN
1765 – 1793, American

HANNAH WEBSTER FOSTER
1758 – 1840, American

The Power of Sympathy/ The Coquette
Introduction and Notes by Carla Mulford

Written in epistolary form and drawn from actual events, Brown's *The Power of Sympathy* (1789) and Foster's *The Coquette* (1797) were two of the earliest novels published in the United States. Both novels reflect the eighteenth-century preoccupation with the role of women as safekeepers of the young country's morality.

384 pp.   0-14-043468-2   **$13.95**

ELIZABETH BARRETT BROWNING
1806 – 1861, British

Aurora Leigh and Other Poems
Edited by John Robert Glorney Bolton and Julia Bolton Holloway

The romantic story of the making of a woman poet, Elizabeth Barrett Browning's epic novel in blank verse, published in 1856, explores women's issues and the relationship of art to politics and social expression. This volume also contains selections of the author's poetry published from 1826 to 1862, including *Casa Guidi Windows* and the British Library manuscript text of *Sonnets from the Portuguese*.

544 pp.   0-14-043412-7   **$12.95**

ROBERT BROWNING
1812 – 1889, British

Selected Poems
Edited with an Introduction and Notes by Daniel Karlin

This edition conveys the intensity, lyric beauty, and vitality of Browning's work through selections from the early *Pippa Passes* (1841), *Dramatic Lyrics* (1842), and *Dramatic Romances and Lyrics* (1845); from the masterpieces *Men and Women* (1855) and *Dramatis Personae* (1864); and from the less familiar works of his later years.

352 pp.   0-14-043726-6   **$12.00**

GEORG BÜCHNER
1813 – 1837, Hessian

Complete Plays, Lenz, and Other Writings
Translated with an Introduction and Notes by John Reddick

Collected in this volume are powerful dramas and psychological fiction by the nineteenth-century iconoclast now recognized as a major figure of world literature. Also included are selections from Büchner's letters and philosophical writings.

368 pp.   0-14-044586-2   **$14.00**

MIKHAIL BULGAKOV
1891 – 1940, Russian

The Master and Margarita
Translated by Richard Pevear and Larissa Volokhonsky with an Introduction by Richard Pevear

An artful collage of grotesqueries, dark comedy, and timeless ethical questions, Bulgakov's devastating satire of Soviet life was written during the darkest period of Stalin's regime and remained unpublished for more than twenty-five years after its completion. This brilliant translation was made from the complete and unabridged Russian text.

432 pp.   0-14-118014-5   **$12.95**

See The Portable Twentieth-Century Russian Reader.

IVAN A. BUNIN
1870 – 1953, Russian
Nobel Prize winner

The Gentleman from San Francisco and Other Stories
Translated with an Introduction by David Richards and Sophie Lund

This collection of seventeen stories hails from one of Russia's great realist writers, a modern heir to Chekhov and Turgenev.

224 pp.   0-14-018552-6   **$15.00**

See The Portable Twentieth-Century Russian Reader.

MIKHAIL BULGAKOV

Described as "a slanderer of Soviet reality," in the official Big Soviet Encyclopaedia, Mikhail Bulgakov graduated with honors as a doctor from Kiev University in 1916, but only three years later gave up his medical practice to pursue writing. His satirical treatment of government officials in his many plays and stories led to growing political censorship and criticism, which became violent toward the end of his career. Poverty-stricken and in despair, Bulgakov wrote a letter to Stalin begging the government to order him out of the country as "there is no hope for any of my works" in Russia. Instead, Bulgakov was granted his second choice, a position as the assistant director and literary consultant to the Moscow Arts Theater, where he could be closely monitored by government officials. Bulgakov died in disgrace at the age of 49.

JOHN BUNYAN
1628 – 1688, British

Grace Abounding to the Chief of Sinners
Edited with an Introduction by W. R. Owens

Bunyan's spiritual autobiography relates his religious awakening and eventual triumph over doubt and despair as it charts the experience of his conversion.

144 pp.   **0-14-043280-9**   **$10.95**

The Pilgrim's Progress
Edited with an Introduction and Notes by Roger Sharrock

Written in prison, Bunyan's chronicle of Christian's pilgrimage to the Celestial City is a powerful allegory of the conflict between religion and society.

384 pp.   **0-14-043004-0**   **$8.95**

JACOB BURCKHARDT
1818 – 1897, Swiss

The Civilization of the Renaissance in Italy
Translated by S. G. C. Middlemore with a New Introduction by Peter Burke and Notes by Peter Murray

In this influential interpretation of the Italian Renaissance, Burckhardt explores the political and psychological forces that marked the beginning of the modern world.

416 pp.   **0-14-044534-X**   **$14.95**

EDMUND BURKE
1729 – 1797, Irish

The Portable Edmund Burke
Edited with an Introduction by Isaac Kramnick

This is the fullest one-volume edition of Burke's thought, with sections devoted to his writings on history and culture, politics and society, the American and French revolutions, and colonialism.

624 pp.   **0-14-026760-3**   **$16.95**

A Philosophical Enquiry into the Origin of Our Ideas of the Sublime and Beautiful
And Other Pre-Revolutionary Writings
Edited with an Introduction by David Womersley

Burke is considered by many to be the father of modern political conservatism but his essay on modern aesthetics influenced innumerable writers of the Romantic period. This volume includes his famous text as well as several of his early political writings to reveal the cross-pollination of Burke's aesthetic and political thinking.

528 pp.   **0-14-043625-1**   **$14.95**

Reflections on the Revolution in France
Edited with an Introduction by Conor Cruise O'Brien

The great debate on the French Revolution was touched off by *Reflections*, which reveals Burke as a much more radical—even revolutionary—thinker than admitted by those who view him as the father of modern conservatism.

400 pp.   **0-14-043204-3**   **$11.00**

See The Portable Enlightenment Reader.

A Little Princess

Edited with an Introduction and Notes by U. C. Knoepflmacher

A young girl's power of imagination and how it transforms her life is at the heart of this rich and resonant novel. Included are excerpts from Burnett's original novella *Sara Crewe* and the stage play, as well as an early story, allowing readers to see how *A Little Princess* evolved.

272 pp. 0-14-243701-8 $10.00

The Secret Garden

Edited with an Introduction and Notes by Alison Lurie

Originally published in 1911, *The Secret Garden* is an extraordinary novel that has influenced writers such as Eliot and Lawrence. The story of the sullen orphan Mary Lennox highlights the transforming powers of love, joy, and nature and of mystical faith and positive thinking.

288 pp. 0-14-243705-0 $7.00

Penguin Readers Guide Available

"One of the most original and brilliant children's books of the century."

—ALISON LURIE

FRANCES BURNEY
1752 – 1840, British

Evelina

Edited with an Introduction and Notes by Margaret Anne Doody

This epistolary portrait of female independence and the intrigues of the social classes introduced an entirely new form of novel—the comedy of manners—when it was published anonymously in 1778.

544 pp. 0-14-043347-3 $11.95

Journals and Letters

Edited by Peter Sabor and Lars E. Troide

Written during a seventy-year period from 1768 to 1839, Frances Burney's letters and journals depict the world in which she lived—London society, the court of Queen Charlotte, France during the Napoleonic wars—and capture the people she encountered in brilliantly candid portraits.

608 pp. 0-14-043624-3 $15.00

ROBERT BURNS
1759 – 1796, Scottish

Selected Poems

Edited by Carol McGuirk

Arranged in probable order of composition, and featuring both lyrics and tunes, this collection of poems and songs written by Burns late in his career reveals his emotional range.

368 pp. 0-14-042382-6 $14.00

EDGAR RICE BURROUGHS
1875 – 1950, American

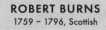

Tarzan of the Apes

Introduction and Notes by John Seelye

This 1914 novel gave birth to one of the most legendary characters in fiction, an ideal image of pure animalistic power at odds with the civilized world.

320 pp. 0-14-018464-3 $8.95

Erewhon

Edited with an Introduction by
Peter Mudford

Butler's tale of a traveler to a remote island, based on his experiences in New Zealand, combines the elements of traditional utopian fiction and the picaresque novel.

272 pp.   0-14-043057-1 $12.00

The Way of All Flesh

Edited by James Cochrane with an
Introduction by Richard Hoggart

With wit, irony, and, sometimes, rancor, Butler savages the smug values and beliefs of a Victorian family.

448 pp.   0-14-043012-1 $12.00

Don Juan

Edited by T. G. Steffan, E. Steffan, and
W. W. Pratt with an Introduction by
T. G. Steffan

In this rambling, exuberant, conversational poem, the travels of Don Juan are used as a vehicle for some of the most lively and acute commentaries on human societies and behavior in the language.

760 pp.   0-14-042216-1 $14.95

Selected Poems

Edited with a Preface by Susan J. Wolfson
and Peter J. Manning

Flamboyant, brilliant, and daring, relishing humor and irony, Byron's poetry reflects European Romanticism in an age of revolutions. Among the poems included are "Childe Harold's Pilgrimage" and "Sardanapalus."

832 pp.   0-14-042381-8 $14.95

See The Portable Romantic Poets.

Chronicle of the Narváez Expedition

Revised and Annotated Translation by
Harold Augenbraum and an Introduction by
Ilan Stavans

The first major narrative detailing the exploration of North America by Spanish conquistadors, Cabeza de Vaca's chronicle describes the nine-year odyssey endured by him and his men after a shipwreck forced them to make a westward journey on foot from present-day Florida to California.

160 pp.   0-14-243707-7 $12.00

The Grandissimes

Introduction by Michael Kreyling

Setting forth formidable arguments for racial equality, Cable's novel of feuding Creole families in early nineteenth-century New Orleans blends post–Civil War social dissent and Romanticism.

384 pp.   0-14-043322-8 $14.95

The Civil War
Together with The Alexandrian War, The African War, and The Spanish War by Other Hands

Translated with an Introduction by
Jane F. Gardner

A general of genius, Caesar was also a vivid and powerful writer. These accounts paint a full and surprisingly fair picture of the great struggle that brought Caesar to power and then caused his death.

360 pp.   0-14-044187-5 $12.95

The Conquest of Gaul
Translated by S. A. Hanford and Revised with a New Introduction by Jane F. Gardner

Caesar's account of the Gallic Wars, although based on fact, also served to impress his contemporaries and justify himself to his enemies. The earliest eye-witness account of Britain and its inhabitants appears in these famous memoirs.

272 pp.   0-14-044433-5 $9.95

See The Portable Roman Reader.

ABRAHAM CAHAN
1860 – 1951, American
(b. Lithuania)

The Rise of David Levinsky
Edited with an Introduction and Notes by Jules Chametzky

Originally published in 1917, this classic of Jewish American literature tells the story of a young immigrant who works his way to success in the garment industry, but is at a loss in matters of love and identity.

544 pp.   0-14-018687-5 $13.95

See American Local Color Writing.

CAO XUEQIN
c. 1715 – 1763, Chinese

The Story of the Stone
Also known as The Dream of the Red Chamber

Divided into five volumes, *The Story of the Stone* charts the glory and decline of the illustrious Jia family. This novel re-creates the ritualized hurly-burly of Chinese family life that would otherwise be lost and infuses it with affirming Buddhist belief.

"Indisputably the greatest masterpiece ...of all the Chinese novels."
—*THE NEW YORK REVIEW OF BOOKS*

The Story of the Stone
Volume 1: The Golden Days (Chapters 1–26)
Translated with an Introduction by David Hawkes

544 pp.   0-14-044293-6 $15.00

The Story of the Stone
Volume 2: The Crab-Flower Club (Chapters 27–53)
Translated with an Introduction by David Hawkes

608 pp.   0-14-044326-6 $13.95

The Story of the Stone
Volume 3: The Warning Voice (Chapters 54–80)
Translated with an Introduction by David Hawkes

640 pp.   0-14-044370-3 $13.95

CAO XUEQIN

Cao Xueqin was born in 1715 into a family that for three generations held the office of Commissioner of Imperial Textiles in Nanking. But calamity overtook them and their property was confiscated. Cao Xueqin was living in poverty near Peking when he wrote his famous novel *The Story of the Stone*, the most popular book in all of Chinese literature. It was not published until thirty years after his death in 1763.

The Story of the Stone
Volume 4: The Debt of Tears
(Chapters 81–98)
Edited by Gao E and Translated with an Introduction by John Minford
400 pp.   0-14-044371-1 $15.00

The Story of the Stone
Volume 5: The Dreamer Awakes
(Chapters 99–120)
Edited by Gao E and Translated with a Preface by John Minford
384 pp.   0-14-044372-X $13.95

LEWIS CARROLL
1832 – 1898, British

Alice's Adventures in Wonderland and Through the Looking-Glass
Edited with an Introduction by Hugh Haughton

Lewis Carroll's incomparable tales about Alice always have intrigued older readers, and the use of puns, parodies, and absurd arguments about meanings and manners brilliantly mock the rules and conventions adults impose on children.
448 pp.   98 b/w drawings
0-14-143976-9 $8.95
Penguin Readers Guide Available

"The two Alices are not books for children, they are the only books in which we become children."

—VIRGINIA WOOLF

The Hunting of the Snark
Edited with an Introduction by Martin Gardner and the Original Illustrations of Henry Holiday

Inspired by the serendipitous line "For the Snark was a Boojum, you see," which occurred to him during a stroll, Lewis Carroll crafted a classic work of nonsense poetry that has intrigued readers for more than a century.
128 pp.   14 b/w illustrations
0-14-043491-7 $9.95

RACHEL L. CARSON
1907 – 1964, American

Under the Sea Wind
Illustrated by Rob Hines

The special mystery and beauty of the sea is the setting for Rachel Carson's portrait of the sea birds and sea creatures that inhabit the eastern coast of North America in this seamless series of riveting adventures along the Atlantic shore, within the open sea, and down into its twilight depths.
304 pp.   0-14-025380-7 $14.00

GIOVANNI GIACOMO CASANOVA
1725 – 1798, Venetian

The Story of My Life
Translated by Stephen Sartarelli and Sophie Hawkins, and Edited with an Introduction by Gilberto Pizzamiglio

Seducer, gambler, necromancer, swashbuckler, spy, self-made gentleman, entrepreneur, and general bon vivant, Casanova lived a life richer and stranger than most fiction. The first new translation since the 1960s, this edition provides the highlights from his twelve volumes in one beautiful, unique volume.
576 pp.   0-14-043915-3 $15.00

"The elegant Sartarelli/Hawkes translation . . . is deliciously transparent, allowing Casanova's flowing storytelling voice . . . to emerge as if English were his own tongue, a major achievement."

—ROBERT COOVER

ROSARIO CASTELLANOS
1925 – 1974, Mexican

The Book of Lamentations
*Translated with an Afterword by
Esther Allen and an Introduction by
Alma Guillermoprieto*

A masterpiece of contemporary Latin
American fiction by Mexico's greatest
twentieth-century woman writer, *The Book
of Lamentations* draws on two centuries of
struggle among the Maya Indians and the
white landowners in the Chiapas region
of southern Mexico. The stark clarity of
Castellanos's vision is beautifully rendered
in Esther Allen's masterful first-ever
English translation.

352 pp.   0-14-118003-X $15.00

BALDESAR CASTIGLIONE
1478 – 1529, Milanese

The Book of the Courtier
*Translated with an Introduction by
George Bull*

Discretion, decorum, nonchalance, and
gracefulness are qualities of the complete
and perfect Italian Renaissance courtier
that are outlined in this series of imaginary
conversations between the principal
members of the court of Urbino in 1507.

368 pp.   0-14-044192-1 $13.95

WILLA CATHER
1873 – 1947, American

Coming, Aphrodite! and Other Stories
*Edited with Notes by
Margaret Anne O'Connor and an
Introduction by Cynthia Griffin Wolff*

Ranging from the simplicity of Cather's
first published story, "Peter" (1892), to
the extraordinary eroticism of "Coming,
Aphrodite!" (1920), this unique selection of
short fiction is an engaging and triumphant
testament to the genius of an American
literary icon.

352 pp.   0-14-118156-7 $12.95

My Ántonia
Introduction and Notes by John J. Murphy

Cather's portrait of a remembered American
girlhood on the Nebraskan prairie at the
end of the nineteenth century alternates
between insightful lyricism and naturalistic
description, as she explores the rich
relationship of Ántonia and the narrator,
Jim Burden.

304 pp.   0-14-018764-2 $9.95

Penguin Readers Guide Available

WILLA CATHER

Born in Virginia in 1873 and raised on a Nebraska ranch, Willa Cather is known
for her beautifully evocative short stories and novels about the American West.
Cather became the managing editor for *McClure*'s magazine in 1906 and lived for
forty years in New York City with her companion, Edith Lewis. In 1922 Cather won
the Pulitzer Prize for *One of Ours*, the story of a Western boy in World War I. In
1933 she was awarded the Prix Femina Americaine "for distinguished literary
accomplishments." She died in 1947.

O Pioneers!

Introduction by Blanche H. Gelfant

The first of Cather's renowned prairie novels, *O Pioneers!* established a new voice in American literature—turning the stories of ordinary Midwesterners and immigrants into authentic literary characters.

224 pp. **0-14-018775-8** **$8.95**

The Song of the Lark

Edited with an Introduction and Notes by Sherrill Harbison

This moving story about an aspiring musician and singer and her devotion to her art is one of Cather's most autobiographical novels. As is characteristic in Cather's work, the western landscape both eloquently represents the characters' inner lives and regenerates their tired imaginations.

480 pp. **0-14-118104-4** **$11.00**

Penguin Readers Guide Available

See The Portable American Realism Reader.

GEORGE CATLIN
1796 – 1872, American

North American Indians

Edited with an Introduction by Peter Matthiessen

From 1831 to 1837, George Catlin traveled extensively among the native peoples of North America studying their habits, customs, and mode of life. Catlin's unprecedented fieldwork culminated in more than five hundred oil paintings and his now-legendary journal, collected here in this one-volume edition, and illustrated with more than fifty reproductions of Catlin's incomparable paintings.

522 pp. **0-14-025267-3** **$16.00**

CATULLUS
c. 84 – c. 54 B.C., Roman (b. Verona)

The Poems of Catullus

Translated with an Introduction by Peter Whigham

These 111 poems introduce the lyric poet Catullus, master of the pungent epigram, who found his inspiration in the glittering Roman society of the late Republic.

256 pp. **0-14-044180-8** **$13.00**

See The Portable Roman Reader.

MARGARET CAVENDISH
c. 1623 – 1673, British

The Blazing World and Other Writings

Edited with an Introduction by Kate Lilley

These remarkable works of the flamboyant Duchess of Newcastle reveal not only a radical feminist, but a transgressor of every literary and sexual role and code. The title piece, depicting a utopia ruled by a warrior queen, is the first work of science fiction ever written.

272 pp. **0-14-043372-4** **$13.00**

BENVENUTO CELLINI
1500 – 1571, Florentine

Autobiography

Translated with an Introduction and Notes by George Bull

With enviable powers of invective and an irrepressible sense of humor, Cellini provides an unrivaled portrait of the manners and morals of the Italy of Michelangelo and the Medici.

496 pp.   0-14-044718-0 $13.00

MIGUEL DE CERVANTES SAAVEDRA
1547 – 1615, Spanish

The Portable Cervantes

Edited and Translated by Samuel Putnam

This collection includes Putnam's acclaimed translation of *Don Quixote*, substantially complete, the two "Exemplary Novels" *Rinconete and Cortadillo* and *Man of Glass*, as well as Cervantes's extraordinary farewell to life from *The Troubles of Persiles and Sigismunda*.

864 pp.   0-14-015057-9 $17.00

*Don Quixote

Translated with Notes by John Rutherford and an Introduction by Roberto González Echevarría

Winner of the Premio Valle Inclàn translation prize

Voted the Greatest Book of All Time by the Nobel Institute

The adventures of Cervantes's idealistic knight-errant and his simple but astute squire, Sancho Panza, is not only a hilarious parody of the romances of chivalry but an exploration of the relationship between the real and the illusionary.

948 pp.   0-14-044804-7 $13.00
(Available January 2003)

MIGUEL DE CERVANTES SAAVEDRA

Miguel de Cervantes Saavedra was born in Alcalé de Henares, Spain, in 1547. As a young man serving in the Spanish wars against the Ottoman Empire, he was captured by the Barbary pirates and sent into slavery in Algeria in 1575. After many attempts at escape, he was finally ransomed in 1580, an act that reduced his family to poverty. Returning to Madrid, Cervantes entered public service (including a stint commandeering supplies for the Spanish Armada) and was so ill-suited to the job that he was jailed for gross irregularities in his accounts. Although his first novel, *La Galatea*, was written in 1585, and he wrote poetry and drama (only two of his thirty plays survive), it was not until the publication of *Don Quixote* in 1605 that Cervantes gained fame as a writer. An immediate success in his native country, the novel soon became a favorite abroad. The intricate, multi-layered structure of the novel, and Cervantes's brilliant exploration of the relationship between art and life, had tremendous impact on the development of the modern novel; the works of writers from Fielding and Smollett to Twain, Dostoyevsky, and even Kafka, all bear traces of the influence of Cervantes's masterpiece.

Exemplary Stories

Translated with an Introduction by
C. A. Jones

Included in this collection are "The Little Gypsy Girl," "Rinconete and Cortadillo," "The Glass Graduate," "The Jealous Extremaduran," "The Deceitful Marriage," and "The Dog's Colloquy."

256 pp.   0-14-044248-0 $10.95

See The Portable Renaissance Reader.

OWEN CHASE

See Thomas Nickerson.

BRUCE CHATWIN
1940 – 1989, British

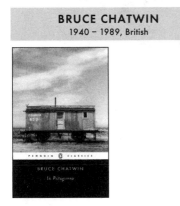

In Patagonia

Introduction by Nicholas Shakespeare

This exquisite account describes Chatwin's journey through "the uttermost part of the earth," that stretch of land at the southern tip of South America, where bandits were once made welcome and Charles Darwin formed part of his theory of evolution.

224 pp.   0-14-243719-0 $14.00

(Available April 2003)

GEOFFREY CHAUCER
c. 1342 – 1400, English

The Portable Chaucer

Edited and translated by
Theodore Morrison

This essential collection contains the complete *The Canterbury Tales* and *Troilus and Cressida* in fresh modern translations, with selections from *The Book of the Duchess, The House of Fame, The Bird's Parliament,* and *The Legend of Good Women,* together with short poems.

624 pp.   0-14-015081-1 $15.95

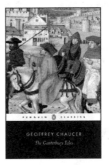

The Canterbury Tales

Translated into Modern English by
Nevill Coghill

The motley members of a five-day pilgrimage from Southwark to Canterbury each tell a story to pass the time. From Knight to Nun and Miller to Monk, these pilgrims from all levels of society reveal a picture of British life in the fourteenth century that is as robust as it is representative. This edition captures the entire body of Chaucer's masterpiece in a thoroughly readable modern translation that preserves the freshness and racy vitality of the original text.

528 pp.   0-14-042438-5 $10.00

(Available February 2003)

The Canterbury Tales
The First Fragment

Edited with an Introduction and Glosses by Michael Alexander

Comprised of the general Prologue and the prologues and tales of the Knight, Miller, Reeve, and Cook, this is the most widely read portion of Chaucer's masterpiece. This unique edition contains the Middle English text on one page and meticulous glosses of Chaucer's language on the facing page.

320 pp.   0-14-043409-7 $9.95

Love Visions

Translated into Modern English with an Introduction and Notes by Brian Stone

Spanning Chaucer's working life, these four poems move from the conventional allegorical "love visions" toward realistic storytelling and provide a marvelous self-portrait. This selection includes "The Book of the Duchess," "The House of Fame," "The Parliament of the Birds," and "The Legend of Good Women."

272 pp.   0-14-044408-4 $11.95

Troilus and Criseyde

Translated into Modern English by Nevill Coghill

Chaucer's depiction of passionate sexual love, his grasp of tragedy, and his sense of the ridiculous hidden in the sublime are all displayed in this poetic retelling of the classical story set during the Trojan War.

336 pp.   0-14-044239-1 $9.95

See The Portable Medieval Reader.
See The Portable Medieval Reader.

ANTON CHEKHOV
1860 – 1904, Russian

The Portable Chekhov

Edited by Avrahm Yarmolinsky

This essential collection of the Russian master's writings contains twenty-eight of his best stories; two complete plays, *The Boor* and *The Cherry Orchard*; and a selection of letters, candidly revealing Chekhov's impassioned convictions on life and art.

640 pp.   0-14-015035-8 $15.95

The Lady with the Little Dog and Other Stories, 1896–1904

Translated by Ronald Wilks with an Introduction by Paul Debreczeny

These eleven stories were written during the last ten years of Chekhov's life: "The Lady with the Little Dog," "The House with the Mezzanine," "My Life," "Peasants," "A Visit to Friends," "Ionych," "About Love,"

ANTON CHEKHOV

Anton Chekhov was born in 1860 at Tanganrog in southern Russia. After a harsh childhood he went to Moscow in 1879 and entered the medical faculty of the university, graduating in 1884. In 1886 Chekhov published his first volume of stories. The next year, his first full-length play, *Ivanov*, was produced in Moscow. He continued to practice medicine while writing many of his best stories. In 1898, Stanislavsky produced *The Seagull* at his newly founded Moscow Art Theater. It was for him that Chekhov wrote *Uncle Vanya* (1900), *The Three Sisters* (1901), and *The Cherry Orchard* (1903). After 1900, when his health began to fail, Chekhov moved to Yalta, where he met Tolstoy and Gorky. In 1901 Chekhov married Olga Knipper, one of the Art Theatre's leading actresses. He died in 1904.

"In the Ravine," "The Bishop," "The Bride,"
and "Disturbing the Balance."
384 pp.   **0-14-044787-3**   **$10.00**

Plays
Ivanov/The Seagull/Uncle Vanya/
Three Sisters/The Cherry Orchard

Translated by Peter Carson with an
Introduction by Richard Gilman

In these vibrant new translations, Chekhov's
dramatic masterpieces portray complex
characters grappling with moral questions.
Though his works baffled his audiences,
Chekhov's sensitive explorations of love,
loss, and time revolutionized the theater.

416 pp.   **0-14-044733-4**   **$9.00**

The Steppe and Other Stories,
1887–1891

Translated by Ronald Wilks with an
Introduction by Donald Rayfield

Written during Chekhov's late twenties and
early thirties, these haunting stories are the
work of a young writer in dialogue with
his masters: Tolstoy, Gogol, and Turgenev.
Included are "The Steppe," "Panpipes,"
"The Kiss," "Verochka," "The Name-day
Party," "A Dreary Story," "Gusev," and
"The Duel."

416 pp.   **0-14-044785-7**   **$10.00**

Ward No. 6 and Other Stories,
1892–1895

Translated by Ronald Wilks with an
Introduction by J. Douglas Clayton

Impressionistic and bold, the nine stories
in this collection frame the middle period
of Chekhov's career: "Ward No. 6," "The
Black Monk," "A Woman's Kingdom,"
"Three Years," "Murder," "The Student,"
"The Grasshopper," "Adriana," and "The
Two Volodyas."

368 pp.   **0-14-044786-5**   **$10.00**

See The Portable Nineteenth-Century
Russian Reader *and* The Portable
Twentieth-Century Russian Reader.

CHARLES W. CHESNUTT
1858 – 1932, American

Conjure Tales and Stories of the
Color Line

Edited with an Introduction by
William Andrews

Chesnutt probed psychological depths in
black people previously unheard of in
Southern regional writing. This important
collection brings together all the stories in
his two published volumes, *The Conjure
Woman* and *The Wife of His Youth*, along
with two uncollected works: "Dave's
Neckliss" and "Baxter's Procustes."

304 pp.   **0-14-118502-3**   **$10.95**

The House Behind the Cedars

Edited with an Introduction by
Donald B. Gibson

An early masterwork among American
literary treatments of miscegenation,
Chesnutt's story is of two young African
Americans who decide to pass for white in
order to claim their share of the American
dream.

304 pp.   **0-14-018685-9**   **$12.95**

The Marrow of Tradition

Edited with an Introduction and Notes by
Eric J. Sundquist

This novel is based on a historically accurate
account of the Wilmington, North Carolina,
"race riot" of 1898, and is a passionate
portrait of the betrayal of black culture in
America, written by an acclaimed African
American writer.

336 pp.   **0-14-018686-7**   **$13.95**

See The Portable American Realism Reader.

G. K. CHESTERTON
1874 – 1936, British

The Man Who Was Thursday
A Nightmare

Introduction by Kingsley Amis

Named after the days of the week for security reasons, the seven members of the Central Anarchist Council vow to destroy the world.

192 pp.   **0-14-018388-4**   **$8.95**

ERSKINE CHILDERS
1870 – 1922 Irish, (b. England)

The Riddle of the Sands

Foreword by Geoffrey Household

First published in 1903, this gripping tale of espionage is "the first and best of spy stories" (*The Times*, London) and a brilliant forerunner to the work of Graham Greene and John Le Carré.

336 pp.   **4 maps**   **0-14-118165-6**   **$7.95**

KATE CHOPIN
1851 – 1904, American

At Fault

Edited with an Introduction and Notes by Bernard Koloski

Both romantic and filled with stark realism, *At Fault* is a love story about the challenge of balancing personal happiness and moral duty. Written at the beginning of Chopin's career, *At Fault* parallels her own life and prefigures her later work, including *The Awakening*.

160 pp.   **0-14-243702-6**   **$10.00**

The Awakening and Selected Stories

Edited with an Introduction by Sandra M. Gilbert

First published in 1899, *The Awakening* shows the transformation of Edna Pontellier, who claims for herself moral and erotic freedom. Other selections include "Emancipation," "At the 'Cadian Ball," and "Désirée's Baby."

288 pp.   **0-14-243709-3**   **$8.00**
(Available February 2003)

Penguin Readers Guide Available

Bayou Folk and A Night in Acadie

Edited with an Introduction and Notes by Bernard Koloski

Here in one volume are the two short-story collections that established Kate Chopin as one of America's best-loved realist writers. Set in New Orleans and rural Louisiana, they anticipate the modern multi-ethnic, gender-sensitive, and sexually charged world of today.

416 pp.   **0-14-043681-2**   **$11.95**

A Vocation and a Voice
Stories

Edited with an Introduction and Notes by Emily Toth

Published for the first time as Chopin intended, this is a collection of her most innovative stories, including "The Story of an Hour," "An Egyptian Cigarette," and "The Kiss."

192 pp.   **0-14-039078-2**   **$10.95**

See American Local Color Writing *and* The Portable American Realism Reader.

Arthurian Romances

Translated with an Introduction and Notes by William W. Kibler; Erec and Enide Translated by Carleton W. Carroll

Fantastic adventures abound in these courtly romances: Erec and Enide, Cligés, The Knight of the Cart, The Knight with the Lion, and The Story of the Grail.

528 pp.   0-14-044521-8 $14.00

See William Bligh.

Murder Trials

Translated with an Introduction by Michael Grant

Cicero's speeches "In Defence of Sextus Roscius of Amerina," "In Defence of Aulus Cluentius Habitus," "In Defence of Gaius Rabirius," "Note on the Speeches in Defence of Caelius and Milo," and "In Defence of King Deiotarus" provide insight into Roman life, law, and history.

368 pp.   0-14-044288-X $13.95

The Nature of the Gods

Translated by Horace C. P. McGregor with an Introduction by J. M. Ross

In De natura deorum, Cicero sets out the ancient Greeks' conclusions about the existence and nature of deities and the extent of their involvement in human affairs.

288 pp.   0-14-044265-0 $14.00

On Government

Translated with an Introduction by Michael Grant

These pioneering writings on the mechanics, tactics, and strategies of government were devised by the Roman Republic's most enlightened thinker.

432 pp.   0-14-044595-1 $13.95

On the Good Life

Translated with an Introduction by Michael Grant

This collection of Cicero's writings discusses duty, friendship, the training of a statesman, and the importance of moral integrity in the search for happiness.

384 pp.   0-14-044244-8 $13.00

Selected Political Speeches

Translated with an Introduction by Michael Grant

The seven speeches in this volume, annotated to supply the relevant political history of the period, include the speeches against the Catiline conspiracy as well as the first "Philippic" against Mark Antony.

336 pp.   0-14-044214-6 $14.00

Selected Works

Translated with an Introduction by Michael Grant

Divided into two parts—"Against Tyranny" and "How to Live"—this selection of Cicero's work reveals the private and public sides of his liberal personality and his opposition to oppressive and unparliamentary methods of government.

272 pp.   0-14-044099-2 $14.00

See The Portable Roman Reader.

WILLIAM CLARK

See Meriwether Lewis.

CARL VON CLAUSEWITZ
1780 – 1831, Prussian

On War
*Edited with an Introduction by
Anatol Rapoport and Translated by
Col. J. J. Graham*

This treatise presents the great Prussian
soldier's views both on total war and on
war as a continuation of foreign policy.

464 pp.   0-14-044427-0 $12.95

JOHN CLELAND
1709 – 1789, British

Fanny Hill
Or, Memoirs of a Woman of Pleasure
Edited with an Introduction by Peter Wagner

This infamous story of a prostitute's rise to
respectability holds a place in the history of
the English novel alongside the works of
Richardson, Fielding, and Smollett.

240 pp.   0-14-043249-3 $10.00

SAMUEL COLERIDGE
1772 – 1834, British

The Portable Coleridge
Edited by I. A. Richards

Faithfully representing all facets of
Coleridge's complex, haunted genius, this
wonderful collection brings together more
than seventy poems, including "The Rime
of the Ancient Mariner," "Christabel," and
"Kubla Khan," as well as letters to friends
and colleagues, selections from *Notebooks*
and *Table Talk*, political and philosophical
writings, literary criticism, and extensive
excerpts from *Biographia Literaria*.

640 pp.   0-14-015048-X $16.95

The Complete Poems
Edited by William Keach

Endowed with a surfeit of imagination and
creativity, Coleridge endlessly revised his
poetry, changing passages, adding new
lines, and even writing several variations
of the same poem. Faced with the challenge
of putting together an authoritative collection, William Keach presents the final
texts of all the poems published during
Coleridge's lifetime and a substantial
selection from the verse still in manuscript
at his death, together with comprehensive,
informative notes on significant variants.

672 pp.   0-14-042353-2 $15.95

Selected Poems
*Edited with an Introduction by
Richard Holmes*

This collection—divided into eight
categories of theme and genre, including
Conversation Poems, Ballads, Hill Walking
Poems, and Confessional Poems—redis-
covers Coleridge as a Romantic autobiographer of tremendous power, daring, and
range.

400 pp.   0-14-042429-6 $12.00

See English Romantic Verse.

WILKIE COLLINS
1824 – 1889, British

Armadale
*Edited with an Introduction and Notes by
John Sutherland*

This intricately plotted Victorian melodrama
draws on the substance and style of the
popular press of the day: fraud, bigamy,

drug addiction, and domestic poisonings all make appearances as Collins chronicles the evil ways of a spectacularly beautiful but unscrupulous woman.

752 pp.   0-14-043411-9 $11.95

The Law and the Lady

Edited with an Introduction by David Skilton

Here Collins introduced one of English literature's earliest woman detectives, Valeria Woodville, who investigates the murder of her husband's first wife in an attempt to prove his innocence.

432 pp.   0-14-043607-3 $10.95

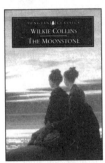

The Moonstone

Edited with an Introduction by Sandra Kemp

The Moonstone, a priceless yellow diamond, is looted from an Indian temple and given to Rachel Verinder on her eighteenth birthday, only to be stolen again that very night.

528pp.   0-14-043408-9 $8.00

Penguin Readers Guide Available

"The first, the longest, and the best of modern English detective novels."

—T. S. ELIOT

No Name

Edited with an Introduction and Notes by Mark Ford

In a tale of courage and confrontation in the world of rigid Victorian society, Collins creates a vivid and disturbing view of the hypocrisy inherent in the upper class.

640 pp.   0-14-043397-X $12.95

The Woman in White

Edited with an Introduction by Matthew Sweet

This thriller, revolving around the identities of two mysterious women, caused great excitement when it was published in 1860 and continues to enthrall.

720 pp.   0-14-143961-0 $7.95

Penguin Readers Guide Available

CARLO COLLODI
1826–1890, Italian, (b. Florence)

Pinocchio

The original Translation by M. A. Murray, revised by G. Tassinari with Illustrations by Charles Folkard and an Introduction by Jack Zipes

Italy's most famous fairy tale recounts the adventures of a mischievous puppet that becomes a boy. This sly and imaginative novel, alternately catastrophic and ridiculous, takes Pinocchio from one predicament to the next, and finally to an optimistic, if uncertain, ending.

224 pp.   0-14-243706-9 $10.00

CHRISTOPHER COLUMBUS
1451 - 1506, Italian, (b. Genoa)

The Four Voyages

Edited and Translated with an Introduction by J. M. Cohen

This volume includes Columbus's letters and logbook and remains the definitive primary source on his voyages to Cuba, Hispaniola, Jamaica, Trinidad, and Central America.

320 pp.   0-14-044217-0 $12.00

The Adventures and The Memoirs of Sherlock Holmes

With an Introduction by Iain Pears and Notes by Ed Glinert

On the docks, in cocaine dens, and in the new suburbs of Victorian London, Holmes unravels case after case—from "A Scandal in Bohemia" to "The Final Problem"—as Dr. Watson records his greatest strokes of brilliance.

576 pp.   **0-14-043771-1**   **$13.00**

The Hound of the Baskervilles

Edited with an Introduction and Notes by Christopher Frayling

The most popular of all Sherlock Holmes stories, *The Hound of the Baskervilles* combines the traditional detective tale with elements of horror and the supernatural. When a dead man is found surrounded by the footprints of a giant hound, blame is placed on a family curse—and it is up to Holmes and Watson to solve the mystery of the legend.

256 pp.   **0-14-043786-X**   **$8.00**

The Lost World and Other Thrilling Tales

Edited with an Introduction and Notes by Philip Gooden

In *The Lost World*, young journalist Edward Malone joins the irascible Professor Challenger on an expedition to a mysterious Jurassic-age plateau untouched by civilization. Also in this volume are *The Poison Belt*, "The Terror of Blue John Gap," and "The Horror of the Heights."

384 pp.   **0-14-043765-7**   **$9.00**

The Sign of Four

With an Introduction by Peter Ackroyd and Notes by Ed Glinert

Contentedly sitting in a cocaine-induced haze, Holmes is forced into action when a distressed and beautiful young woman comes begging his help. Every year since the disappearance of her father, Miss Morstan has received a rare and lustrous pearl. Now, summoned to meet her anonymous benefactor, she consults Holmes and Watson.

160 pp.   **0-14-043907-2**   **$7.00**

ARTHUR CONAN DOYLE

Born in Edinburgh in 1859, Sir Arthur Conan Doyle was educated at Stonyhurst, and later studied medicine at Edinburgh University, where he became the surgeon's clerk to Professor Joseph Bell, whose diagnostic method provided the model for the science of deduction perfected by Sherlock Homes. Conan Doyle set up as a doctor at Southsea, and it was while waiting for patients that he began to write. Sherlock Holmes first appeared in *A Study in Scarlet* in 1887. The Holmes stories attracted such a following that Conan Doyle felt the character overshadowed his other work and killed him off in "The Final Problem" (1893), but public demand compelled Conan Doyle to restore the detective to life. Conan Doyle himself died in 1930.

A Study in Scarlet

With an Introduction by Iain Sinclair and Notes by Ed Glinert

In the debut of literature's most famous sleuth, a dead man is discovered in a bloodstained room in Brixton. The only clues are a wedding ring, a gold watch, a pocket edition of Boccaccio's *Decameron*, and a word scrawled in blood on the wall. With this investigation begins the partnership of Holmes and Watson.

192 pp.   0-14-043908-0 $7.00

The Valley of Fear and Selected Cases

With an Introduction by Charles Palliser and Notes by Ed Glinert

A man with a bullet in his head, a secret message, and a bizarre series of clues that have Scotland Yard stumped put Holmes on the trail of the evil Moriarty. Along with the novella *The Valley of Fear*, this collection includes ten of Holmes's most intriguing cases from *The Return of Sherlock Holmes* (1905) and *His Last Bow* (1917).

448 pp.   0-14-043772-X $11.00

CONFUCIUS
551 – 479 B.C., Chinese

The Analects

Translated with an Introduction by D. C. Lau

The only reliable account of the philosophy of the legendary Chinese sage, the Lun-yü (*Analects*) constitute a collection of Confucius's sayings compiled by his pupils.

256 pp.   0-14-044348-7 $10.95

See The Portable World Bible.

JOSEPH CONRAD
1857 – 1924, British
(b. Poland)

The Portable Conrad

Edited by Morton Dauwen Zabel

This anthology includes the fictions *Typhoon, The Nigger of the "Narcissus," Heart of Darkness,* and *The Secret Sharer*; selections from Conrad's essays; and letters to Henry James, John Galsworthy, and others.

768 pp.   0-14-015033-1 $18.00

Chance

Neglected by her bankrupt father and rejected by her governess, Flora, desperate, takes refuge at sea on Captain Anthony's ship in this unrelenting novel of emotional isolation.

368 pp.   0-14-018654-9 $6.95

JOSEPH CONRAD

Born in Poland as Józef Teodor Konrad Korzeniowski in 1857, Joseph Conrad led an itinerant life until the mid-1890s, first in exile in Russia with his family and then as a seaman. During the course of his maritime career, he worked as a gunrunner, tried to commit suicide by shooting himself in the chest, and sailed throughout Asia and on the Congo River. Subsequently, he used these experiences in many of his stories. Ending his career as a seaman in 1894, he married Jessie George in 1896 and retired to Kent. Known particularly for his masterpieces *Heart of Darkness, Nostromo,* and *Lord Jim,* many of his works concern men struggling with their consciences in exotic and dangerous locales.

Heart of Darkness

Edited with an Introduction and Notes by Robert Hampson

Marlow, a seaman and wanderer, travels to the heart of the African continent in search of a corrupt man named Kurtz. Instead he discovers a horrible secret in this exploration of the subconscious and the grim reality of imperialism. This edition includes more than seventy pages of critical commentary, together with Conrad's "The Congo Diary," the record of his 1890 journey upon which the novel is based.

224 pp.   **0-14-018652-2**   **$7.95**

Lord Jim

Edited by Cedric Watts and Robert Hampson with an Introduction and Notes by Cedric Watts

Conrad's powerful portrait of a young idealist whose one moment of weakness marks his life forever probes the nature of innocence and experience, heroism and cowardice.

384 pp.   **0-14-018092-3**   **$5.95**

The Nigger of the "Narcissus"

Edited with an Introduction and Notes by Cedric Watts

In his third novel and first major work, Conrad explores the themes of political and psychological subversion when the "closed society" on a ship is threatened by a storm and by mutiny.

208 pp.   **0-14-018094-X**   **$12.95**

Nostromo

Edited with an Introduction and Notes by Martin Seymour-Smith

Conrad's pessimistic worldview colors this novel depicting the brutality of Latin American politics and the tragedies that inevitably ensue.

480 pp.   **0-14-018371-X**   **$10.00**

The Secret Agent

Edited with an Introduction and Notes by Martin Seymour-Smith

A black satire of British society, this chilling tale features amoral characters on both sides of the law—fatuous civil servants and corrupt policemen, bomb-carrying terrorists and sleazy pornographers.

272 pp.   **0-14-018096-6**   **$11.00**

The Shadow-Line

Edited with an Introduction by Jacques Berthoud

A young captain in crisis at sea must wrestle with his isolation and his conscience to cross the "shadow-line" between youth and adulthood. Written at the beginning of World War I, this is Conrad's attempt to open people's eyes to the meaning of war.

160 pp.   **0-14-018097-4**   **$10.95**

Tales of Unrest

Conrad exhibits his tenacious grasp of expression and hard experience gained from years at sea in this collection, which includes "Karain: A Memory," "The Idiots,"

"An Outpost of Progress," "The Return," and "The Lagoon."

208 pp.   0-14-018036-2 $8.95

Typhoon and Other Stories
Edited with an Introduction, Notes, and Appendix by Paul Kirschner

Originally published in 1903, this volume, written as Conrad bids farewell to his life as a seaman, contains "Typhoon," "Falk A Remembrance," "Amy Foster," and "Tomorrow."

320 pp.   0-14-018257-8 $9.00

Under Western Eyes
Edited with an Introduction and Notes by Paul Kirschner

Conrad deftly depicts the political turmoil in Russia in 1911 and its psychological repercussions in this novel about a student unwittingly caught in revolutionary intrigue.

400 pp.   0-14-018849-5 $11.00

Victory
Edited with an Introduction by Robert Hampson

A story of rescue and violent tragedy set in the Malayan archipelago, *Victory* combines high adventure with a sensitive portrayal of three drifters.

416 pp.   0-14-018978-5 $11.00

Youth/Heart of Darkness/ The End of the Tether
Edited with an Introduction and Notes by John Lyon

These three novels, originally published together, form a subtle, somewhat skeptical portrait of the "ages of man." Combining the traditional elements of adventure stories with psychological insights, these works demonstrate why Conrad has been hailed as a vital link between Victorian literature and the birth of the modern novel.

384 pp.   0-14-018513-5 $9.00

Adolphe
Translated with an Introduction by Leonard Tancock

This chronicle of the love affair between a young man and an older woman is based on the author's own stormy affair with Madame de Staël.

128 pp.   0-14-044134-4 $13.00

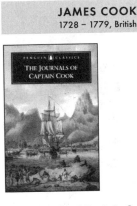

The Journals of Captain Cook
Selected and Edited with Introductions by Philip Edwards

In three expeditions between 1768 and 1779, Captain Cook charted the entire coast of New Zealand and the east coast of Australia, and brought back detailed descriptions of Tahiti, Tonga, and a host of previously unknown islands in the Pacific including the Hawaiian islands. This selection preserves the spirit and rhythm of the full narrative, as well as Cook's idiosyncratic spelling.

672 pp   17 maps   0-14-043647-2 $9.95

JAMES FENIMORE COOPER
1789 – 1851, American

The Deerslayer
Introduction by Donald E. Pease

In this acclaimed depiction of life during America's westward movement, part of *The Leatherstocking Tales*, Cooper describes the young manhood of Natty Bumppo, who remains one of the most significant characters in American literature.

384 pp.   **0-14-039061-8**   **$10.95**

The Last of the Mohicans
Introduction by Richard Slotkin

Tragic, fast-paced, and stocked with the elements of a classic Western adventure, this novel takes Natty Bumppo and his Indian friend Chingachgook through hostile Indian territory during the French and Indian War.

688 pp.   **0-14-039024-3**   **$9.95**

The Pathfinder
Introduction and Notes by Kay Seymour House

The fourth novel in *The Leatherstocking Tales* is a "romance," the story of Natty Bumppo's unsuccessful courtship of a young woman during the French and Indian War.

496 pp.   **0-14-039071-5**   **$12.00**

The Pioneers
Introduction and Notes by Donald A. Ringe

The first of *The Leatherstocking Tales* introduces the mythical hero Natty Bumppo in a portrait that contrasts the natural codes of Bumppo to the rigid legal and social structures of a new settlement.

448 pp.   **0-14-039007-3**   **$11.00**

The Prairie
Introduction by Blake Nevius

The final novel in Cooper's epic, *The Prairie* depicts Natty Bumppo at the end of his life, still displaying his indomitable strength and dignity.

384 pp.   **0-14-039026-X**   **$13.00**

The Spy
Introduction and Notes by Wayne Franklin

An historical adventure reminiscent of Sir Walter Scott's *Waverley* romances, Cooper's novel centers on Harvey Birch, a common man wrongly suspected of being a spy for the British.

464 pp.   **0-14-043628-6**   **$15.00**

PIERRE CORNEILLE
1606 – 1684, French

The Cid/Cinna/The Theatrical Illusion
Translated with an Introduction by John Cairncross

The Cid, Corneille's masterpiece set in medieval Spain, was the first great work of French classical drama; *Cinna*, written three years later in 1641, is a tense political drama, while *The Theatrical Illusion*, an earlier work, is reminiscent of Shakespeare's exuberant comedies.

288 pp.   **0-14-044312-6**   **$13.00**

MALCOLM COWLEY
1898 – 1989, American

Exile's Return
A Literary Odyssey of the 1920s

Introduction by Donald W. Faulkner

Hemingway, Fitzgerald, Dos Passos, and their Lost Generation confrères are memorably brought to life in Cowley's memoir.

352 pp.   0-14-018776-6 $14.95

"Far and away the best book about this generation."

—*THE NEW YORK TIMES*

STEPHEN CRANE
1871 – 1900, American

The Portable Stephen Crane
Edited by Joseph Katz

This essential collection of Crane's work includes three complete novels, *Maggie: A Girl of the Streets, George's Mother, The Red Badge of Courage*; nineteen short stories; and essays, letters, and poems.

576 pp.   0-14-015068-4 $15.95

Maggie: A Girl of the Streets
And Other Tales of New York

Edited with an Introduction by Larzer Ziff

This unflinching portrayal of the squalor and brutality of turn-of-the-century New York caused a scandal upon its initial publication in 1893. This volume also includes twelve other tales and sketches written between 1892 and 1896.

288 pp.   0-14-043797-5 $8.95

The Red Badge of Courage and Other Stories

Edited with an Introduction by Pascal Covici, Jr.

Here is one of the greatest novels ever written about war and its psychological effects on the individual soldier. This edition also includes the short stories "The Open Boat," "The Bride Comes to Yellow Sky," "The Blue Hotel," "A Poker Game," and "The Veteran."

304 pp.   0-14-039081-2 $8.95

See The Portable American Realism Reader.

J. HECTOR ST. JOHN DE CRÈVECOEUR
1735 – 1813, American
(b. France)

Letters from an American Farmer and Sketches of Eighteenth-Century America

Edited with an Introduction by Albert E. Stone

America's physical and cultural landscape is captured in these two classics of American history. *Letters* provides an invaluable view of the pre-Revolutionary and Revolutionary eras; *Sketches* details in vivid prose the physical setting in which American settlers created their history.

496 pp.   0-14-039006-5 $13.95

QUENTIN CRISP
1908 – 1999, American
(b. England)

The Naked Civil Servant

Preface by Michael Holroyd

Crisp describes his life with uninhibited exuberance in this classic autobiography. He came out as a gay man in 1931, when the slightest sign of homosexuality shocked public sensibilities, and he did so with provocative flamboyance, determined to spread the message that homosexuality did not exclude him or anyone else from the human race.

224 pp.   **0-14-118053-6**   **$12.95**

SOR JUANA INÉS DE LA CRUZ
1648 – 1695, Mexican

Poems, Protest, and a Dream
Selected Writings

Translated with Notes by Margaret Sayers Peden and an Introduction by Ilan Stavans

La Respuesta a Sor Filotea, the most famous prose work of Sor Juana Inés de la Cruz, is a passionate defense of the rights of women to study, teach, and write. Also included in this bilingual collection by Latin America's finest baroque poet is the epistemological poem "Primero Sueño," as well as autobiographical sonnets, religious poetry, secular love poems, playful verses, and lyrical tributes to New World culture.

304 pp.   **0-14-044703-2**   **$14.00**

QUOBNA OTTOBAH CUGOANO
c.1757 – unknown, African

Thoughts and Sentiments on the Evil of Slavery

Edited with an Introduction and Notes by Vincent Carretta

Thoughts and Sentiments, the most radical assault published by a writer of African descent on slavery, was Cugoano's response to the hypocrisy of Enlightenment Europe's attitude toward slavery. This is the only available edition of a neglected classic and includes Cugoano's correspondence with Edmund Burke, King George III, and William Pitt.

224 pp.   **0-14-044750-4**   **$11.95**

"A masterful achievement... Carretta's edition restores this important, but little known, author to his rightful place as a central figure in the Black Atlantic tradition of the eighteenth century."

—HENRY LOUIS GATES, JR

E. E. CUMMINGS
1894 – 1962, American

The Enormous Room
Edited with an Introduction and Glossary by Samuel Hynes

Drawn from Cummings's unexpected confinement in a French concentration camp, this rambunctious modern story reflects the essential paradox of his experience: to lose everything—all comforts, possessions, all rights and privileges—is to become free, and so to be saved.

384 pp.   0-14-118124-9 $13.00

"When a book like *The Enormous Room* manages to emerge from the morass of print we flounder in, it is time to take off your new straw hat and jump on it."
—JOHN DOS PASSOS

QUINTUS CURTIUS RUFUS
c. 1st cent. A.D., Roman

The History of Alexander
Translated by John Yardley with an Introduction and Notes by Waldemar Heckel

This history of Alexander's life provides by far the most plausible and haunting portrait of him: a brilliantly realized image of a man ruined by constant good fortune in his youth.

352 pp.   0-14-044412-2 $13.00

RICHARD HENRY DANA, JR.
1815 – 1882, American

Two Years Before the Mast
A Personal Narrative of Life at Sea
Edited with an Introduction and Notes by Thomas Philbrick

Dana's account of his passage as a common seaman from Boston around Cape Horn to California, and back, is a remarkable portrait of the seagoing life. Bringing to the public's attention for the first time the plight of the most exploited segment of the American working class, he forever changed readers' romanticized perceptions of life at sea.

576 pp.   0-14-039008-1 $11.95

DANTE
1265 – 1321, Florentine

The Portable Dante
Translated and Edited by Mark Musa

The Portable Dante captures the scope and fire of Dante's genius as thoroughly as any single volume can with the complete verse translations of *The Divine Comedy* and *La Vita Nuova*.

720 pp.   0-14-023114-5 $17.00

DANTE ALIGHIERI

Dante Alighieri was born in Florence in 1265 to a noble but impoverished family. At twenty, he married Gemma Donati, by whom he had four children. He had first met his muse Bice Portinari, whom he immortalized as Beatrice, in 1274, and when she died in 1290 he sought distraction by studying philosophy and theology and by writing *La Vita Nuova*. During this time he became involved in the strife between the Guelfs and the Ghibellines, becoming a prominent White Guelf. When the Black Guelfs came to power in 1302 Dante was condemned to exile. He took refuge first in Verona and after wandering from place to place, as far as Paris, he settled in Ravenna. There he completed *The Divine Comedy*, which he had begun in about 1308, if not later. Dante died in Ravenna in 1321.

The Divine Comedy
Volume 1: Inferno

Translated with an Introduction, Notes, and Commentary by Mark Musa

This vigorous new blank-verse translation of the poet's journey through the circles of Hell recreates for the modern reader the rich meanings that Dante's poem had for his contemporaries while preserving his simple, natural style and capturing the swift movement of the original Italian verse.

432 pp.   0-14-243722-0 $11.00
(Available January 2003)

The Divine Comedy
Volume 2: Purgatory

Translated with an Introduction, Notes, and Commentary by Mark Musa

400 pp.   0-14-044442-4 $12.00

The Divine Comedy
Volume 3: Paradise

Translated with an Introduction, Notes, and Commentary by Mark Musa

456 pp.   0-14-044443-2 $12.00

The Divine Comedy
Volume 1: Hell

Translated with an Introduction by Dorothy L. Sayers

Sayers's revered translation attempts to reveal Dante through his classic work as a poet of vivid personality: sublime, intellectual, humorous, simple, and tender.

352 pp.   0-14-044006-2 $12.00

The Divine Comedy
Volume 2: Purgatory

Translated with an Introduction by Dorothy L. Sayers

392 pp.   0-14-044046-1 $12.00

The Divine Comedy
Volume 3: Paradise

Translated by Dorothy L. Sayers and Barbara Reynolds with an Introduction by Barbara Reynolds

400 pp.   0-14-044105-0 $11.95

La Vita Nuova

Translated with an Introduction by Barbara Reynolds

This series of astonishing and tender love poems to Beatrice is interspersed with Dante's own explanations of their sources and detailed analyses of their structure.

128 pp.   0-14-044216-2 $11.00

CHARLES DARWIN
1809 – 1882, British

The Portable Darwin

Edited by Duncan M. Porter and Peter W. Graham

This essential collection includes selections from *The Origin of Species, The Voyage of the* Beagle, and *The Descent of Man*, as well as many of Darwin's scientific papers, travel writings, letters, and a family memorial.

592 pp.   0-14-015109-5 $16.00

Autobiographies

Edited by Michael Neve and Sharon Messenger with an Introduction by Michael Neve

Comprising a fragment Darwin wrote at the age of twenty-nine and the longer "Recollections" written in his later years, *Autobiographies* shows the great scientist weighing his career and private life in an engaging and revealing self-portrait.

112 pp.   0-14-043390-2 $11.00

The Origin of Species

Edited with an Introduction by J. W. Burrow

The foundation of our current understanding about the place of humanity in the universe, this scientific account of Darwin's evolutionary view of the world challenged contemporary beliefs about Divine Providence and the fixity of species.

480 pp.   0-14-043205-1 $10.95

The Voyage of the *Beagle*
Charles Darwin's Journal of Researches

Edited and Abridged with an Introduction by Janet Browne and Michael Neve

This shortened version of Darwin's journal of his five-year voyage on the HMS *Beagle* provides a profusion of detail about natural history and geology and illuminates the local people, politics, and customs of the places he visited.

448 pp.   0-14-043268-X $13.00

ELIZABETH DAVID
1914 – 1992, British

"Probably the greatest food writer we have."

—JAMES BEARD

French Provincial Cooking

Foreword by Julia Child

First published in 1962, David's culinary odyssey through provincial France forever changed the way we think about food. This delightful exploration of the traditions of French cooking includes recipes.

544 pp.   28 pp. b/w illustrations
0-14-118153-2 $16.00

Italian Food

Foreword by Julia Child

One of the first books to demonstrate the range of Italian cuisine, this volume distinguishes the complex traditions of Tuscany, Sicily, Lombardy, Umbria, and many other regions.

384 pp.   20 pp. b/w illustrations
0-14-118155-9 $15.00

ROBERTSON DAVIES
1913 – 1995, Canadian

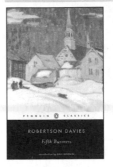

Fifth Business

With an Introduction by Gail Godwin

The first novel of Davies' celebrated Deptford Trilogy, *Fifth Business* stands alone as a remarkable story told by a rational man who discovers that the marvelous is only another aspect of the real.

288 pp.   0-14-118615-1 $14.00

Penguin Readers Guide Available

"A mature, accomplished, and altogether remarkable book, one of the best...it simply cannot be ignored."

—*THE WASHINGTON POST BOOK WORLD*

DANIEL DEFOE
1660 – 1731, British

A Journal of the Plague Year

Edited by Anthony Burgess and Christopher Bristow with an Introduction by Anthony Burgess

The shocking immediacy of Defoe's description of plague-racked London makes this one of the most convincing accounts of the Great Plague of 1665 ever written.

256 pp.   0-14-043015-6 $10.00

Moll Flanders

Edited with an Introduction by David Blewett

This tale of Moll Flanders's glorious, picaresque progress through vice, poverty, mishaps, and strange coincidences is an exuberant panorama of eighteenth-century England.

464 pp.   **0-14-043313-9**   **$8.95**

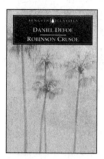

*Robinson Crusoe

Edited with an Introduction by John Richetti

Robinson Crusoe runs away to sea and after a number of adventures is shipwrecked on an uninhabited island. There he remains for twenty years with his friendly cannibal servant, Man Friday, until he is rescued and returned to England. This tale is of considerable moral significance; it sets up tension between God's purpose and Crusoe's very human impulses.

288 pp.   **0-14-143982-3**   **$8.00**

Roxana

Edited by David Blewett

Defoe's last novel, *Roxana*, depicts the decline and defeat of a woman tempted by the glamour of immortality.

416 pp.   **0-14-043149-7**   **$11.95**

JOHN W. DE FOREST
1826 – 1906, American

Miss Ravenel's Conversion from Secession to Loyalty

Edited with an Introduction and Notes by Gary Scharnhorst

Drawing on his own combat experience with the Union forces, De Forest crafted a riveting war novel whose honesty and gritty realism surpassed its contemporaries and anticipated the realistic war writings of Hemingway, Mailer, and Tim O'Brien.

544 pp.   **0-14-043757-6**   **$14.95**

"One of the best American novels ever written."
—WILLIAM DEAN HOWELLS

THOMAS DE QUINCEY
1785 – 1859, British

Confessions of an English Opium Eater

Edited with an Introduction by Alethea Hayter

De Quincey's powerful evocation of his constant and bitter struggle against the incapacity and torpor of opium use brings to life the "celestial" dreams and terrifying nightmares that transport and destroy the addict.

232 pp.   **0-14-043061-X**   **$12.00**

RENÉ DESCARTES
1596 – 1650, French

Discourse on Method and Related Writings

Translated with an Introduction and Notes by Desmond M. Clarke

This superb translation of Descartes's seminal contribution to modern philosophy and science puts the work in context by including extracts from his correspondence, the *Rules for Guiding One's Intelligence*, and *The World*.

256 pp.   **0-14-044699-0**   **$7.95**

Meditations and Other Metaphysical Writings

Translated with an Introduction by Desmond M. Clarke

Descartes's definitive statement on the foundations of his whole philosophy is brought together with extensive selections from the *Objections and Replies*, relevant correspondence, and other metaphysical writings from the period.

256 pp.   0-14-044701-6 $9.95

See The Portable Enlightenment Reader.

BERNAL DÍAZ DEL CASTILLO
1492 – c. 1581, Spanish

The Conquest of New Spain

Translated with an Introduction by J. M. Cohen

Fifty years after the startling defeat of the Aztecs by Hernán Cortés and his small band of adventurers, Díaz writes a magnificent account of his experience as a soldier in Cortés's army.

416 pp.   0-14-044123-9 $13.00

CHARLES DICKENS
1812 – 1870, British

*American Notes for General Circulation

Edited with an Introduction by Patricia Ingham

The youthful, still-rough United States of 1842 is vividly recalled in this journal of Dickens's famous tour, offering a fascinating view of the New World by one of the Old World's greatest writers and social thinkers.

352 pp.   0-14-043649-9 $13.00

Barnaby Rudge

Edited with an Introduction and Notes by Gordon W. Spence

In this superb novel about individuals caught in the horrors of the rebellion of apprentices against their masters, Dickens dramatizes his fascination with private murder and public violence.

768 pp.   0-14-043728-2 $10.95

Bleak House

Edited with an Introduction and Notes by Nicola Bradbury and Original Illustrations by Hablot K. Browne ("Phiz")

Part romance, part melodrama, part detective story, this novel centers around the interminable land inheritance suit of Jarndyce and Jarndyce and spreads out among a web of relationships in every level of society from the simple-minded but self-important Sir Leicester Dedlock to Jo the street sweeper. Its story is a metaphor for the decay and corruption at the heart of British society.

1,088 pp.   0-14-143972-6 $10.95

The Christmas Books
Volume 1: A Christmas Carol/The Chimes
Edited with an Introduction and Notes by Michael Slater

A Christmas Carol, with its unique blend of comedy and horror and the delightful grotesque, Scrooge, continues to mark our celebrations of Christmas. *The Chimes* is a provocative satire of how the wealthy celebrate New Year's Eve.

272 pp.   0-14-043068-7 $7.95

David Copperfield
Edited with an Introduction and Notes by Jeremy Tambling

Written in the form of an autobiography and intimately rooted in Dickens's own life, this is the evergreen story of a young man growing to maturity in both affairs of the world and affairs of the heart.

912 pp.   0-14-043494-1 $7.95

Penguin Readers Guide Available

*Dombey and Son
Edited with an Introduction and Notes by Andrew Sanders

Paul Dombey is a proud, heartless London merchant who runs his domestic affairs like a business. Rich in plot, language, and social commentary, this novel explores the possibility of redemption through familial love.

992 pp.   0-14-043546-8 $9.00

Great Expectations
Edited with an Introduction by David Trotter and Notes by Charlotte Mitchell

The orphan Pip's terrifying encounter with an escaped convict on the Kent marshes, and his mysterious summons to the house of Miss Havisham and her cold, beautiful ward Estella, form the prelude to his "great expectations." How Pip comes into a fortune, what he does with it, and what he discovers through his secret benefactor are the ingredients of his struggle for moral redemption.

560 pp.   0-14-143956-4 $8.00
(Available January 2003)

Penguin Readers Guide Available

CHARLES DICKENS

Charles Dickens was born in Portsmouth on February 7, 1812, the second of eight children. His father, a government clerk, was imprisoned for debt and Dickens was sent to work at the age of twelve. He became a reporter of parliamentary debates for the *Morning Chronicle* and began to publish sketches in various periodicals. *The Pickwick Papers* were published in 1836–37 and became a publishing phenomenon and Dickens's characters the center of a popular cult. He died on June 9, 1870. Dickens's popularity during his lifetime was exceptional but, as the distinguished literary critic Walter Allen said, his influence continues to be felt and "his work has become part of the literary climate within which Western man lives."

Hard Times

Edited with an Introduction by
Kate Flint

With its vivid depiction of Coketown's tall chimneys and its evocations of the dismal conditions of oppressed workers, *Hard Times* is certainly an "industrial novel." While it conveys deep concern for children, family, and home life, it is a heartfelt satire as well, targeting utilitarianism, self-help doctrines, and the mechanization of the mid-Victorian soul.

384 pp.   0-14-143967-X $8.00

Little Dorrit

Edited with an Introduction and Notes by
Stephen Wall and Helen Small

In one of the supreme masterpieces of his maturity, Dickens portrays a world of hypocrisy and shame, of exploiters and parasites, in a penetrating study of the psychology of imprisonment.

928 pp.   40 line drawings   1 map
0-14-043492-5   8.95

Martin Chuzzlewit

Edited with an Introduction and Notes by
Patricia Ingham and Original Illustrations
by Hablot K. Browne ("Phiz")

Moving from sunny farce to the grimmest reaches of criminal psychology, this study of selfishness and hypocrisy follows the lives of two brothers with very different fates.

864 pp.   38 b/w illustrations
0-14-043614-6 $10.95

*The Mystery of Edwin Drood

Edited with an Introduction and Notes by
David Paroissien

Unfinished at the time of Dickens's death, this novel explores the dark opium underworld and the uneasy and violent fantasies of its inhabitants.

432 pp.   0-14-043926-9 $8.00

Nicholas Nickleby

Edited with an Introduction by
Mark Ford

Around the central story of Nicholas Nickleby and the misfortunes of his family, Dickens creates a gallery of colorful characters: the muddle-headed Mrs. Nickleby, the gloriously theatrical Crummles, their protégée Miss Petowker, the pretentious Mantalinis, and the mindlessly cruel Squeers and his wife.

864 pp.   39 b/w illustrations
0-14-043512-3 $7.95

*The Old Curiosity Shop

Edited with an Introduction by
Norman Page

This novel contains some of Dickens's most bizarre characters, including the lecherous dwarf Quilp, as well as his most sentimental creation, the innocent Little Nell, who is destroyed by an evil world.

352 pp.   0-14-043742-8 $10.00

*Oliver Twist

Edited with an Introduction by
Philip Horne

This story of Oliver, a boy of unknown parentage who escapes a workhouse and embarks on a life of crime, shows how the lack of compassion in privileged society helps to make poverty a nursery of crime.

464 pp.   0-14-143974-2 $7.00

Our Mutual Friend

Edited with an Introduction and Notes by
Adrian Poole and Illustrations by
Marcus Stone

With a cast that embraces the "accumulated scum of humanity," this novel, the last Dickens completed before his death, probes into the crimes and guilt of dead fathers and its impact on a generation of sons and daughters.

928 pp.   0-14-043497-6 $10.95

The Pickwick Papers

Edited with an Introduction by
Mark Wormald

The story of the adventures of the charming, portly Sam Weller and his Pickwick Club catapulted the twenty-four-year-old Dickens to fame. This edition contains the original 1837 illustrations.

848 pp.   44 b/w illustrations   2 maps
0-14-043611-1 $9.95

Pictures from Italy
1850–1870

Edited with an Introduction and Notes by
Kate Flint

This thrilling travelogue—with Dickens's prolific powers of description—is the result of encounters with Italy's colorful street life, the visible signs of its richly textured past, and its urban desolation.

272 pp.   0-14-043431-3 $13.00

Selected Journalism
1850–1870

Edited with an Introduction and Notes by
David Pascoe

This collection showcases Dickens's much-admired talent for bringing touches of imagination and entertaining insights to factual accounts of life in London.

688 pp.   0-14-043580-8 $15.95

Selected Short Fiction

Edited with an Introduction and Notes by
Deborah A. Thomas

Divided into three sections—"Tales of the Supernatural," "Impressionistic Sketches," and "Dramatic Monologues"—this volume reveals Dickens's recurring concerns and places them clearly in the context of related elements in his novels.

368 pp.   0-14-043103-9 $8.95

Sketches by Boz

Edited with an Introduction by
Dennis Walder and Original Illustrations by
George Cruikshank

Dickens's first book, published when he was twenty-four, *Sketches by Boz* is a wonderful miscellany of reportage, observation, fancy, and fiction—all centering on the teeming metropolis of London. With its episodic structure, improvisational flourishes, comic invention, and cast of odd and eccentric characters, it introduces all the elements characteristic of Dickens's great novels.

688 pp.   0-14-043345-7 $15.00

CHARLES DICKENS
A Tale of Two Cities

A Tale of Two Cities

Edited with an Introduction and Notes by
Richard Maxwell

In this stirring tale of the French Revolution, Dickens reveals much about his own "psychological revolution," examining his fears and innermost conflicts through the actions of Charles Darnay, Sydney Carton, and Lucie Manette.

528 pp.   17 b/w illustrations
0-14-143960-2 $6.95

DENIS DIDEROT
1713 – 1784, French

Jacques the Fatalist and His Master
Translated by Michael Henry with an Introduction and Notes by Martin Hall

In this revolutionary novel, a leading figure of the Enlightenment celebrates the unpredictable nature of man and the world as he considers the behavior of the moral being and the philosophical dilemma of free will and determinism.

264 pp.   **0-14-044472-6**   **$12.95**

The Nun
Translated with an Introduction by Leonard Tancock

Conventional Christianity is sharply criticized in a tale about a woman confined to a convent against her will.

192 pp.   **0-14-044300-2**   **$12.00**

Rameau's Nephew and D'Alembert's Dream
Translated with Introductions by Leonard Tancock

In the form of dialogues, Diderot attacks stale conventions and offers a surprisingly modern view of life, sex, and morals.

240 pp.   **0-14-044173-5**   **$12.95**

See The Portable Enlightenment Reader.

CASSIUS DIO
c. 163 – 235, Roman

The Roman History
The Reign of Augustus
Translated by Ian Scott-Kilvert with an Introduction by John Carter

Following Rome's long road to peace after decades of civil war, Cassius Dio provides the fullest account of the reign of the first emperor in Books 50 through 60 of his Roman History.

368 pp.   **0-14-044448-3**   **$14.95**

JOHN DONNE
1572 – 1631, English

The Complete English Poems
Edited by A. J. Smith

Written in the natural rhythms of the speaking voice, John Donne's love poetry is considered some of the greatest of all time.

680 pp.   **0-14-042209-9**   **$15.00**

See The Metaphysical Poets.

JOHN DOS PASSOS
1896 – 1970, American

Three Soldiers
Introduction and Notes by Townsend Ludington

Based on his personal experiences in France during the First World War, Dos Passos's novel is a fierce denunciation of the military.

400 pp.   **0-14-118027-7**   **$11.00**

FYODOR DOSTOYEVSKY
1821 – 1881, Russian

The Brothers Karamazov
Translated with an Introduction and Notes by David McDuff

This striking new translation of Dostoyevsky's masterful drama of parricide and family rivalry chronicles the murder of Fyodor Karamazov and the subsequent investigation and trial. This excellent translation recaptures the sound, tone, and rough humor of the original, and includes extensive notes.

960 pp.   **0-14-044924-8**   **$14.00**

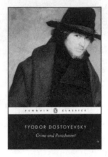

Crime and Punishment

Translated with an Introduction and Notes by David McDuff

Dostoyevsky's masterpiece of modern literature is a study in the psychology of the criminal mind, an indictment of social conditions, and an engrossing portrait of Raskolnikov's Russia.

656 pp.   0-14-044913-2 $13.00
(Available January 2003)

Penguin Readers Guide Available

The Devils

Translated with an Introduction by David Magarshack

Denounced by radical critics as the work of a reactionary, this powerful story of Russian terrorists who plot destruction only to murder one of their own seethes with provocative political opinions.

704 pp.   0-14-044035-6 $12.00

The Gambler/Bobok/A Nasty Story

Translated with an Introduction by Jessie Coulson

Conveying all the intensity and futility of an obsession, *The Gambler* is based on Dostoyevsky's firsthand experience; "Bobok" and "A Nasty Story" are two of the author's best darkly comic stories.

240 pp.   0-14-044179-4 $12.00

The House of the Dead

Translated with an Introduction by David McDuff

The four years Dostoyevsky spent in a Siberian prison inform this portrait of convicts, their diverse stories, and prison life, rendered in almost documentary detail.

368 pp.   0-14-044456-4 $10.95

The Idiot

Translated with an Introduction by David Magarshack

At the center of a novel that has the plot of a thriller, Dostoyevsky portrays the Christlike figure of Prince Myshkin, bringing readers face-to-face with human suffering and spiritual compassion.

624 pp.   0-14-044054-2 $12.00

Netochka Nezvanova

Translated with an Introduction by Jane Kentish

Written as a serial, this never-completed first publication treats many of the themes that dominate Dostoyevsky's later great novels.

176 pp.   0-14-044455-6 $12.00

Notes from the Underground/ The Double

Translated with an Introduction by Jessie Coulson

In *Notes from the Underground*, Dostoyevsky portrays a nihilist who probes into the dark underside of man's nature; *The Double* is Dostoyevsky's classic study of a psychological breakdown.

288 pp.   0-14-044252-9 $8.95

Poor Folk and Other Stories

Translated with an Introduction and Notes by David McDuff

Dostoyevsky's first great literary triumph, the novella *Poor Folk* is presented here, along with "The Landlady," "Mr. Prokharchin," and "Polzunkov."

288 pp.   0-14-044505-6 $9.95

The Village of Stepanchikovo

Translated with an Introduction by Ignat Avsey

This work introduces a Dostoyevsky

unfamiliar to most readers, revealing his unexpected talents as a humorist and satirist. While its lighthearted tone and amusing plot make it a joy to read, it also contains the prototypes of characters who appear in his later works.

224 pp.   0-14-044658-3 $12.00

See The Portable Nineteenth-Century Russian Reader.

FREDERICK DOUGLASS
1818 – 1895, American

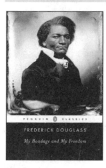

My Bondage and My Freedom

Edited with an Introduction and Notes by John David Smith

Ex-slave Frederick Douglass's second autobiography—written after ten years of reflection following his legal emancipation in 1846 and his break with his mentor William Lloyd Garrison—catapulted Douglass into the international spotlight as the foremost spokesman for American blacks, both freed and slave.

384 pp.   0-14-043918-8 $13.00
(Available February 2003)

Narrative of the Life of Frederick Douglass, an American Slave

Edited with an Introduction by Houston A. Baker, Jr.

The preeminent example of the American slave narrative, Douglass's personal account of life in the pre–Civil War American South is a telling indictment of the institution of slavery and of the people and the country that allowed it to flourish.

160 pp.   0-14-039012-X $8.95

Great Books Foundation Readers Guide Available

ARTHUR CONAN DOYLE
1859 – 1930, Scottish

See Conan Doyle.

FREDERICK DOUGLASS

Born Frederick Augustus Washington Bailey in 1818 in Tuckahoe, Maryland, Frederick Douglass changed his surname to conceal his identity after escaping slavery in 1838 and making his way to Philadelphia and New York. Having been taught to read by the wife of one of his former owners, Douglass wrote later that literacy was his "pathway from slavery to freedom," and in 1845 he published his instantly bestselling *Narrative of the Life of Frederick Douglass, an American Slave*, followed by *My Bondage and My Freedom* (1855) and *Life and Times of Frederick Douglass* (1881, 1892). Beginning a long career in journalism in 1847, he later held several appointed positions in the United States Government. Renowned as the foremost African American advocate against slavery and segregation of his time, he died in Washington, D.C., in 1895, and after lying in state in the nation's capital, was buried in the Mount Hope Cemetery in Rochester, New York.

THEODORE DREISER
1871 – 1945, American

Jennie Gerhardt
Edited with an Introduction and Notes by James L. W. West III

This unexpurgated edition of Dreiser's 1911 novel about a woman compromised by birth and fate not only restores passages critical of society but offers a stronger heroine and a clearer picture of the immigrant milieu into which she—and Dreiser—were born.

432 pp.   0-14-018710-3 $14.00

Sister Carrie
Introduction by Alfred Kazin

This subversive landmark novel, restored and unexpurgated, portrays the social world of turn-of-the-century United States through the story of a woman who becomes the mistress of a wealthy man.

496 pp.   0-14-018828-2 $12.95

See The Portable American Realism Reader.

JOHN DRYDEN
1631 – 1700, English

Selected Poems
Edited with an Introduction and Notes by Steven N. Zwicker and David Bywaters

This authoritative edition of Dryden's broad career of poetic achievements grasps the finest works of his political and spiritual imagination, including "Annus Mirabilis," "Absalom and Achitophel" and "The Hind and the Panther."

592 pp.   0-14-043914-5 $14.00

W. E. B. DU BOIS
1868 – 1963, American

The Souls of Black Folk
Introduction by Donald B. Gibson and Notes by Monica M. Elbert

Social reformer and activist W. E. B. Du Bois expresses his passionate concern for the future of his race in this 1903 collection of essays depicting the psychological effects of segregation on American society. This classic exploration of the moral and intellectual issues surrounding the perception of blacks within American society remains an important document of our social and political history.

288 pp.   0-14-018998-X $9.95

See The Portable Harlem Renaissance Reader.

ALEXANDRE DUMAS
1802 – 1870, French

The Count of Monte Cristo
Translated with an Introduction and Notes by Robin Buss

This is the quintessential novel of revenge, complete with a mysterious and implacable hero who will stop at nothing to punish the men who betrayed him and brought about his unjust imprisonment. It is a tale of nonstop adventure, intrigue, and excitement.

1,136 pp.   0-14-044926-4 $12.95

The Man in the Iron Mask

*Translated by Joachim Neugroschel with an
Introduction by Francine du Plessix Gray*

The celebrated conclusion of Dumas's cycle
of the Musketeers concerns a mysterious
masked prisoner whose fate is entangled
with a corrupt king, and the Musketeers
must fight through their conflicting loyalties.

448 pp.   0-14-043924-2 $13.00

(Available April 2003)

The Three Musketeers

*Translated with an Introduction by
Lord Sudley*

Based on historic fact, this is the stirring,
romantic story of d'Artagnan, Athos,
Porthos, and Aramis, and their fight to
preserve the honor of their Queen.

720 pp.   0-14-044025-9 $11.00

GERALD DURRELL
1925 – 1994, British

My Family and Other Animals

When the Durrell family can no longer
endure the damp, gray English climate, they
do what any sensible family would do: sell
their house and relocate to the sun-soaked
Greek island of Corfu. There, ten-year-old
Gerry pursues his interest in natural history
with a joyful passion, revealing the engrossing, hidden world of the island's fauna.

272 pp.   0-14-028902-X $14.00

MEISTER ECKHART
c. 1260 – 1327, German

Selected Writings

*Edited and Translated with an
Introduction by Oliver Davies*

Including some works translated into
English for the first time, this volume illuminates the German Dominican Meister
Eckhart's synthesis of traditional Christian
belief and Greek metaphysics, yielding a
boldly speculative philosophy founded on
"oneness" of the universe and on a God at
once personal and transcendent.

336 pp.   0-14-043343-0 $13.95

ALEXANDRE DUMAS (*PÈRE*)

Alexandre Dumas was born in 1802 at Villers-Cotterêts. His father, the illegitimate
son of a marquis, was a general in the Revolutionary armies, but died when Dumas
was only four. Brought up in straitened circumstances and receiving very little
education, he nevertheless entered the household of the future king, Louis-Phillipe,
and began reading voraciously. Later he entered the *cénacle* of Charles Nodier and
began to write. In 1829 he embarked on twenty years of successful playwriting, and
in 1839 he turned his attention to writing historical novels, the most successful of
which were *The Count of Monte Cristo* (1844–5) and *The Three Musketeers* (1844).
In addition to his many novels, Dumas wrote travel books, children's stories, and
his *Mémoires*, which describe most amusingly his early life, his entry into Parisian
literary circles, and the 1830 Revolution. He died in 1870.

The Absentee

Edited with an Introduction by Heidi Thompson

Maria Edgeworth's sparkling satire about an Anglo-Irish family—more concerned with London society than their duties and responsibilities to those who live and work on their Irish estates—is also a landmark novel of morality and social realism.

320 pp.   **0-14-043645-6**   **$10.95**

Castle Rackrent and Ennui

Edited with an Introduction by Marilyn Butler

These are two stylish novels of Anglo-Irish relations: *Castle Rackrent* is an Irish family history unreliably narrated by a loyal servant; *Ennui* is a "confession" by an aristocrat caught up in Ireland's 1798 revolution.

368 pp.   **0-14-043320-1**   **$13.00**

Ormond

Edited with an Introduction and Notes by Claire Connolly

Blending issues of moral development with questions about the shape of Ireland's political future, Edgeworth emphasizes the importance of education and upbringing, as opposed to inheritance and lineage, in the tale of Harry Ormond, a handsome orphan determined to make his way in the world.

352 pp.   **0-14-043644-8**   **$12.00**

Two Lives of Charlemagne

Translated with an Introduction by Lewis Thorpe

Einhard offers a factual account of Charlemagne's personal life and his achievements in warfare, learning, art, and statesmanship, while Notker's anecdotal approach presents Charlemagne as a near-legendary figure.

240 pp.   **0-14-044213-8**   **$14.00**

Adam Bede

Edited with an Introduction by Stephen Gill

The story of a beautiful country girl's seduction by a local squire and the bitter consequences is told with Eliot's peculiar, haunting power.

608 pp.   **0-14-043121-7**   **$8.95**

Daniel Deronda

Edited with an Introduction and Notes by Terence Cave

In *Daniel Deronda*, her remarkable final novel, Eliot set out to come to terms with the British Jews, a society-within-a-society of which her contemporaries seemed to be either oblivious or contemptuous. Eliot weaves her plot strands intimately, infusing them with her insights about human nature and daring the readers of *Middlemarch* and *Adam Bede* to consider realms of experience completely new to the Victorian novel.

848 pp.   **0-14-043427-5**   **$9.95**

Felix Holt: The Radical

Edited with an Introduction and Notes by Lynda Mugglestone

Esther Lyon, the heroine, must choose between two men—one of independent wealth and one who is a political rascal—while also deciding her fate as a woman.

576 pp.   **0-14-043435-6**   **$12.95**

The Lifted Veil and Brother Jacob

Edited with an Introduction by Sally Shuttleworth

The two novellas in this volume—one Gothic, the other satiric—offer a dark counterpoint to the warm humanism of Eliot's novels.

160 pp.   **0-14-043517-4**   **$9.00**

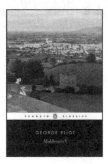

Middlemarch

Edited with an Introduction and Notes by Rosemary Ashton

This superb novel, Eliot's finest achievement, portrays the shape and texture of a rising provincial town of the 1830s through the remarkable story of determined heroine Dorothea Brooke—an idealist and a woman of conviction trapped in an agonizing marriage to the egotistical Mr. Casaubon.

880 pp.   **0-14-143954-8**   **$10.00**

(Available April 2003)

The Mill on the Floss

Edited with an Introduction and Notes by A. S. Byatt

This affectionate and perceptive portrayal of childhood and adolescence in rural England features an imaginative heroine whose spirit closely resembles Eliot's own.

696 pp.   **0-14-143962-9**   **$8.95**

Romola

Edited with an Introduction by Dorothea Barrett

Published in 1863, *Romola* probes into the issues of gender and learning and of desire and scholarship.

688 pp.   **0-14-043470-4**   **$10.95**

Scenes of Clerical Life

Edited with an Introduction and Notes by Jennifer Gribble

These stories constitute Eliot's fictional debut and contain what became her enduring themes: the impact of religious controversy and social change in provincial life, and the power of love to transform the lives of individual men and women.

416 pp.   **1 map**   **0-14-043638-3**   **$8.95**

"The exquisite truth and delicacy, both of the humour and the pathos of those stories, I have never seen the like of."

—CHARLES DICKENS

Silas Marner

Edited with an Introduction and Notes by David Carroll

In a novel that combines the emotional and moral satisfaction of a fairy tale with the realism and intelligence that are her hallmarks, Eliot counterpoints Silas's experiences with those of Godfrey Cass, the rich squire who is Eppie's father.

240 pp.   **0-14-143975-0**   **$6.95**

T. S. ELIOT
1888 – 1965, British
(b. America)
Nobel Prize winner

The Waste Land and Other Poems

Edited with an Introduction and Notes by Frank Kermode

This new edition collects all of the poems published in Eliot's first three volumes of verse, including "The Love Song of J. Alfred Prufrock," "Portrait of a Lady," "Gerontion," "Sweeney Among the Nightingales," and "Whispers of Immortality." Along with *The Waste Land*, as Frank Kermode writes in his Introduction, "the early poems establish what the later poems confirm: taken together, they constitute a strong claim for Eliot's primacy among twentieth-century poets in English."

144 pp.   0-14-243731-X $8.00
(Available March 2003)

RALPH WALDO EMERSON
1803 – 1882, American

The Portable Emerson

Edited by Carl Bode and Malcolm Cowley

This essential guide to Emerson comprises essays, poems, journals, and letters. Includes Emerson's first book, *Nature*, in its entirety; "The American Scholar," "Self-Reliance," and "The Poet."

720 pp.   0-14-015094-3 $16.95

Selected Essays

Edited with an Introduction by Larzer Ziff

This sampling includes fifteen essays that highlight the formative and significant ideas of this central American thinker: "Nature," "The American Scholar," "An Address Delivered Before the Senior Class in Divinity College, Cambridge," "Man the Reformer," "History," "Self-Reliance," "The Over-Soul," "Circles," "The Transcendentalist," "The Poet," "Experience," "Montaigne: Or, the Skeptic," "Napoleon: Or, the Man of the World," "Fate," and "Thoreau."

360 pp.   0-14-243762-X $13.00
See Nineteenth-Century American Poetry *and* The Portable Romanic Poets.

FRIEDRICH ENGELS
1820 – 1895, German

The Condition of the Working Class in England

Edited with a Foreword by Victor Kiernan

Introducing ideas further developed in *The Communist Manifesto*, this savage indictment of the bourgeoisie studies British factory, mine, and farm workers—graphically portraying the human suffering born of the Industrial Revolution.

304 pp.   0-14-044486-6 $13.95
See Karl Marx.

OLAUDAH EQUIANO
c. 1735 – 1797, British
(b. West Africa)

The Interesting Narrative and Other Writings

Edited with an Introduction and Notes by Vincent Carretta

An account of the slave trade by a native African, former slave, and loyal British subject, *The Interesting Narrative* is both an exciting, often terrifying, adventure story and an important precursor to such famous nineteenth-century slave narratives as Frederick Douglass's autobiography.

368 pp.   0-14-043485-2 $10.95

ERASMUS
c. 1469 – 1536, Dutch

Praise of Folly

*Translated by Betty Radice with an
Introduction and Notes by A. H. T. Levi*

The best introduction to the work of
Erasmus, this is one of the finest masterpieces of the sixteenth century, superbly
translated and reflecting the latest scholarly
research.

256 pp. 0-14-044608-7 $10.95

WOLFRAM VON ESCHENBACH
c. 1170 – c. 1220, Bavarian

Parzival

Translated by A. T. Hatto

A prose translation of Wolfram von
Eschenbach's thirteenth-century narrative
poem recreates and completes the story of
the Holy Grail, left unfinished by Chrétien
de Troyes.

448 pp. 0-14-044361-4 $14.00

Willehalm

*Translated by Marion E. Gibbs and
Sidney M. Johnson*

A martial epic and a tragic romance, this is
the story of the consequences of Willehalm's elopement with Giburc, written by
the greatest narrative poet of the German
Middle Ages.

320 pp. 0-14-044399-1 $18.00

EURIPIDES
c. 484 – 406 B.C., Greek

Alcestis and Other Plays

*Translated by John Davie with an
Introduction and Notes by
Richard Rutherford*

Euripides was the first of the great Greek
tragedians to depict the figures of ancient
mythology as fallible human beings.
Shocking to his contemporaries, the four
plays in this collection—*Alcestis, Medea,
The Children of Heracles,* and *Hippolytus*—
are uncannily modern not only in their
insights but also in their realistic portraits
of women, both good and evil.

240 pp. 0-14-044643-5 $11.00

The Bacchae and Other Plays

*Translated with an Introduction by
Philip Vellacott*

Four plays—*Ion* and *Helen* in prose and
The Bacchae and *The Women of Troy*
with dialogue rewritten in verse—depict
the guilt and suffering of war, and the
subsequent loss of faith.

256 pp. 0-14-044044-5 $11.00

Electra and Other Plays

*Translated by John Davie with an
Introduction by Richard Rutherford*

Written in the period from 426 to 415 B.C.,
during the fierce struggle for supremacy
between Athens and Sparta, these five
plays are haunted by the horrors of war,
and in particular its impact on women.
Included are: *Andromache, Electra, Hecabe,
Suppliant Women,* and *Trojan Women.*

220 pp. 0-14-044668-0 $9.95

Heracles and Other Plays

Translated by John Davie with an Introduction by Richard Rutherford

The dramas that Euripides wrote toward the end of his life are remarkable for their stylistic innovation and adventurous plots. In the plays in this collection—*Heracles, Cyclops, Iphigenia Among the Taurians, Ion,* and *Helen*—he weaves plots full of startling shifts of tone and exploits the comic potential found in traditional myth.

416 pp.   0-14-044725-3 $11.00

Medea and Other Plays

Translated with an Introduction by Philip Vellacott

Euripides was the first playwright to use the chorus as commentator, to put contemporary language into the mouths of heroes, and to interpret human suffering without reference to the gods. These verse translations of *Medea, Hecuba, Electra,* and *Mad Heracles* capture all the brilliance of his work.

208 pp.   0-14-044929-9 $10.00

Orestes and Other Plays

Translated with an Introduction by Philip Vellacott

Spanning the last twenty-four years of Euripides's career, this volume includes *The Children of Heracles, Andromache, The Suppliant Women, The Phoenician Women, Orestes,* and *Iphigenia in Aulis.*

448 pp.   0-14-044259-6 $11.00

See The Portable Greek Reader.

EUSEBIUS
c. 260 – c. 339, Palestinian

The History of the Church

Edited and Revised with an Introduction by Andrew Louth and Translated by G. A. Williamson

A clear, readable translation of the ten books of Bishop Eusebius's *Ecclesiastical History* —the only surviving record of the Church during its crucial first three hundred years —this edition recounts the martyrdoms, heresies, schisms, and proceedings that led to Nicaea and other great church councils.

440 pp.   0-14-044535-8 $15.95

RICHARD FARIÑA
1937 – 1966, American

Been Down So Long It Looks Like Up to Me

Introduction by Thomas Pynchon

In this classic novel of the 1960s—an unerring, corrosively comic depiction of a campus in revolt—Fariña evokes the period as precisely, wittily, and poignantly as F. Scott Fitzgerald captured the Jazz Age.

352 pp.   0-14-018930-0 $15.00

JAMES T. FARRELL
1904 – 1979, American

Studs Lonigan

Introduction by Ann Douglas

The renowned trilogy of the youth, early manhood, and death of Studs Lonigan is here collected in one volume.

912 pp.   0-14-118673-9 $20.00

> **"Farrell was perhaps the most powerful naturalist who ever worked in the American tradition."**
> —ALFRED KAZIN

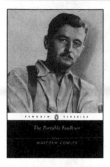

The Portable Faulkner

Edited by Malcolm Cowley

In prose of biblical grandeur and feverish intensity, William Faulkner reconstructed the history of the American South as a tragic legend of courage and cruelty, gallantry and greed, futile nobility and obscene crimes. This essential collection offers a panorama of life in Yoknapatawpha County by means of stories and episodes from ten of Faulkner's books, including "The Bear," "Spotted Horses," and "Old Man"; as well as the Nobel Prize Address, a chronology of the Compsons, and a unique map surveyed by Faulkner himself.

768 pp.   0-14-243728-X $16.00
(Available March 2003)

"The job is splendid. . . . By God, I didn't know myself what I had tried to do, and how much I had succeeded."

—WILLIAM FAULKNER

Ruth Hall
A Domestic Tale of the Present Time

Introduction and Notes by
Susan Belasco Smith

In *Ruth Hall*, one of the bestselling novels of the 1850s, Fanny Fern drew heavily on her own experiences: the death of her first child and her beloved husband, a bitter estrangement from her family, and her struggle to make a living as a writer. Written as a series of short vignettes and snatches of overheard conversations, it is as unconventional in style as in substance and strikingly modern in its impact.

384 pp.   0-14-043640-5 $13.00

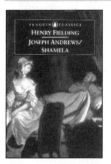

Joseph Andrews/Shamela

Edited with an Introduction by
Judith Hawley

Joseph Andrews, Fielding's first full-length novel, is the story of a young man's determination to save his virtue—and one of the richest satires ever written. In *Shamela*, a brilliant parody of Samuel Richardson's *Pamela*, a virtuous servant girl long resists her master's advances and is eventually "rewarded" with marriage.

432 pp.   0-14-043386-4 $9.95

Tom Jones
Edited with an Introduction by
R. P. C. Mutter

A novel rich in incident and coincidence, this picaresque tale of a lusty, handsome young man and his amorous adventures mocks the literary—and moral—conventions of Fielding's time.

912 pp.   0-14-043009-1 $8.95

SARAH FIELDING
1710 – 1768, English

The Adventures of David Simple
Edited with an Introduction and Notes by
Linda Bree

Both a witty satire of eighteenth-century London and a serious examination of the moral and social issues facing men and women of the day, this novel tells the story of one man's search for truth, honesty, and friendship in a corrupt world.

336 pp.   0-14-043747-9 $14.00

F. SCOTT FITZGERALD
1896 – 1940, American

The Beautiful and Damned
Introduction by Kermit Vanderbilt

It is the vivid depiction of life amid the glitter of Jazz Age New York that transforms the now-familiar stories about F. Scott and Zelda Fitzgerald's early marriage—as well as Fitzgerald's impressions of several well-known literary figures—into a captivating work of fiction.

448 pp.   0-14-118087-0 $10.00

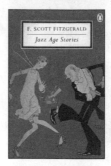

Jazz Age Stories
Edited with an Introduction and Notes by
Patrick O'Donnell

An original collection of Fitzgerald's greatest tales from the "Roaring '20s," *Jazz Age Stories* includes "Bernice Bobs Her Hair," "The Ice Palace," and "A Diamond as Big as the Ritz."

400 pp.   0-14-118048-X $9.95

This Side of Paradise
Edited with an Introduction and Notes by
Patrick O'Donnell

The story of Amory Blaine's adolescence and undergraduate days at Princeton, *This Side of Paradise* captures the essence of an American generation struggling to define itself in the aftermath of World War I and the destruction of the "old order."

320 pp.   0-14-018976-9 $9.95

GUSTAVE FLAUBERT
1821 – 1880, French

Bouvard and Pécuchet
with The Dictionary of Accepted Ideas
Translated with an Introduction by
A. J. Krailsheimer

Unfinished at the time of Flaubert's death in 1880, *Bouvard and Pécuchet* features two Chaplinesque figures in a farce that mocks bourgeois stupidity and the banality of intellectual life in France.

336 pp.   0-14-044320-7 $19.00

Flaubert in Egypt

Edited and Translated with an Introduction by Francis Steegmuller

At once a classic of travel literature and a penetrating portrait of a "sensibility on tour," *Flaubert in Egypt* wonderfully captures the young writer's impressions during his 1849 voyages. Using diaries, letters, travel notes, and the evidence of Flaubert's traveling companion, Maxime Du Camp, Francis Steegmuller reconstructs his journey through the bazaars and brothels of Cairo and down the Nile to the Red Sea.

240 pp.   **0-14-043582-4**   **$14.00**

*Madame Bovary

Translated with an Introduction by Geoffrey Wall and a Preface by Michèle Roberts

Flaubert's landmark story unfolds the desperate love affair of Emma Bovary, the bored provincial housewife who abandons her husband in defiance of bourgeois values.

320 pp.   **0-14-044912-4**   **$10.00**

(Available January 2003)

Salammbô

Translated with an Introduction by A. J. Krailsheimer

An epic story of lust, cruelty, and sensuality, this historical novel is set in Carthage in the days following the First Punic War with Rome.

288 pp.   **0-14-044328-2**   **$12.95**

Sentimental Education

Translated with an Introduction by Robert Baldick

Flaubert skillfully recreates the fiber of his times and society in this novel of a young man's romantic attachment to an older woman.

432 pp.   **0-14-044141-7**   **$8.00**

Three Tales

Translated with an Introduction by Robert Baldick

In *A Simple Life*, Flaubert recounts the life of a pious servant girl; in *The Legend of St. Julian*, Hospitaller gives insight into medieval mysticism; and *Hérodias* is a powerful story of the martyrdom of St. John the Baptist.

128 pp.   **0-14-044106-9**   **$9.95**

GUSTAVE FLAUBERT

Born in Rouen in 1821, Gustave Flaubert was the son of a brilliant surgeon and grew to be strongly critical of bourgeois society. He quit law school in 1841 after being diagnosed with epilepsy and devoted himself to writing. His stormy affair with the poet Louise Colet ended after nine years in 1855. His masterpiece *Madame Bovary*, based on two different true stories, was published the next year, and Flaubert narrowly escaped being convicted for immorality due to its daring content. His work reflects his passion for poetic prose and, at the same time, relentless objectivity. Flaubert counted among his friends George Sand, Turgenev, Zola, and his protégé Maupassant.

THEODOR FONTANE
1819 – 1898, Prussian

*Effi Briest
Translated by Hugh Rorrison and Helen Chambers

This story of a woman's adultery and its consequences is a stunning portrait of the rigidity of the Prussian aristocracy in the mid–nineteenth century.

256 pp.   0-14-044766-0 $13.00

"I recommend *Effi Briest*. . . . First-class —uplifting, shaming, beautiful enough to make you weep."

—THOMAS MANN

FORD MADOX FORD
1873 – 1939, British

The Fifth Queen
With an Introduction by A. S. Byatt

This masterful example of historical fiction is Ford's acclaimed portrait of Henry VIII's controversial fifth Queen, the beautiful, clever, and outspoken Katherine Howard.

608 pp.   0-14-118130-3 $12.95

Penguin Readers Guide Available

The Good Soldier

Ford explores the deceptions of Edward Ashburnham, an impeccable British gentleman and soldier with an overbearing ruthlessness in affairs of the heart.

240 pp.   0-14-018081-8 $11.00

Parade's End
Introduction by Robie Macaulay

Published in four parts from 1924 to 1928, Ford's extraordinary novel centers on Christopher Tietjens, an officer and a gentleman, whose tale is told from the secure, orderly world of Edwardian England and follows him into the horrors of the First World War.

840 pp.   0-14-118661-5 $18.00

"A breathtaking, Herculean project . . . An achievement of the order of Proust's *Remembrance of Things Past*."

—THE NEW YORK TIMES

E. M. FORSTER
1879 – 1970, British

"One of the wisest and the warmest, one of the gentlest and yet one of the most sharp-edged, of the great modern English writers."

—MALCOLM BRADBURY

Howards End
Edited with an Introduction and Notes by David Lodge

A chance acquaintance bringing together the prosperous bourgeois Wilcox family and the clever, cultured, and idealistic Schlegel sisters sets in motion a chain of events that will entangle three families and their aspirations for personal and social harmony.

352 pp.   0-14-118213-X $11.00

Penguin Readers Guide Available

A Room with a View

Edited with an Introduction and Notes by Malcolm Bradbury

Lucy Honeychurch is torn between the expectations of her world and the passionate yearnings of her heart. Within this sparkling love story, Forster has couched a perceptive examination of class structure and a penetrating social comedy.

256 pp.   0-14-118329-2 $9.95

Penguin Readers Guide Available

Selected Stories

Edited with an Introduction and Notes by David Leavitt and Mark Mitchell

The twelve stories in this collection are rich in irony and often feature violent events, discomforting coincidences, and other disruptive happenings that throw the characters' perceptions and beliefs off balance. Included are "The Story of a Panic," "The Machine Stops," "The Eternal Moment," and others.

224 pp.   0-14-118619-4 $13.00

HANNAH WEBSTER FOSTER

See William Hill Brown.

GEORGE FOX
1624 – 1691, English

The Journal

Edited with an Introduction and Notes by Nigel Smith

The fascinating autobiographical account of struggles, hardships, and successes from the father of Quakerism is presented in an edition that enhances the coherence of the main narrative while retaining the immediacy and excitement of the original. Extracts from Fox's letters and travelogues and William Penn's Preface to the first printed edition supplement the main text.

576 pp.   0-14-043399-6 $16.00

ANATOLE FRANCE
1844 – 1924, French
Nobel Prize winner

The Gods Will Have Blood

Translated with an Introduction by Frederick Davies

Set during the French Revolution in the fifteen months preceding the fall of Robespierre, this novel by Nobel Prize winner Anatole France powerfully re-creates the Terror—a period of intense and virtually indiscriminate violence.

256 pp.   0-14-010457-0 $12.95

BENJAMIN FRANKLIN
1706 – 1790, American

The Autobiography and Other Writings

Edited with an Introduction by Kenneth A. Silverman

Tracing his rise from a printer's apprentice to an internationally famous scientist, inventor, statesman, legislator, and diplomat, Franklin distills the complex and passionate intellectual strivings of his life into a persona extolling industry and sober virtue. Also included here are selections from Franklin's essays and letters.

320 pp.   0-14-243760-3 $8.00

See The Portable Enlightenment Reader.

JAMES FRAZER
1854 – 1941, Scottish

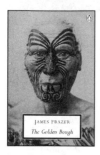

The Golden Bough
Abridged Edition

Introduction by George W. Stocking, Jr.

A monumental study of magic, folklore, and religion, *The Golden Bough* draws on the myths, rites and rituals, totems and taboos, and customs of ancient European civilizations and primitive cultures throughout the world. Frazer's ideas had a far-reaching impact on the course of modern anthropology, philosophy, and psychology, and on the writing of literary figures such as D. H. Lawrence, Ezra Pound, and T. S. Eliot.

944 pp.   0-14-018931-9 $14.95

"Perhaps no book has had so decisive an effect upon modern literature."

—LIONEL TRILLING

HAROLD FREDERIC
1856 – 1898, American

The Damnation of Theron Ware

Introduction by Scott Donaldson

A candid inquiry into the intertwining of religious and sexual fervor, and a telling portrait of the United States at the end of the nineteenth century, this novel foreshadows the rise of naturalism in American literature.

512 pp.   0-14-039025-1 $13.95

MARY E. WILKINS FREEMAN
1852 – 1930, American

A New England Nun and Other Stories

Edited with an Introduction and Notes by Sandra A. Zagarell

"Regionalist" writer Freeman began her career when writing was becoming the first culture industry and her work appeared in many popular magazines. This collection showcases her many modes—romantic, gothic, and psychologically symbolic—as well as her use of humor and irony and comprises fifteen stories and the novella *The Jamesons*.

320 pp.   0-14-043739-8 $12.95

JEAN FROISSART
c. 1337 – c. 1410, French

Chronicles

Selected and Translated with an Introduction by Geoffrey Brereton

This selection from Froissart's *Chronicles* forms a vast panorama of Europe, from the deposition of Edward II to the downfall of Richard II.

496 pp.   0-14-044200-6 $14.00

ROBERT FROST
1874 – 1963, American

Early Poems
A Boy's Will, North of Boston, Mountain Interval, and Other Poems

Edited with an Introduction and Notes by Robert Faggen

This volume presents Frost's first three books, masterful and innovative collections that contain some of his best-known poems, including "Mowing," "Mending Wall," "After Apple-Picking," "Home Burial," "The Oven Bird," "Birches," and "The Road Not Taken."

288 pp.   0-14-118017-X $9.95

Carpenter's Gothic

This story of raging comedy and despair centers on the tempestuous marriage of an heiress and a Vietnam veteran.

272 pp.   0-14-118222-9 $13.95

Great Books Foundation Readers Guide Available

"Everything in this compelling and brilliant vision of America—the packaged sleaze, the incipient violence, the fundamentalist furor, the constricted sexuality—is charged with the force of a volcanic eruption."

—WALTER ABISH

JR

Introduction by Frederick R. Karl

The hero of this novel of epic comedy and satire is an eleven-year-old capitalist who parlays Navy surplus forks and some defaulted bonds into a vast empire of free enterprise. Winner of the National Book Award in 1976.

752 pp.   0-14-018707-3 $20.00

The Recognitions

Introduction by William H. Gass

First published in 1955 and considered one of the most profound works of fiction of this century, *The Recognitions* tells the story of a painter-counterfeiter who forges out of love, not larceny, in an age when the fakes have become indistinguishable from the real.

976 pp.   0-14-018708-1 $24.00

Letters to Father
Suor Maria Celeste to Galileo, 1623–1633

Translated and Annotated by Dava Sobel

Placed in a convent at the age of thirteen (where she was renamed Suor Maria Celeste), Virginia Galilei, Galileo's eldest daughter, wrote to her father continually. The letters span a dramatic decade that included the Thirty Years' War, the bubonic plague, and the development of Galileo's own universe-changing discoveries, but though they touch on these events, the letters mostly focus on the details of everyday life that connect this fascinating father and daughter. All 124 surviving letters are here translated into English.

208 pp.   0-14-243715-8 $13.00
(Available January 2003)

ELIZABETH GASKELL
1810 – 1865, British

Cranford/Cousin Phillis

Edited with an Introduction and Notes by Peter J. Keating

Both *Cranford*, an affectionately ironic and understated depiction of an early Victorian country town, and *Cousin Phillis*, the story of an unfulfilled love affair, are concerned with the transition from old values to new.

368 pp.   **0-14-043104-7**   **$12.00**

Gothic Tales

Edited by Laura Kranzler

In these nine strange and wonderful tales, Gaskell—best known for books about middle-class life in country villages—used spine-tingling, supernatural elements to explore human frailties and the dualities in everyday life.

416 pp.   **0-14-043741-X**   **$12.00**

The Life of Charlotte Brontë

Edited with an Introduction and Notes by Elisabeth Jay

Novelist Elizabeth Gaskell drew on her friendship with the author of *Jane Eyre*, *Shirley*, and *Villette* to write this compelling psychological portrait of Brontë, whose controversial works belied the reclusive life she led.

544 pp.   **0-14-043493-3**   **$15.00**

Mary Barton

Edited with an Introduction and Notes by MacDonald Daly

A powerful depiction of industrial strife and class conflict in Manchester in the 1840s, Elizabeth Gaskell's first novel won widespread attention and established her reputation as a writer concerned with social and political issues.

464 pp.   **0-14-043464-X**   **$7.95**

North and South

Edited with an Introduction and Notes by Patricia Ingham

Gaskell's great portrait of vastly differing conditions in England's industrial north and rural south explores the exploitation of the working class and links the plight of workers with that of women.

480 pp.   **0-14-043424-0**   **$10.00**

Ruth

Edited with an Introduction by Angus Easson

Overturning the conventional assumption that a woman once seduced is condemned to exclusion from respectable society, Gaskell draws a heroine whose emotional honesty, innate morality, and the love she shares with her illegitimate son are sufficient for redemption.

432 pp.   **0-14-043430-5**   **$10.00**

Wives and Daughters

Edited with an Introduction and Notes by Pam Morris

This is Gaskell's comic tale of the coming-of-age of two very different stepsisters and of men and women constantly, if unintentionally, at cross-purposes. Beneath the nostalgic domesticity of *Wives and Daughters* readers will discover the same acute insights that have won Gaskell's earlier, more controversial novels new readership.

720 pp.   **0-14-043478-X**   **$13.95**

Omensetter's Luck

With an Afterword by the Author

The quirky, impressionistic, and breath-takingly original story of an ordinary community galvanized by the presence of an extraordinary man, *Omensetter's Luck* (1966) has been called the "most important work of fiction by an American in this literary generation" (Richard Gilman, *The New Republic*).

320 pp.   **0-14-118010-2**   **$14.00**

The Beggar's Opera

Edited by Bryan Loughrey and T. O. Treadwell with an Introduction by Bryan Loughrey

This witty parody of Italian opera, featuring the denizens of the British underworld, was performed more than any other play during the eighteenth century.

128 pp.   **0-14-043220-5**   **$8.95**

The History of the Kings of Britain

Translated with an Introduction by Lewis Thorpe

This heroic epic of the twelfth century, describing such half-legendary kings as Cymbeline, Arthur, and Lear inspired Malory, Spenser, Shakespeare, and many other writers.

384 pp.   **0-14-044170-0**   **$15.00**

The History and Topography of Ireland

Translated with an Introduction and Notes by John O'Meara

Arguably the most authoritative primary source for what is known about medieval Ireland, this lively history by a twelfth-century Norman describes the land's topography, natural resources, and inhabitants in vivid detail.

144 pp.   **maps**   **0-14-044423-8**   **$12.95**

The Journey Through Wales/ The Description of Wales

Translated with an Introduction by Lewis Thorpe

The Journey, an accurate and comprehensive history of twelfth-century Wales, is filled with lively anecdotes and folklore; *The Description* offers a fascinating picture of the life of ordinary Welshmen.

336 pp.   **0-14-044339-8**   **$13.95**

EDWARD GIBBON
1737 – 1794, British

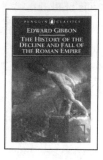

The History of the Decline and Fall of the Roman Empire

Edited with an Introduction and Appendices by David Womersley

Inspired by a visit to Rome in 1764, Edward Gibbon spent twenty years weaving together his epic chronicle. This definitive three-volume edition presents a complete unmodernized text, the author's own comments and notes, and his famous *Vindication*.

The History of the Decline and Fall of the Roman Empire
Volume I

Edited with an Introduction and Appendices by David Womersley

Launches the history by describing the Empire during the Age of Trajan and the Antonines.

1,120 pp.   0-14-043393-7 $24.95

The History of the Decline and Fall of the Roman Empire
Volume II

Edited with an Introduction and Appendices by David Womersley

Includes two of Gibbon's most subtle portraits, those of Constantine and Julian the Apostate.

1,008 pp.   0-14-043394-5 $24.95

The History of the Decline and Fall of the Roman Empire
Volume III

Edited with an Introduction and Appendices by David Womersley

Examines the enfeebled state of the Byzantine Empire and the spread of Islam.

1,184 pp.   0-14-043395-3 $24.95

The History of the Decline and Fall of the Roman Empire

Abridged with a New Introduction by David Womersley

Based on Womersley's three-volume Penguin Classics edition, this abridgement contains complete chapters from all three volumes, linked by extended bridging passages, vividly capturing the architecture of Gibbon's masterwork.

848 pp.   0-14-043764-9 $16.00

> **"Womersley has produced a wholly new edition...which is a fitting monument to the greatest of all English historians."**
> —NIALL FERGUSON

EDWARD GIBBON

Edward Gibbon was born in 1737, in Putney, and was the only child of his parents to survive infancy. Although his education was frequently interrupted by ill health, he was finally able to study Greek and French in Lausanne, Switzerland. It was while he was in Rome in 1764 that he first conceived the work that was to become *The History of the Decline and Fall of the Roman Empire*. The first volume of his famous *History* was published in 1776, the second and third appeared in 1781, and the final three in 1788. He died while on a visit to his friend Lord Sheffield, who later edited Gibbon's autobiographical papers and published them in 1796.

STELLA GIBBONS
1902 – 1989, British

Cold Comfort Farm
First published to great acclaim in 1932, and now recognized as one of the funniest books ever written, this witty parody mocks the melodrama, earthly sensuality, and use of symbolism found in the works of Thomas Hardy, D. H. Lawrence, and other popular "country-life" novels of the period.
240 pp.   0-14-018869-X $13.00

ANDRÉ GIDE
1869 – 1951, French
Nobel Prize winner

The Immoralist
Translated by David Watson with an Introduction by Alan Sheridan

This new translation of Nobel Laureate André Gide's masterpiece presents the confessional account of a man seeking the truth of his own nature as he awakens sexually and morally.
144 pp.   0-14-218002-5 $10.00

CHARLOTTE PERKINS GILMAN
1860 – 1935, American

Herland, The Yellow Wall-Paper, and Selected Writings
Edited with an Introduction by Denise D. Knight

Gilman used the utopian form, satire, and fantasy powerfully to critique women's place in society. This volume collects her classic story, "The Yellow Wall-Paper," her most famous novel, *Herland*, and a selection of her poetry and other short fiction.
384 pp.   0-14-118062-5 $11.00

See Four Stories by American Women.

GEORGE GISSING
1857 – 1903, British

New Grub Street
Edited with an Introduction by Bernard Bergonzi

Through Edwin Reardon, a struggling novelist, and his friends on Grub Street—Milvain, a journalist, and Yule, an embittered critic—Gissing brings to life the literary climate of 1880s London.
560 pp.   0-14-043032-6 $12.95

The Odd Women
Introduction by Elaine Showalter

A refreshing antidote to Victorian novels celebrating romantic love and marriage, *The Odd Women* is a dramatic look at the actual circumstances, options, and desires of women, told with psychological and political realities that are astonishingly contemporary.
416 pp.   0-14-043379-1 $11.95

Caleb Williams

Edited with an Introduction and Notes by Maurice Hindle

A psychological detective novel about power, *Caleb Williams* was an imaginative contribution to the radical cause in the British debate on the French Revolution.

448 pp. 0-14-043256-6 **$14.00**

JOHANN WOLFGANG VON GOETHE
1749 – 1832, German (b. Frankfurt-am-Main)

Elective Affinities

Translated with an Introduction by R. J. Hollingdale

Condemned as immoral when it was first published, this novel reflects the conflict Goethe felt between his respect for the conventions of marriage and the possibility of spontaneous passion.

304 pp. 0-14-044242-1 **$13.00**

Faust, Part 1

Translated with an Introduction by Philip Wayne

Goethe's masterpiece dramatizes the struggle of modern man to solve the mysteries of energy, pleasure, and the creation of life.

208 pp. 0-14-044012-7 **$8.95**

Faust, Part 2

Translated with an Introduction by Philip Wayne

Rich in allusion and allegory, *Faust, Part 2* explores philosophical themes that obsessed Goethe throughout his life.

288 pp. 0-14-044093-3 **$12.00**

Italian Journey

Translated with an Introduction by W. H. Auden and Elizabeth Mayer

Goethe's account of his passage through Italy from 1786 to 1788 is a great travel chronicle as well as a candid self-portrait of a genius in the grip of spiritual crisis.

512 pp. 0-14-044233-2 **$13.95**

Maxims and Reflections

Translated by Elizabeth Stopp and Edited with an Introduction by Peter Hutchinson

These 1,413 reflections reveal only some of his deepest thoughts on art, ethics, literature, and natural science but also his immediate reactions to books, chance encounters, and his administrative work.

208 pp. 0-14-044720-2 **$13.00**

Selected Verse

Translated with an Introduction by David Luke

This dual-language edition of nearly three hundred poems draws from every period of Goethe's work, and includes substantial portions of *Faust*.

368 pp. 0-14-042074-6 **$14.00**

The Sorrows of Young Werther

Translated with an Introduction and Notes by Michael Hulse

Based partly on Goethe's unrequited love for Charlotte Buff, this novel of pathological sensibility strikes a powerful blow against Enlightenment rationalism.

144 pp. 0-14-044503-X **$10.95**

See Romantic Fairy Tales.

VINCENT VAN GOGH
1853 – 1890, Dutch

The Letters of Vincent van Gogh
Edited and Selected with an Introduction by Ronald de Leeuw and Translated by Arnold Pomerans

This volume reinstates passages omitted from early editions of van Gogh's letters and includes, whenever possible, the wonderful pen-and-ink sketches he added to his written messages. Winner of the PEN/Book-of-the-Month Club Translation Prize.

560 pp.   **0-14-044674-5**   **$14.95**

NIKOLAI GOGOL
1809 – 1852, Russian

Dead Souls
Translated with an Introduction by David Magarshack

The hero of this satiric masterpiece is Gogol's most beguiling and devilish creation, a man who buys dead serfs. Gogol's attempts to continue the story in two more books obsessed him, eventually driving him to madness and death.

384 pp.   **0-14-044113-1**   **$10.95**

Diary of a Madman and Other Stories
Translated with an Introduction by Ronald Wilks

These five stories, "Diary of a Madman," "The Overcoat," "How Ivan Ivanovich Quarelled with Ivan Nikiforovich," "Ivan Fyodorovich Shponka and His Aunt," and "The Nose," demonstrate Gogol's peculiar and strikingly original imagination.

192 pp.   **0-14-044273-1**   **$9.95**

See The Portable Nineteenth-Century Russian Reader.

OLIVER GOLDSMITH
1728 – 1774, British

The Vicar of Wakefield
Edited with an Introduction and Notes by Stephen Coote

This charming comedy is an artful send-up of the literary conventions of Goldsmith's time—the pastoral scene, the artificial romance, the stoic bravery of the hero—culminating in a highly improbable denouement.

224 pp.   **0-14-043159-4**   **$7.95**

IVAN GONCHAROV
1812 – 1891, Russian

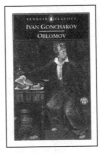

Oblomov
Translated with an Introduction by David Magarshack

Goncharov's detached yet sympathetic portrait of the humdrum life of his ineffectual and slothful hero is a tragicomedy created through painstaking accumulation of seemingly insignificant details alongside a sympathetic analysis of his character.

496 pp.   **0-14-044040-2**   **$14.00**

MAXIM GORKY
1868 – 1936, Russian

My Childhood

Translated with an Introduction by Ronald Wilks

The first part of Gorky's celebrated autobiography, this volume records with charm and poignancy the childhood of extreme poverty and brutality that deepened Gorky's understanding of the "ordinary Russian," an experience that would influence some of his greatest works.

240 pp.   0-14-018285-3 $13.95

See The Portable Twentieth-Century Russian Reader.

SIR EDMUND GOSSE
1849 – 1928, British

Father and Son

Edited with an Introduction and Notes by Peter Abbs

An account of the religious fanaticism surrounding his upbringing, Gosse's novel also serves as a brilliant and moving document of Victorian social and intellectual history.

224 pp.   0-14-018276-4 $11.95

GOTTFRIED VON STRASSBURG
c. 12th – 13th cent., German

Tristan

Translated with an Introduction by A. T. Hatto

This medieval version of the legendary romance between Tristan and Isolde portrays Tristan as a sophisticated pre-Renaissance man.

384 pp.   0-14-044098-4 $15.00

ULYSSES S. GRANT
1822 – 1885, American

Personal Memoirs

Introduction and Notes by James M. McPherson

Grant's memoirs demonstrate the intelligence, intense determination, and laconic modesty that made him the Union's foremost commander.

704 pp.   0-14-043701-0 $14.95

"Perhaps the most revelatory autobiography of high command to exist in any language."

—JOHN KEEGAN

HENRY GREEN
1905 – 1973, British

"Green's remains the most interesting and vital imagination in English fiction in our time."

—EUDORA WELTY

Loving/Living/Party Going

Introduction by John Updike

This volume brings together three of Henry Green's intensely original novels: *Loving* brilliantly contrasts the lives of servants and masters in an Irish castle during World War II; *Living* those of workers and owners in a Birmingham iron foundry; *Party Going* presents a party of wealthy travelers stranded by fog in a London railway hotel while throngs of workers await trains in the station below.

528 pp.   0-14-018691-3 $14.95

GRAHAM GREENE
1904 – 1991, British

"Graham Greene was in a class by himself....He will be read and remembered as the ultimate chronicler of twentieth-century man's consciousness and anxiety."

—WILLIAM GOLDING

The Portable Graham Greene
Edited by Philip Stratford

This rich cross-section of Greene's vast body of work includes the complete novels *The Third Man* and *The Heart of the Matter*, along with short stories, travel writings, essays, criticism, and memoirs.

672 pp.   0-14-023359-8 $16.95

Brighton Rock
Greene's chilling exposé of violence and gang warfare in the prewar British under-world features Pinkie, a protagonist who is the embodiment of evil.

256 pp.   0-14-018492-9 $12.95

A Burnt-Out Case
A world-famous architect, who has lost interest in his life and art, anonymously begins work at a leper colony in order to cure his "disease of the mind."

200 pp.   0-14-018539-9 $13.00

The Captain and the Enemy
Greene's last novel is a fascinating tale of adventure and intrigue that follows an Englishman from his boyhood with an odd surrogate family to Panama where he becomes involved in gun smuggling and betrayal.

208 pp.   0-14-018855-X $13.00

Collected Short Stories
Previously published in three volumes — *May We Borrow Your Husband?*, *A Sense of Reality*, and *Twenty-One Stories*—these thirty-seven stories reveal Greene in a range of contrasting moods, sometimes cynical and witty, sometimes searching and philosophical.

368 pp.   0-14-018612-3 $13.95

The Comedians
Three men meet on a ship bound for Haiti, a world in the grip of the corrupt "Papa Doc" and his sinister secret police, the Tontons Macoute.

288 pp.   0-14-018494-5 $14.00

GRAHAM GREENE

Graham Greene was born in England in 1904 and died in 1991 in Switzerland. He studied at the Berkhamsted School, where his father was headmaster, before entering Balliol College, Oxford. In 1926 Greene became a journalist for the *Nottingham Journal* and converted to Catholicism to be closer to his future wife, Vivien Dayrell-Browning. His first novel, *The Man Within*, was published three years later. *The Quiet American, Our Man in Havana*, and *Orient Express* are among his numerous provocative, exotically suspenseful, and often hilarious explorations of the corruption of the human spirit. Many of his novels have been adapted successfully to the screen.

The End of the Affair

A love affair, abruptly and inexplicably broken off, prompts the grief-stricken novelist Maurice Bendrix to hire a private detective to discover the cause.

192 pp.   **0-14-018495-3**   **$13.00**

England Made Me

A tour de force of moral suspense, this is the story of a confirmed liar and cheat whose untimely discovery of decency may cost him not only his job but also his life.

208 pp.   **0-14-018551-8**   **$14.00**

A Gun for Sale

Raven's cold-blooded killing of the Minister of War is an act of violence with chilling repercussions, not just for Raven himself but for the nation as a whole.

208 pp.   **0-14-018540-2**   **$14.00**

The Heart of the Matter

The terrifying depiction of a man's awe of the Church and Greene's ability to portray human motive and to convey such a depth of suffering make *The Heart of the Matter* one of his most enduring and tragic novels.

272 pp.   **0-14-018496-1**   **$12.95**

Journey Without Maps

This chronicle of Greene's journey through Liberia in the 1930s is at once vivid reportage and a powerful document of spiritual hunger and renewal.

256 pp.   **0-14-018579-8**   **$14.00**

The Last Word and Other Stories

These twelve stories, spanning from 1923 to 1989, represent the quintessential Graham Greene. Rich in gallows humor, they have the power both to move and to entertain.

160 pp.   **0-14-118157-5**   **$11.95**

The Lawless Roads

This story of Greene's visit to Mexico emerged after he was commissioned to find out how ordinary people had reacted to the brutal anticlerical purges of President Calles.

224 pp.   **0-14-018580-1**   **$14.00**

Loser Takes All

This superb story offers up a tale of an unsuccessful accountant's second try at luck and love.

128 pp.   **0-14-018542-9**   **$13.00**

The Man Within

The themes of betrayal, pursuit, and the search for peace run through Greene's first published novel about a smuggler who takes refuge from his avengers.

224 pp.   **0-14-018530-5**   **$15.00**

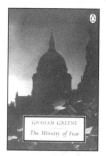

The Ministry of Fear

This is a complex portrait of the shadowy inner landscape of Arthur Rowe—torn apart with guilt over mercifully murdering his sick wife—and the terrifying and phantasmagoric landscape of England during the Blitz.

224 pp.   **0-14-018536-4**   **$13.00**

Our Man in Havana

In this comic novel, Wormwold tries to keep his job as a secret agent in Havana by filing bogus reports based on Lamb's *Tales from Shakespeare* and dreaming up military installations from vacuum-cleaner designs.

224 pp.   0-14-018493-7 $12.95

The Power and the Glory

Introduction by John Updike

Set in a terror-ridden Mexican state, Greene's masterpiece is a compelling depiction of a "whisky priest" struggling to overcome physical and moral cowardice and find redemption.

240 pp.   0-14-243730-1 $14.00
(Available March 2003)

The Quiet American

While the French Army in Indo-China grapples with the Vietminh, a young and high-minded American based in Saigon begins to channel economic aid to a "Third Force" —leading him to blunder into a complex political and cultural world he seems not to understand fully, with disastrous and violent results.

192 pp.   0-14-018500-3 $13.00

Stamboul Train

Set on the Orient Express, this suspense thriller involves the desperate affair between a pragmatic Jew and a naïve chorus girl entangled in lust, duplicity, and murder.

224 pp.   0-14-018532-1 $12.95

The Third Man and The Fallen Idol

This edition pairs two thrillers: Greene's legendary *The Third Man* and *The Fallen Idol*, in which a small boy discovers the deadly truths of the adult world.

160 pp.   0-14-018533-X $12.00

Travels with My Aunt

Henry Pulling's dull suburban life is interrupted when his septuagenarian Aunt Augusta persuades him to travel the world with her in her own inimitable style.

272 pp.   0-14-018501-1 $14.00

Twenty-One Stories

Some of the stories included here are comic, others are wryly sad. They can be deeply shocking or hauntingly tragic. Whatever the mood, each one is compellingly entertaining.

224 pp.   0-14-018534-8 $14.00

GREGORY OF TOURS
539 – 594, Frankish

A History of the Franks

Translated with an Introduction by Lewis Thorpe

This colorful narrative of French history in the sixth century is a dramatic and detailed portrait of a period of political and religious turmoil.

720 pp.   0-14-044295-2 $15.95

ZANE GREY
1872 – 1939, American

Riders of the Purple Sage
Introduction by Jane Tompkins

A great drama of psyche and landscape, Zane Grey's bestselling 1912 adventure romance is the definitive Western novel, with popular appeal and distinct codes of chivalry and toughness.

304 pp.   **0-14-018440-6**   **$9.95**

JACOB GRIMM
1785 – 1863, German

WILHELM GRIMM
1786 – 1859, German

Selected Tales
Translated with an Introduction and Notes by David Luke

Sixty-five selections from *Kinder-und Hausmärchen* provide a representative sample of the folktale motifs that have fascinated children and adults around the world for centuries.

432 pp.   **0-14-044401-7**   **$12.95**

H. RIDER HAGGARD
1856 – 1925, British

She
Edited with an Introduction by Patrick Brantlinger

"She" is Ayesha, the mysterious white queen of a Central African Tribe—and the goal of three English gentlemen, who must face shipwreck, fever, and cannibals in their quest to find her hidden realm. *She* has enthralled the imaginations of generations of readers who remain fascinated by its representations of dangerous women, adventuring men, and unexplored Africa.

368 pp.   **0-14-043763-0**   **$9.00**

"Full of hidden meaning . . . the eternal feminine, the immorality of our emotions."
—SIGMUND FREUD

RICHARD HAKLUYT
c. 1552 – 1616, English

Voyages and Discoveries
Edited and Abridged with an Introduction by Jack Beeching

In this work of Hakluyt—a Renaissance diplomat, scholar, and spy—lies the beginnings of geography, economics, ethnography, and the modern world itself.

448 pp.   **0-14-043073-3**   **$14.00**

ALEXANDER HAMILTON

See James Madison.

KNUT HAMSUN
1859 – 1952, Norwegian
Nobel Prize winner

Hunger

Translated with an Introduction and Notes by Sverre Lyngstad

First published in Norway in 1890, *Hunger* probes into the depths of consciousness with frightening and gripping power. Like the works of Dostoyevsky, it marks an extraordinary break with Western literary and humanistic traditions.

224 pp. 0-14-118064-1 $13.00

"The classic novel of humiliation, even beyond Dostoyevsky... Lyngstad's translation restores to the English-speaking reader one of the cold summits in modern prose literature."

—GEORGE STEINER

Mysteries

Translated with an Introduction and Notes by Sverre Lyngstad

Johan Nilsen Nagel is a mysterious stranger who suddenly turns up in a small Norwegian town one summer—and just as suddenly disappears. The novel creates a powerful sense of Nagel's stream-of-thought as he increasingly withdraws into the torture chamber of his own subconscious psyche.

352 pp. 0-14-118618-6 $14.00

Pan
From Lieutenant Thomas Glahn's Papers

Translated with an Introduction and Notes by Sverre Lyngstad

A remarkable new translation of Hamsun's portrait of a man rejecting the claims of bourgeois society for a Rousseauian embrace of Nature and Eros.

224 pp. 0-14-118067-6 $11.00

THOMAS HARDY
1840 – 1928, British

Desperate Remedies

Edited with an Introduction and Notes by Mary Rimmer

Blackmail, murder, and romance are among the ingredients of Hardy's first published novel, which appeared anonymously in 1871. In its depiction of country life and insight into psychology and sexuality, it already bears the unmistakeable imprint of Hardy's genius.

512 pp. 1 map 0-14-043523-9 $15.00

The Distracted Preacher and Other Tales

Edited with an Introduction and Notes by Susan Hill

Hardy captures the provincial experiences of his native Dorset and environs in eleven of his best and most representative stories, including "The Withered Arm," "Barbara of the House of Grebe," "The Son's Veto," and "A Tragedy of Two Ambitions."

368 pp. 0-14-043124-1 $11.00

Far from the Madding Crowd

Edited with an Introduction and Notes by Rosemarie Morgan with Shannon Russell

In this tale of rural romance—and Hardy's most humorous novel—the capricious and willful Bathsheba Everdene is wooed by three very different men and comes to comprehend the true nature of generosity, humility, and, ultimately, love.

480 pp. 0-14-143965-3 $7.95

The Hand of Ethelberta

Edited with an Introduction and Notes by Tim Dolin and Illustrations by George du Maurier

This tale of an opportunistic yet ultimately loyal adventuress, who begins life humbly and ends as the wife of a rakish aristocrat, will surprise readers of Hardy's more familiar, and darker, Wessex novels.

512 pp.   0-14-043502-6 $13.95

Jude the Obscure

Edited with an Introduction and Notes by Dennis Taylor

In this haunting love story, the stonemason Jude Fawley and Sue Brideshead, both having left earlier marriages, find happiness in their relationship. Ironically, when tragedy tests their union, it is Sue, the modern emancipated woman, who proves unequal to the challenge. This edition reprints the 1895 text with Hardy's Postscript of 1912.

528 pp.   1 map   0-14-043538-7 $7.95
Penguin Readers Guide Available

A Laodicean

Edited with an Introduction and Notes by John Schad

Hardy's experience as a professional architect shines through in the meticulous, highly visual descriptions of towns and buildings in this novel. Using the restoration of a castle as a framework, Hardy considers the ancient analogy between architecture and philosophy.

512 pp.   0-14-043506-9 $11.00

The Mayor of Casterbridge

Edited with an Introduction and Notes by Keith Wilson

Thomas Hardy's fascination with the dualities inherent in human nature is at the root of this depiction of a man who overreaches the limits allowed by society. Using the device of classic tragedy—the downfall of a man caused by the whims of chance and his own fatal flaws—Hardy took the British novel in a new direction and emerged as not only the last Victorian novelist but the first modern one.

448 pp.   20 b/w illustrations   2 maps
0-14-143978-5 $7.95

A Pair of Blue Eyes

Edited with an Introduction and Notes by Pamela Dalziel

Clearly based on Hardy's relationships with his family, his fiancée, and his closet male friend, this story of a classic love triangle between Elfride Swancourt, Stephen Smith, and Henry Knight explores how lovers fall victim, in different ways, to society's assumptions about class and gender.

448 pp.   0-14-043529-8 $10.00

The Pursuit of the Well-Beloved and The Well-Beloved

Edited with an Introduction by Patricia Ingham

Containing the 1892 serial version and the version that appeared in book form in 1897, this volume not only brings one of Hardy's lesser-known works to the public but also sheds light on Hardy's tendency to interweave either/or variations in his plots and fashion a "series of screenings," as he himself described in *Jude the Obscure*.

416 pp.   3 maps   0-14-043519-0 $9.95

"Hardy is among the greatest poets, and this authoritative selection represents him wonderfully."

—JOHN HOLLANDER

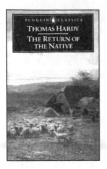

The Return of the Native

*Edited with Notes by Tony Slade and an
Introduction by Penny Boumelha*

One of Hardy's classic statements about
modern love, courtship, and marriage,
The Return of the Native explores the
impersonal forces and eternal verities
that control the lives of Eustacia Vye and
Clym Yeobright, the returning "native."

**496 pp.   2 b/w illustrations   2 maps
0-14-043518-2 $8.95**

Selected Poems

*Edited with an Introduction and Notes by
Robert Mezey*

This generous selection of nearly two
hundred poems will help readers recognize
Hardy as one of the greatest poets of the
twentieth century.

192 pp.   0-14-043699-5 $8.95

Tess of the D'Urbervilles

*Edited with Notes by Tim Dolin and an
Introduction by Margaret R. Higonnet*

Tess's seduction, hopeful marriage, and
cruel abandonment compose an unforgettable novel that exhibits the hallmarks of
Hardy's best art: a keen sense of tragedy and
a sharp critique of social hypocrisy. This
edition of Hardy's most moving and poetic
novel includes as appendices Hardy's Pref-
aces, a map, illustrations, and episodes censored from the *Graphic* periodical version.

**512 pp.   3 b/w illustrations   2 maps
0-14-043514-X $7.95**

Two on a Tower

*Edited with an Introduction and Notes by
Sally Shuttleworth*

Hardy's most complete treatment of the
theme of love across the divides of age and
class, *Two on a Tower* was first published in
1882 and charts the tragic romance of Lady
Viviette Constantine and Swithin St. Cleve.

336 pp.   0-14-043536-0 $10.95

The Withered Arm and Other Stories

*Edited with an Introduction by
Kristen Brady*

These nine short stories constitute some of
Hardy's finest early work and foreshadow
his later novels in their controversial sexual
politics, their refusal of romantic structures,
and their elegiac pursuit of past, lost loves.

464 pp.   0-14-043532-8 $11.95

The Woodlanders

*Edited with an Introduction and Notes by
Patricia Ingham*

In this portrait of four people caught up in
a web of intense, often unrequited passion,
Hardy explores the complexity of sexual
feelings and the roles of social class, gender,
and evolutionary survival.

464 pp.   1 map   0-14-043547-6 $7.95

See The Penguin Book of First
World War Poetry.

JOEL CHANDLER HARRIS
1848 – 1908, American

Uncle Remus
His Songs and His Sayings
*Edited with an Introduction by
Robert Hemenway*

The dialect, lore, and flavor of black life in the nineteenth-century South is portrayed as it appeared to Georgia-born Joel Chandler Harris in Uncle Remus's "Legends of the Old Plantation."

288 pp.   0-14-039014-6 $10.95

See American Local Color Writing *and* The Portable American Realism Reader.

BRET HARTE
1836 – 1902, American

The Luck of Roaring Camp and Other Writings
*Edited with an Introduction by
Gary Scharnhorst*

More than any other writer, Harte was at the forefront of western American literature. This volume brings together all of his best-known pieces, as well as a selection of his poetry, lesser-known essays, and three of his hilarious Condensed Novels—parodies of James Fenimore Cooper, Charles Dickens, and Sir Arthur Conan Doyle.

320 pp.   0-14-043917-X $12.00

See The Portable American Realism Reader.

JAROSLAV HAŠEK
1883 – 1923, Czech

The Good Soldier Švejk
*Translated with an Introduction by
Cecil Parrott and Illustrations by Josef Lada*

This novel portrays the "little man" fighting officialdom and bureaucracy with the only weapons available to him—passive resistance, subterfuge, native wit, and dumb insolence.

784 pp.   0-14-018274-8 $14.95

NATHANIEL HAWTHORNE
1804 – 1864, American

The Portable Hawthorne
Edited by Malcolm Cowley

This essential Hawthorne collection contains the complete Scarlet Letter and additional selections from *The House of Seven Gables* and the unfinished *Dolliver Romance*, as well as thirteen short stories, excerpts from the notebooks, letters, and a chronology of Hawthorne's life.

704 pp.   0-14-015038-2 $16.95

The Blithedale Romance
*Introduction and Notes by
Annette Kolodny*

In language that is suggestive and often erotic, Hawthorne offers a superb depiction of a utopian community that cannot survive the individual passions of its members.

304 pp.   0-14-039028-6 $7.95

The House of the Seven Gables
*Edited with an Introduction and Notes by
Milton R. Stern*

This enduring novel of crime and retribution is a psychological drama that vividly reflects the social and moral values of New England in the 1840s.

352 pp.   0-14-039005-7 $8.95

The Marble Faun

Introduction and Notes by
Richard H. Brodhead

Set in Rome, Hawthorne's tale of the influence of European culture on American morality echoes *The Scarlet Letter* in its concern with the nature of transgression and guilt.

480 pp.   **0-14-039077-4**   **$9.95**

The Scarlet Letter

Introduction by Nina Baym with Notes by
Thomas E. Connolly

Hawthorne's novel of guilt and redemption in pre-Revolutionary Massachussetts provides vivid insight into the social and religious forces that shaped early America.

272 pp.   **0-14-243726-3**   **$6.00**
(Available January 2003)

Selected Tales and Sketches

Selected with an Introduction by
Michael J. Colacurcio

Displaying Hawthorne's understanding of the distinctly American consciousness, these thirty-one short fictions of the early nineteenth century include "Young Goodman Brown," "The Minister's Black Veil," and "Rappaccini's Daughter."

488 pp.   **0-14-039057-X**   **$10.95**

GEORG WILHELM FRIEDRICH HEGEL
1770 – 1831, German (b. Stuttgart)

Introductory Lectures on Aesthetics

Translated by Bernard Bosanquet with an
Introduction and Commentary by
Michael Inwood

Hegel's writings on art—and his profound conclusion that art was in terminal decline—have had a broad impact on our culture.

240 pp.   **0-14-043335-X**   **$14.00**

See German Idealist Philosophy.

HÉLOÏSE

See Abélard.

O. HENRY
1862 – 1910, American

Selected Stories

Edited with an Introduction by
Guy Davenport

Compiled here are eighty classic stories—about con men, tricksters, and innocent deceivers, about fate, luck, and coincidence—by one of the great masters of American literary comedy and the short-story form. Included are "The Ransom of Red Chief," "A Retrieved Reformation," and "The Rose of Dixie."

384 pp.   **0-14-018688-3**   **$13.95**

GEORGE HERBERT
1593 – 1633, English

The Complete English Poems

Edited with an Introduction and Notes by
John Tobin

The Temple, Herbert's masterpiece of worldly anguish and divine transcendence; his uncollected English verse; *A Priest to the Temple* (prose); and selections from Herbert's Latin poetry with translations form the basis of this volume.

496 pp.   **0-14-042348-6**   **$16.00**

See The Metaphysical Poets.

HERODOTUS
c. 490 – c. 425 B.C., Greek

The Histories

Translated by Aubrey de Sélincourt and Revised with an Introduction and Notes by John M. Marincola

Written during a period of increasing conflict between Sparta and Athens, these compelling descriptions of great battles, rulers, and political upheavals attempt to recapture the glorious past of a unified Greece.

672 pp.   0-14-044908-6 $12.00

See The Portable Greek Historians.

HESIOD
c. 8th cent. B.C., Greek

THEOGNIS
c. 6th cent. – 5th cent. B.C., Greek

Hesiod and Theognis

Translated with Introductions and Notes by Dorothea Wender

Together these two poets—Hesiod, the epic poet, and Theognis, the elegist—offer a superb introduction to the life and thought of ancient Greece.

176 pp.   0-14-044283-9 $12.00

See The Portable Greek Reader.

HERMANN HESSE
1877 – 1962, Swiss (b. Germany)
Nobel Prize winner

Siddhartha

Translated by Joachim Neugroschel with an Introduction by Ralph Freedman

This deluxe edition of Hesse's most beloved novel tells of a young Brahmin's quest that takes him from a life of decadence through asceticism to transcendent wisdom.

176 pp.   0-14-243718-2 $12.00
(Available January 2003)

Siddhartha

Translated by Joachim Neugroschel with an Introduction by Ralph Freedman

Set in India, *Siddhartha* is the story of a young Brahmin's search for ultimate reality after meeting with the Buddha.

176 pp.   0-14-118123-0 $7.00

HERMANN HESSE

Hermann Hesse was born into a family of strict Pietist missionaries in Calw, a small southern German town in the northern Black Forest, in July 1877. He spent World War I in Bern, Switzerland, working under the auspices of the Red Cross. After the war and a psychological crisis, Hesse removed himself to the small town of Montagnola in Italian-speaking Switzerland where he lived out the rest of his life in seclusion. There, in the relative peace of rural surroundings, he created his best-known work: *Siddhartha* (1922), *Steppenwolf* (1927), *Narcissus and Goldmund* (1930), *Journey into the East* (1932), and *The Glass Bead Game* (1943). He received many important honors, including the Nobel Prize for Literature in 1946. Hesse died in 1962.

THOMAS WENTWORTH HIGGINSON
1823 – 1911, American

Army Life in a Black Regiment and Other Writings

Edited with an Introduction and Notes by R. D. Madison

Colonel Higginson's stirring account of his wartime experiences as the leader of the first regiment of emancipated slaves "has some claim to be the best written narrative to come from the Union during the Civil War" (Henry Steele Commager). This edition of *Army Life* features a selection of Higginson's essays, including "Nat Turner's Insurrection" and "Emily Dickinson's Letters."

352 pp.   0-14-043621-9 $14.00

HILDEGARD OF BINGEN
1089 – 1179, German

Selected Writings

Translated with an Introduction by Mark Atherton

Hildegard, the "Sybil of the Rhine," was a Benedictine nun and one of the most prolific and original women writers of the Middle Ages. This volume brings together writings that show her to be a visionary, a wide-ranging thinker, and an early proponent of a holistic approach to life.

320 pp.   0-14-043604-9 $13.00

See Medieval Writings on Female Spirituality.

THOMAS HOBBES
1588 – 1679, British

Leviathan

Edited with an Introduction by C. B. Macpherson

Written amid the turmoil of the English civil war, Hobbes's apologia for the emergent seventeenth-century mercantile society speaks directly to twentieth-century minds in its concern for peace, systematic analysis of power, and elevation of politics to the status of a science.

736 pp.   0-14-043195-0 $9.95

ERNST THEODOR HOFFMANN
1776 – 1822, Prussian

The Life and Opinions of the Tomcat Murr

Translated and Annotated by Anthea Bell with an Introduction by Jeremy Adler

Hoffman was a follower of Cervantes and Sterne, a pioneering "magical realist," fascinated by Gothic horror. This bizarre double narrative is a supreme example of literary bravado that reveals Hoffman as the greatest of German storytellers.

384 pp.   0-14-044631-1 $12.95

The Tales of Hoffmann

Selected and Translated with an Introduction by R. J. Hollingdale

Eight of Hoffmann's best and best-known tales are retold in this collection —among them "Mademoiselle de Scudery," "Doge and Dogeressa," and "The Sandman," which forms the basis for the first half of Offenbach's opera.

416 pp.   0-14-044392-4 $12.00

FRIEDRICH HÖLDERLIN
1770 – 1843, German (b. Lauffen)

Selected Poems and Fragments

Edited by Jeremy Adler and Translated with a New Preface and Introduction by Michael Hamburger

Though his literary talents were scarcely known to his contemporaries, Friedrich Hölderlin has emerged today as one of Europe's supreme poets. In this superb bilingual selection, Michael Hamburger has produced the definitive English version of a giant of German literature.

240 pp.   0-14-042416-4 $16.00

Robert Fagles's Translations of Homer

*with Introductions and Notes
by Bernard Knox*

The Iliad

Fagles combines his talents as poet and scholar to present this masterful, elegant translation of the stirring story of the Trojan War and the rage of Achilles.

672 pp.   0-14-044592-7 $9.95

The Iliad

This handsome deluxe edition of Fagles's finely tuned translation brings the horror and heroism of the Trojan War into sharp relief.

704 pp.   0-14-027536-3 $15.95

"An astonishing performance. There is no modern version of the whole *Iliad* which is better or as good, and this should now become the standard translation for a new generation."

—PETER LEVI

The Odyssey

Odysseus's ten-year voyage home to Ithaca after the Trojan War is a timeless human story of moral endurance. In this elegantly packaged edition, Fagles has captured the energy and poetry of Homer's original in bold, contemporary idiom.

560 pp.   0-14-026886-3 $14.95

Great Books Foundation Readers Guide Available

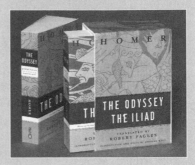

The Iliad and The Odyssey Boxed Set

The deluxe editions of Fagles's magnificent translations of Homer are here combined in a beautifully designed boxed set.

1,264   0-14-771255-6 $30.90

HOMER

The Greeks believed that *The Iliad* and *The Odyssey* were composed by a single poet whom they named Homer. Nothing is known of his life. While seven Greek cities claim the honor of being his birthplace, ancient tradition and the dialect and locational knowledge of the poems place him in Ionia, located in the eastern Aegean. His birthdate is undocumented as well, though most modern scholars now place the composition of *The Iliad* and *The Odyssey* between 725 and 675 B.C. The subject of Homer's epics involves the Trojan War, generally dated around 1200 B.C., but they actually reflect the eighth-century world of the Eastern Mediterranean; a world of dramatic growth and expansion, emerging out of the Dark Ages that followed the collapse of the Mycenaen civilization in the twelfth century.

The Iliad
A New Prose Translation

Translated with an Introduction by Martin Hammond

This prose translation captures the emotional power and the dramatic tension of the first and greatest literary achievement of Greek civilization.

416 pp.   0-14-044444-0 $12.00

The Iliad

Translated by E. V. Rieu

The original highly-acclaimed translation by E. V. Rieu, editor of Penguin Classics from 1944 to 1964.

480 pp.   0-14-044014-3 $9.95

The Odyssey

Translated by E. V. Rieu with a Revised Translation by D. C. H. Rieu and a New Introduction by Peter Jones

Odysseus's perilous ten-year voyage from Troy to his home in Ithaca is recounted in a revised translation that captures the swiftness, drama, and worldview of the Greek original.

448 pp.   0-14-044556-0 $9.95

See The Portable Greek Reader.

The Prisoner of Zenda and Rupert of Hentzau

With an Introduction and Notes by Gary Hoppenstand

The ever-popular *The Prisoner of Zenda* and the darker, more dramatic *Rupert of Hentzau* are full of swashbuckling feats of heroism as well as witty ironies that brilliantly satirize late nineteenth-century European politics.

400 pp.   0-14-043755-X $7.95

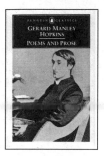

Poems and Prose

Edited and Selected by W. H. Gardner

This edition contains verse wrought from the creative tensions and paradoxes of a poet-priest who strove to evoke the spiritual essence of nature sensuously. Besides such poems as "The Wreck of the Deutschland," "The Windhover," and "God's Grandeur," this collection includes the "terrible sonnets," numerous journal entries, and Hopkins's letters to Robert Bridges.

272 pp.   0-14-042015-0 $14.95

The Complete Odes and Epodes

Translated with Notes by W. G. Shepherd and an Introduction by Betty Radice

The elusive personality and ironic philosophy of Horace are exemplified in seventeen epodes, 103 odes, and *The Centennial Hymn*.

256 pp.   0-14-044422-X $13.95

See The Portable Roman Reader *and* Classical Literary Criticism.

HORACE
65 – 8 B.C., Roman

PERSIUS
34 – 62, Roman

The Satires of Horace and Persius
Translated with an Introduction and Notes by Niall Rudd

The broad range of the controversial Roman poetic form the satura is illustrated in eighteen satires and twenty-three epistles of Horace and six metaphorical essays of the Stoic critic Persius, presented in modern verse translation.

304 pp.   0-14-044279-0 $12.95

WILLIAM DEAN HOWELLS
1837 – 1920, American

A Hazard of New Fortunes
Introduction by Phillip Lopate

Set against a vividly depicted background of fin de siècle New York, *A Hazard of New Fortunes* is both a memorable portrait of an era and a profoundly moving study of human relationships.

464 pp.   0-14-043923-4 $14.00

A Modern Instance
Introduction by Edwin H. Cady

The story of a philandering, dishonest Boston journalist and the woman who divorces him, this is the first serious treatment of divorce in American writing and a powerful example of realism in literature.

480 pp.   0-14-039027-8 $14.00

The Rise of Silas Lapham
Introduction by Kermit Vanderbilt

The social and moral questions posed by the Gilded Age of American business are chronicled in this tale of a newly rich New England family.

352 pp.   0-14-039030-8 $12.00

See The Portable American Realism Reader.

VICTOR HUGO
1802 – 1885, French

Les Misérables
Translated with an Introduction by Norman Denny

Including unforgettable descriptions of the Paris sewers, the Battle of Waterloo, and the fighting at the barricades during the July Revolution, this is at once a thrilling narrative and a vivid social document.

1,248 pp.   0-14-044430-0 $11.95

Penguin Readers Guide Available

Notre-Dame of Paris

Translated with an Introduction by
John Sturrock

Hugo's powerful evocation of Paris in 1482 and the tragic tale of Quasimodo, the hunchback of Notre-Dame, has become a classic example of French romanticism.

496 pp.   **0-14-044353-3**   **$11.95**

Selected Poems

Translated by Brooks Haxton

A brilliant new bilingual edition of Hugo's finest work: love poems, historical tableaux, elegy and idyll, including his incomparable "Boaz Asleep," which Proust acclaimed the most beautiful poem of the nineteenth century.

80 pp.   **0-14-243703-4**   **$12.00**

ALEXANDER VON HUMBOLDT
1769 – 1859, German (b. Berlin)

Personal Narrative of a Journey to the Equinoctial Regions of the New Continent

Abridged and Translated with an Introduction and Notes by Jason Wilson and a Historical Introduction by Malcolm Nicolson

With *Personal Narrative*, the German scientist and explorer Alexander von Humboldt invented the art of travel writing. Translated into English for the first time since 1851, this edition demonstrates

Humboldt's extraordinary ability to present scientific observations and information in an entertaining, engaging style. His book, imbued with the spirit of nineteenth-century romanticism, profoundly influenced Charles Darwin and other Victorian scientists.

400 pp.   **0-14-044553-6**   **$13.95**

DAVID HUME
1711 – 1776, Scottish

Dialogues Concerning Natural Religion

Edited with an Introduction and Notes by Martin Bell

Modeled on Cicero's *De natura deorum*, this classic treatise on natural religion portrays the eighteenth-century conflict between scientific theism and philosophical skepticism. Hume savages the traditional arguments for the existence of God and suggests that the only religion that can

VICTOR HUGO

Victor Hugo was the most forceful, prolific, and versatile of French nineteenth-century writers. He wrote Romantic costume dramas, many volumes of lyrical and satirical verse, political and other journalism, criticism, and several novels, the best known of which are *Les Misérables* (1862) and the *Notre-Dame de Paris* (1831). A royalist and conservative as a young man, Hugo later became a committed social democrat; during the Second Empire of Napoleon III he was exiled from France and lived in the Channel Islands. He returned to Paris in 1870 and remained a great public figure until his death: his body lay in state under the Arc de Triomphe before being buried in the Panthéon.

stand up to serious scrutiny is one that is rationally and philosophically derived by the human mind.

160 pp.   0-14-044536-6 $10.95

See The Portable Enightenment Reader.

A Treatise of Human Nature
Edited with an Introduction by Ernest C. Mossner

The first work of this influential philosopher is an unprecedented extension of the Copernican revolution in science to the realm of philosophy.

688 pp.   0-14-043244-2 $12.95

ELSPETH HUXLEY
1907 – 1997, Kenyan (b. England)

The Flame Trees of Thika
Memories of an African Childhood

Huxley's eloquent 1959 memoir ranks in beauty and power with Isak Dinesen's *Out of Africa*. As pioneering settlers in Kenya, Huxley's family discovered—the hard way —the world of the African. With an extraordinary gift for detail and a keen sense of humor, Huxley recalls her childhood in a land that was as harsh as it was beautiful.

288 pp.   0-14-118378-0 $14.00

"The secret of this book's compulsive attraction is the meeting of the fresh field and the innocent eye."

—MARY RENAULT

Red Strangers
Introduction by Richard Dawkins

Epic in its scale, *Red Strangers* is the thoroughly engrossing novel of four generations of a Kikuyu family whose lifestyle and culture were dramatically and damagingly transformed by the forces of colonization in Africa.

432 pp.   0-14-118205-9 $15.00

J.-K. HUYSMANS
1848 – 1907, French

Against Nature
Translated by Robert Baldick

This chronicle of the exotic practices and perverse pleasures of a hero, who is a thinly disguised version of the author, was condemned by the public as a work of alarming depravity—and was much admired by Oscar Wilde.

224 pp.   0-14-044086-0 $14.00

The Damned (Là-Bas)
Translated with an Introduction and Notes by Terry Hale

A masterpiece of French decadent literature, J.-K. Huysmans's gaudy, shocking, and largely autobiographical novel was condemned upon publication and just as quickly achieved cult status, with its portrayal of erotic devilry in fin-de-siècle Paris.

320 pp.   0-14-044767-9 $8.00

HENRIK IBSEN
1828 – 1906, Norwegian

Brand
A Version for the Stage by Geoffrey Hill

The story of a minister driven by faith to risk the death of his wife and child, *Brand* pits a man of vision against the forces of ignorance and venality.

176 pp.   0-14-044676-1 $11.00

A Doll's House and Other Plays

*Translated with an Introduction by
Peter Watts*

From *The League of Youth*, his first venture
into realistic social drama, to *A Doll's
House*, a provocative portrait of a woman's
struggle for freedom, to the family tensions
depicted in *The Lady from the Sea*, Ibsen is
concerned with the individual's conflicts
with society.

336 pp.   0-14-044146-8 $10.95

Ghosts and Other Plays

*Translated with an Introduction and Notes
by Peter Watts*

Incisive, critical, and controversial, *Ghosts*
and *A Public Enemy* depict the negative
effects of social rigidity on individual
lives; *When We Dead Awaken*, Ibsen's last
play, is a story of internal turmoil that can
be read as the dramatist's comments on his
lifework.

304 pp.   0-14-044135-2 $9.95

Hedda Gabler and Other Plays

*Translated with an Introduction and Notes
by Una Ellis-Fermor*

The Pillars of the Community and *The Wild
Duck* show Ibsen's preoccupation with
problems of personal and social morality;
Hedda Gabler, the latest of these plays, is
both a drama of individual conflict and a
partial return to social themes.

368 pp.   0-14-044016-X $8.95

The Master Builder and Other Plays

*Translated with an Introduction by
Una Ellis-Fermor*

The four plays collected here—*The Master
Builder, Rosmersholm, Little Eyolf,* and *John
Gabriel Borkman*—were written late in
Ibsen's career and reflect his then growing
interests in internal conflicts and the
dangers of self-deception.

384 pp.   0-14-044053-4 $7.95

Peer Gynt

*Translated with an Introduction by
Peter Watts*

This high-spirited poetical fantasy, based
on Norwegian folklore, is the story of
an irresponsible, lovable hero. After its
publication, Ibsen abandoned the verse
form for more realistic prose plays.

224 pp.   0-14-044167-0 $8.95

HENRIK IBSEN

Henrik Ibsen was born at Skien, Norway, in 1828. His family went bankrupt when
he was a child, and he struggled with poverty for many years. His first ambition
was medicine, but he abandoned this to write and to work in theater. A scholarship
enabled him to travel to Rome in 1864. In Italy he wrote *Brand* (1866), which
earned him a state pension, and *Peer Gynt* (1867), for which Grieg later wrote the
incidental music. These plays established his reputation. From *The League of Youth*
(1869) onward, Ibsen renounced poetry and wrote prose drama. He supported in
his plays many crucial issues of his day, such as the emancipation of women. Plays
like *Ghosts* (1881) and *A Doll's House* (1879) caused a critical uproar.

SAINT IGNATIUS OF LOYOLA
1491 – 1556, Spanish

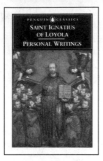

Personal Writings
Translated with Introductions and Notes by Joseph A. Munitiz and Philip Endean

The founder of the Jesuit order, Ignatius Loyola was one of the most influential figures of the Counter-Reformation. The works in this volume—*Reminiscences, The Spiritual Diary, The Spiritual Exercises*, and selected letters—shed light on the more private aspects of Ignatius's life and beliefs.

464 pp.   0-14-043385-6 $13.95

GILBERT IMLAY
1754 – 1828, American

The Emigrants
Edited with an Introduction by W. M. Verhoeven and Amanda Gilroy

Imlay's delightful epistolary adventure of 1793, set on the American frontier, was one of the first American novels. The trials of an emigrant family in the Ohio River Valley of Kentucky contrast the decadence of Europe with the utopian promise of the American West. Its sensational plots also dramatize the novel's surprising feminist allegiances.

400 pp.   0-14-043672-3 $12.95

ELIZABETH INCHBALD
1753 – 1821, British

A Simple Story
Edited with an Introduction by Pamela Clemit

In scenes charged with understated erotic tension, this novel tells the stories of the flirtatious Miss Milner who falls in love with her guardian, a Catholic priest and aristocrat, and of their daughter who, banished from her father's sight, desperately craves his love.

368 pp.   0-14-043473-9 $20.00

WASHINGTON IRVING
1783 – 1859, American

The Legend of Sleepy Hollow and Other Stories
With an Introduction and Notes by William L. Hedges

Irving's delightful 1819 miscellany of essays and sketches includes the two classic tales "The Legend of Sleepy Hollow" and "Rip Van Winkle."

368 pp.   0-14-043769-X $8.95

HARRIET JACOBS
c. 1813 – 1897, American

Incidents in the Life of a Slave Girl
Written by Herself

Edited with an Introduction and Notes by Nell Irvin Painter

Jacobs's haunting, evocative memoir of her life as a slave in North Carolina and her final escape and emancipation is one of the most important books ever written documenting the traumas and horrors of slavery—and the particular experiences of female slaves—in the antebellum South. This edition also includes "A True Tale of Slavery," written by Jacobs's brother, John, for a London periodical.

240 pp.   0-14-043795-9 $10.95

HENRY JAMES
1843 – 1916, British (b. American)

The Portable Henry James
Edited by Morton Dauwen Zabel

This essential selection includes three novellas, *The Turn of the Screw, The Beast in the Jungle*, and *The Pupil*; three short stories, literary criticism, travel writing, and letters.

704 pp.   0-14-015055-2 $15.95

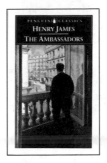

The Ambassadors
Introduction and Notes by Harry Levin

One of Henry James's three final novels, this tale, set in Paris, is a finely drawn portrait of a man's late awakening to the importance of morality.

520 pp.   0-14-043233-7 $5.95

The American
Introduction and Notes by William Spengemann

This story of an American millionaire rejected by the family of the European aristocrat he loves is James's first novel to dramatize the social relationship between the Old World and the New.

392 pp.   0-14-039082-0 $11.95

HENRY JAMES

Henry James was born into a brilliant family in New York City in 1843. In 1875, James moved to Europe, eventually settling in England. His fourth novel, *Daisy Miller*—a story about a naïve American girl visiting the Continent—became a runaway bestseller when it was published in 1879. His tale of the supernatural, *The Turn of the Screw*, created a sensation when it appeared in 1898 in *Collier's Weekly*. In it, as in his other works, James explored the interaction between innocence and corrupt experience. He was one of the first writers in the English language to embrace stream-of-consciousness writing and greatly influenced the works of writers such as James Joyce, Virginia Woolf, Joseph Conrad, and Edith Wharton. James died in 1916.

The Aspern Papers and The Turn of the Screw

Introduction and Notes by Anthony Curtis

Set in a palazzo in Venice, *The Aspern Papers* tells of the confrontation between an elderly woman and a charming young man; in *The Turn of the Screw*, the story of a governess and her charges, James conjures up inexplicable terrors.

272 pp.   0-14-043224-8 $5.95

The Awkward Age

Introduction and Notes by Ronald Blythe

This study of innocence exposed to corrupting influences has been praised for its natural dialogue and the delicacy of feeling it conveys.

328 pp.   0-14-043297-3 $8.95

The Bostonians

Edited by Richard Lansdown

In this story of a Mississippi lawyer and a radical feminist vying for exclusive possession of a beautiful woman, James explores what it means to be fully human, for both men and women.

480 pp.   0-14-043766-5 $9.00

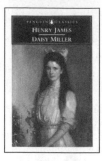

Daisy Miller

Edited with an Introduction by Geoffrey Moore and Notes by Patricia Crick

James's first novel to reach great popularity, this is also the first of his timeless portraits of American women.

128 pp.   0-14-043262-0 $5.95

The Europeans

Edited with an Introduction by Tony Tanner and Notes by Patricia Crick

This subtle examination of the effect of two slightly raffish Europeans upon their cousins in rural Boston in 1830 was published the year after James's *The American*.

576 pp.   0-14-043232-9 $7.95

The Figure in the Carpet and Other Stories

Edited with an Introduction and Notes by Frank Kermode

James's first short story, launched in 1864, was followed, throughout his varied literary career, by nearly a hundred more. This sampling includes "The Author of Beltraffio," "The Lesson of the Master," "The Private Life," "The Middle Years," "The Death of the Lion," "The New Time," "The Figure in the Carpet," and "John Delavoy."

464 pp.   0-14-043255-8 $12.95

The Golden Bowl

Introduction by Gore Vidal and Notes by Patricia Crick

A work unique among James's novels in that things come out happily for the characters, this is the story of the alliance between Italian aristocracy and American millionaires.

576 pp.   **0-14-043235-3**   **$8.95**

Italian Hours

Edited with an Introduction and Notes by John Auchard

In these essays on travels in Italy, written from 1872 to 1909, Henry James explores art and religion, political shifts and cultural revolutions, his own ambivalent reactions to the transformations of nineteenth-century Europe, and the nature of travel itself.

416 pp.   **0-14-043507-7**   **$13.95**

A Life in Letters

Edited by Philip Horne

Henry James and his beliefs, views, and art come to life in this fully annotated selection from his eloquent correspondence with the likes of Henry Adams, Edith Wharton, Robert Louis Stevenson, and H. G. Wells, as well as presidents, prime ministers, bishops, painters and more.

704 pp.   **0-14-043516-6**   **$16.00**

"Henry James was not only the greatest novelist in the English language, but also the greatest letter writer. . . . [These letters] are robust, funny, dignified, gossipy, informative, entertaining and, above all, beautifully written."

—JOHN BANVILLE

The Portrait of a Lady

Edited with an Introduction by Geoffrey Moore and Notes by Patricia Crick

Regarded by many critics as James's masterpiece, this is the story of Isabel Archer, an independent American heiress captivated by the languid charms of an Englishman.

688 pp.   **0-14-143963-7**   **$9.95**

Penguin Readers Guide Available

The Princess Casamassima

Edited with an Introduction by Derek Brewer and Notes by Patricia Crick

A young man involved in the world of revolutionary politics falls in love with the beautiful Princess Casamassima and finds he must make a choice between his honor and his desires.

608 pp.   **0-14-043254-X**   **$13.95**

Roderick Hudson

Edited with an Introduction by Geoffrey Moore and Notes by Patricia Crick

In his first full-length novel James writes with verve and passion about an egotistical young sculptor and the mentor who tries to help him develop his talents.

400 pp.   **0-14-043264-7**   **$9.95**

Selected Tales

Edited with an Introduction by John Lyon

In these nineteen haunting, witty, and beautifully drawn tales that span his career, James explores the Old World and the New, as well as money, class, and art. Included are "Daisy Miller," "The Lesson of the Master," "The Figure in the Carpet," and "The Real Thing."

704 pp.   **0-14-043694-4**   **$13.00**

The Spoils of Poynton

Edited with an Introduction by David Lodge and Notes by Patricia Crick

In this study of irreducible ambiguity, a family quarrel unfolds when a mother and son disagree on whom he should marry, and one of the potential brides will not make her true feelings known.

256 pp.   0-14-043288-4 $10.95

The Tragic Muse

Introduction and Notes by Philip Horne

James explores the tensions between the artistic life and worldly temptations in a novel that is at once satiric and serious. He muses on the concept of "art for art's sake," on the vagaries of society's infatuation with the artist, and, as he writes in his Preface, on "the personal consequences of the art-appetite raised to intensity, swollen to voracity."

576 pp.   0-14-043389-9 $14.95

Washington Square

Introduction and Notes by Brian Lee

This early novel, set in New York, is a spare and intensely moving story of divided loyalties and innocence betrayed.

224 pp.   0-14-043226-4 $7.95

What Maisie Knew

Edited with an Introduction and Notes by Paul Theroux and Additional Notes by Patricia Crick

In creating a portrait of a young girl raised in a world of intrigue and betrayal, James sketches with subtle irony the actions and motives of her corrupt adult companions.

288 pp.   0-14-043248-5 $9.95

The Wings of the Dove

Edited with an Introduction by John Bayley and Notes by Patricia Crick

The story of Milly Theale, a rich, lonely, and gravely ill young woman searching for happiness, this beautifully written novel deals with human greed and human tragedy.

520 pp.   0-14-043263-9 $9.95

See The Portable American Realism Reader.

WILLIAM JAMES
1842 – 1910, American

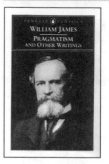

Pragmatism and Other Writings

Edited with an Introduction and Notes by Giles Gunn

This volume presents in its entirety James's seminal set of lectures in which he argues for the "reasonableness of ordinary experience" and selections from his other formative works, *The Meaning of Truth, Psychology, The Will to Believe,* and *Talks to Teachers on Psychology.*

368 pp.   0-14-043735-5 $14.95

The Varieties of Religious Experience
A Study in Human Nature

Edited with an Introduction by Martin E. Marty

In this synthesis of religion and psychology, James discusses conversion, repentance, and other religious experiences in terms of the individual experience rather than the precepts of organized religion.

576 pp.   0-14-039034-0 $13.00

JOHN JAY

See James Madison.

THOMAS JEFFERSON
1743 – 1826, American

The Portable Thomas Jefferson
Edited by Merrill D. Peterson

This volume presents a broad view of Jefferson in the fullness of his thought and imagination, including his famous essays, notes, state papers and addresses, including the Declaration of Independence; and letters to George Washington, James Madison, John Adams, and others.

640 pp.   **0-14-015080-3**   **$15.95**

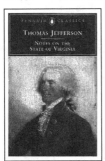

Notes on the State of Virginia
Edited with an Introduction and Notes by Frank Shuffelton

Jefferson's chronicle of the natural, social, and political history of Virginia is at once a scientific discourse, an attempt to define America, and a brilliant examination of the idea of freedom.

400 pp.   **0-14-043667-7**   **$14.00**

See The Portable Enlightenment Reader.

JEROME K. JEROME
1859 – 1927, British

Three Men in a Boat and Three Men on the Bummel
Edited with an Introduction and Notes by Jeremy Lewis

Three Men in a Boat is the beloved comic account of three friends and a dog as they experience misadventures on a "relaxing" river jaunt. Jerome's heroes proved so popular that he brought them back for an equally picaresque bicycle tour of Germany in *Three Men on the Bummell.*

400 pp.   **0-14-043750-9**   **$9.95**

SARAH ORNE JEWETT
1849 – 1909, American

The Country of the Pointed Firs and Other Stories
Edited with an Introduction by Alison Easton

Modeled in part on Flaubert's sketches of life in provincial France, *The Country of the Pointed Firs* is a richly detailed portrait of a seaport on the Maine coast as seen through the eyes of a summer visitor. Jewett celebrates the friendships shared by the town's women, interweaving conversations and stories about poor fishermen and retired sea captains, thus capturing the spirit of community that sustains the declining town.

304 pp.   **0-14-043476-3**   **$8.95**

See *American Local Color Writing* and *Four Stories by American Women.*

JAMES WELDON JOHNSON
1871 – 1938, American

"James Weldon Johnson's name stirs up emotions which are contained only by tremendous control....Aptly, deeply, with love and humor and a powerful rhyming tongue, he has told our story and sung our song."

—MAYA ANGELOU

The Autobiography of an Ex-Colored Man

Edited with an Introduction and Notes by William L. Andrews

First published in 1912, Johnson's pioneering fictional "memoir" is an unprecedented analysis of the social causes and artistic consequences of a black man's denial of his heritage.

304 pp.   **0-14-018402-3**   **$9.95**

Complete Poems

Edited with an Introduction by Sondra Kathryn Wilson

This volume brings together all of Johnson's published works, a number of previously unpublished poems, and reflections on his pioneering contributions to recording and celebrating the African American experience.

352 pp.   **0-14-118545-7**   **$14.00**

God's Trombones
Seven Negro Sermons in Verse

Illustrated by Aaron Douglas

The inspirational sermons of the old Negro preachers are set down as poetry in this classic collection.

64 pp.   **0-14-018403-1**   **$10.00**

Lift Every Voice and Sing
Selected Poems

This selection brings together more than forty poems including "Lift Every Voice and Sing"—Johnson's most famous lyric and now embraced as the African American National Anthem.

112 pp.   **0-14-118387-X**   **$9.95**

See The Portable Harlem Renaissance Reader.

SAMUEL JOHNSON
1709 – 1784, English

The History of Rasselas, Prince of Abissinia

Edited with an Introduction by D. J. Enright

The pilgrimage of Rasselas from Abissinia to Egypt is used as a vehicle for Johnson's musings on such wide-ranging subjects as flying machines, poetry, marriage, and madness.

160 pp.   **0-14-043108-X**   **$9.95**

Selected Writings

Edited with an Introduction and Notes by Patrick Crutwell

Generous selections from Johnson's major works include *A Journey to the Western Islands of Scotland, The Dictionary of the English Language*, and *The Lives of the English Poets*, as well as portions of his journals, letters, and papers.

576 pp.   **0-14-043033-4**   **$14.95**

SAMUEL JOHNSON
1709 – 1784, English

JAMES BOSWELL
1740 – 1795, Scottish

A Journey to the Western Islands of Scotland/The Journal of a Tour to the Hebrides

Edited with an Introduction and Notes by Peter Levi

The remarkable friendship between Johnson and Boswell is celebrated in these complementary journals written during their tour of Scotland in 1773. Abridged.

272 pp.   **0-14-043221-3**   **$14.95**

See James Boswell.

JEAN DE JOINVILLE
c. 1224 – 1317, French

GEOFFROI DE VILLEHARDOUIN
c. 1150 – c. 1218, French

Chronicles of the Crusades

Translated with an Introduction by M. R. B. Shaw

These two famous Old French chronicles were composed by soldiers who took part in the Holy Wars and offer both eyewitness accounts of the battles and pictures of life in the East.

368 pp.   **0-14-044124-7**   **$13.95**

See The Portable Medieval Reader.

BEN JONSON
1572 – 1637, English

The Complete Poems

Edited with a Preface and Notes by George Parfitt

Nearly 400 works display the characteristic blend of classical and contemporary ideals that imbues Jonson's work, including *Epigrams, The Forest, Underwoods: Miscellaneous Poems, Horace, The Art of Poetry,* and *Timber: Or Discoveries.*

640 pp.   **0-14-042277-3**   **$14.95**

Three Comedies

Edited by Michael Jameison

Shakespeare's nearest rival created in *Volpone* and *The Alchemist* hilarious portraits of cupidity and chicanery, while in *Bartholomew Fair* he portrays his fellow Londoners at their most festive—and most bawdy.

496 pp.   **0-14-043013-X**   **$11.95**

See The Metaphysical Poets.

FLAVIUS JOSEPHUS
c. 37 – c. 100, Roman (b. Jerusalem)

The Jewish War
Revised Edition

Translated by G. A. Williamson and Revised with an Introduction, Notes, and Appendices by E. Mary Smallwood

Josephus depicts in vivid detail the Jewish rebellion of A.D. 66, supplying much of the available information on first-century Palestine.

512 pp.   **0-14-044420-3**   **$14.95**

The Portable James Joyce
Edited by Harry Levin

This essential collection contains four of the six books on which Joyce's reputation is founded—*A Portrait of the Artist As a Young Man, Collected Poems, Exiles* (Joyce's only drama), and *Dubliners*—as well as generous samplings from *Finnegans Wake* and *Ulysses*.

768 pp.   **0-14-015030-7**   **$16.95**

Dubliners
Introduction and Notes by Terence Brown

In these stories about the men and women of the struggling lower middle class and their anxious desires for respectability, Joyce creates an exacting portrait of and a lament for his native city and Irish culture.

368 pp.   **0-14-018647-6**   **$9.95**

Great Books Foundation Readers Guide Available

Finnegans Wake
With an Introduction by John Bishop

Written in a fantastic dream-language, forged from polyglot puns and portmanteau words, the *Wake* features some of Joyce's most inventive writing.

672 pp.   **0-14-118126-5**   **$16.95**

"Joyce's masterpiece...if aesthetic merit were ever again to center the canon *Finnegans Wake* would be as close as our chaos could come to the heights of Shakespeare and Dante."

—HAROLD BLOOM

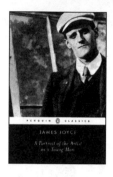

A Portrait of the Artist as a Young Man
Introduction and Notes by Seamus Deane

Joyce's rich and complex coming-of-age story of the artist Stephen Dedalus—one of the great portraits of modern "Irishness"—is a tour de force of style and technique.

384 pp.   **0-14-243724-4**   **$9.00**
(Available April 2003)

JAMES JOYCE

Born in Dublin in 1882 and educated by Jesuits, James Joyce moved to the Continent after graduating from the University of Dublin. While he was teaching English abroad, many of his closest friends were among the more than 500 Irish patriots killed by the British in the Easter Rebellion. Although he would never live in Ireland again, his works describe and reflect his homeland in both dialect and setting. His epic novel *Ulysses*, one of the supreme masterpieces of twentieth-century literature, was published in Paris in 1922 and banned as obscene in the United States until 1933. In 1940, Joyce fled Paris to Zurich, where he died the following year.

JULIAN OF NORWICH
c. 1342 – c. after 1416, English

Revelations of Divine Love
Translated by Elizabeth Spearing with an Introduction and Notes by A. C. Spearing

The first known woman writing in English, Julian of Norwich identified the female nature of Christ's suffering, the mother-hood of God, and, using images from domestic daily life, emphasized the homeliness of God's love. Including both the long and short versions of the *Revelations*, this translation from the Middle English preserves Julian's directness of expression and the rich complexity of her thoughts.

240 pp.   **0-14-044673-7**   **$11.95**

See Medieval Writings on Female Spirituality.

CARL JUNG
1875 – 1961, Swiss

The Portable Jung
Edited by Joseph Campbell

This comprehensive collection of writings by the epoch-shaping Swiss psychoanalyst includes his pioneering studies of the structure of the psyche, as well as inquiries into the psychology of spirituality and creativity, and Jung's hugely influential "On Synchronicity."

704 pp.   **0-14-015070-6**   **$17.00**

JUSTINIAN I
483 – 565, Roman

The Digest of Roman Law
Theft, Rapine, Damage, and Insult
Translated with an Introduction by C. F. Kolbert

Codified by Justinian I and published under his aegis in A.D. 533, this celebrated work of legal history forms a fascinating picture of ordinary life in Rome.

192 pp.   **0-14-044343-6**   **$15.00**

JUVENAL
c. 55 – 138, Roman

Sixteen Satires
Third Edition
Translated with an Introduction and Notes by Peter Green

Whores, fortune-tellers, shameless sycophants, aging flirts, and debauched officials populate Juvenal's Rome and he sternly puts into exquisite relief the splendor and squalor of his infamous times. In this edition, Green substantially revises and updates his celebrated translation.

320 pp.   **0-14-044704-0**   **$10.95**

See The Portable Roman Reader.

FRANZ KAFKA
1883 – 1924, Czech
(b. Austro-Hungary)

The Transformation ("Metamorphosis") and Other Stories
Translated from the German and Edited by Malcolm Pasley

This collection of all the works published during Kafka's lifetime includes "The Transformation," Kafka's famous story of a man who wakes to find himself trapped in the body of an insect; "The Meditation"; "The Stoker," a fragment from a novel set in America; "Before the Law," the only part of *The Trial* published during Kafka's lifetime; "In the Penal Colony"; and "A Fasting Artist."

256 pp.   **0-14-018478-3**   **$10.95**

BANNA KANUTE
d. 1994, Gambian

See Bamba Suso.

JOHN KEATS
1795 – 1821, British

The Complete Poems
Second Edition
Edited by John Barnard

In addition to all the poems and plays known to be written by the archetypal romantic poet, this edition includes long extracts from Keats's letters, his annotations to *Paradise Lost*, and two poems and a play fragment that have been attributed to him.

760 pp.   0-14-042210-2 $15.00

Selected Poems
Edited with an Introduction and Notes by John Barnard

This beautifully repackaged edition of Keats's most treasured poems illustrates both the rapid development of his poetic skills and his preoccupying themes of love, art, sorrow, the natural world, and the nature of the imagination. *Selected Poems* includes "On First Looking into Chapman's Homer," "Endymion," and "La Belle Dame Sans Merci."

256 pp.   0-14-043725-8 $11.00

See The Portable Romantic Poets.

MARGERY KEMPE
c. 1373 – c. 1438, British

The Book of Margery Kempe
Translated with an Introduction by Barry Windeatt

This earliest known British autobiography is a remarkable and touching record of the author's difficult pilgrimage from madness to Christian faith.

336 pp.   0-14-043251-5 $12.95

See Medieval Writings on Female Spirituality *and* The Portable Medieval Reader.

JACK KEROUAC
1922 – 1969, American

The Portable Jack Kerouac
Edited by Ann Charters

This omnibus presents selections from Kerouac's "Legend of Duluoz" novels, along with poetry, letters, and essays on Buddhism, writing, and the Beat Generation.

656 pp.   0-14-017819-8 $15.95

"Kerouac's work represents the most extensive experiment in language and literary form undertaken by an American writer of his generation."

—ANN DOUGLAS,
THE NEW YORK TIMES BOOK REVIEW

On the Road
Introduction by Ann Charters

The novel that defined the Beat generation, this exuberant tale of Sal Paradise and Dean Moriarty traversing the United States swings to the rhythms of the 1950s.

352 pp.   0-14-243725-5 $14.00
(Available January 2003)

See The Portable Beat Reader.

One Flew Over the Cuckoo's Nest

*With a Preface and Illustrations
by the author an Introduction by
Robert Faggen*

Boisterous, ribald, and ultimately shattering,
Ken Kesey's unforgettable story of a mental
ward and its inhabitants is the seminal novel
of the 1960s and a counterculture classic.

320 pp.   0-14-118122-2 $14.00
(Available in January 2003)

See The Portable Sixties Reader *and*
The Portable Western Reader.

The Economic Consequences of the Peace

Introduction by Robert Lekachman

One of the great economic and political
works of our time, Keynes's brilliant and
prescient analysis of the economic effects
of the Treaty of Versailles offered vehement
opposition to a reparations policy that
would stifle the German economy in the
aftermath of World War I.

336 pp.   0-14-018805-3 $17.00

Either/Or
A Fragment of Life

*Translated and Abridged with an
Introduction and Notes by Alastair Hannay*

The first major work by the precursor of
existentialism examines the philosophical
choice between aesthetic and romantic life
versus ethical and domestic life, and offers
profound observations on the meaning of
choice itself. Sheltering behind the persona
of a fictitious editor, Kierkegaard brings
together a diverse range of material, including reflections on Mozart and the famous
"Seducer's Diary."

640 pp.   0-14-044577-3 $16.95

KEN KESEY

Ken Kesey was born in 1935 and grew up in Oregon. He graduated from the
University of Oregon and later studied at Stanford with Wallace Stegner, Malcolm
Cowley, Richard Scowcroft, and Frank O' Connor. *One Flew Over the Cuckoo's Nest*,
his first novel, was published in 1962, and his second novel, *Sometimes a Great
Notion*, followed in 1964. His other books include *Kesey's Garage Sale, Demon Box,
Caverns* (with O. U. Levon), *The Further Inquiry, Sailor Song,* and *Last Go Round*
(with Ken Babbs). His two children's books are *Little Trickster the Squirrel Meets
Big Double the Bear* and *The Sea Lion.* Kesey died in 2001.

Fear and Trembling

Translated with an Introduction by Alastair Hannay

Abraham's unreserved submission to God's will provides the focus for this religious and ethical polemic. Originally written under the pseudonym of Johannes de Silentio, this is a key work in the psychology of religious belief.

160 pp.   **0-14-044449-1**   **$14.00**

A Literary Review

Translated with an Introduction by Alastair Hannay

Ostensibly a straightforward commentary on the work of a contemporary novelist, Kierkegaard's incisive essay developed concepts of religion, nihilism, and post-modernism that remain relevant to current debates on identity, addiction, and social conformity.

160 pp.   **0-14-044801-2**   **$13.00**

Papers and Journals
A Selection

Translated with an Introduction and Notes by Alastair Hannay

Drawn from Kierkegaard's private papers and journals, this meticulously edited volume of philosophical musings, theoretical arguments, and descriptions of everyday life sheds light on the conflicts that gave birth to his radical observations on the nature of choice, offers insights into his rejection of conventional Christianity and the formation of his belief in the "leap of faith," and reveals the moral intensity with which he lived his life.

688 pp.   **0-14-044589-7**   **$15.00**

The Sickness unto Death

Translated with an Introduction and Notes by Alastair Hannay

Arguing that true Christianity exists only in accordance with free will, Kierkegaard's stern treatise attacks Hegelianism and the established Church, and breaks ground for existentialism and modern theology.

320 pp.   **0-14-044533-1**   **$13.95**

RUDYARD KIPLING
1865 – 1936, British (b. India)
Nobel Prize winner

The Portable Kipling

Edited by Irving Howe

This essential volume of Kipling's writings contains selections from *The Jungle Books* and *Soldiers Three* as well as more than twenty stories, fifty poems, and three essays.

736 pp.   **0-14-015097-8**   **$16.95**

RUDYARD KIPLING

Rudyard Kipling was born in Bombay in 1865. During his time at the United Services College, he began to write poetry, privately publishing *Schoolboy Lyrics* in 1881. The following year he started work as a journalist in India, and while there produced a body of work, stories, sketches, and poems—including "Mandalay" "Gunga Din," and "Danny Deever"—which made him an instant literary celebrity when he returned to England in 1889. While living in Vermont with his wife, an American, Kipling wrote *The Jungle Books, Just So Stories,* and *Kim*—which became widely regarded as his greatest long work, putting him high among the chroniclers of British expansion. Kipling returned to England in 1902, but he continued to travel widely and write, though he never enjoyed the literary esteem of his early years. In 1907, he became the first British writer to be awarded the Nobel Prize. He died in 1936.

The Jungle Books
*Edited with an Introduction by
Daniel Karlin*

Kipling's knowledge of and love for the
jungle animates these delightful fables,
many featuring Mowgli the wolf boy. Both
The Jungle Book and *The Second Jungle
Book* are included in this volume.

384 pp.   0-14-018316-7 $9.00

Just So Stories
Edited with an Introduction by Peter Levi

Linked by poems and scattered with
Kipling's own illustrations, these imaginative fables were inspired by the author's
empathy with the animal world and his
delight with the foibles of human nature.

128 pp.   0-14-018351-5 $5.95

Kim
*Edited with an Introduction by
Edward W. Said*

The story of a young boy who moves
through two cultures, *Kim* captures India's
opulent, exotic landscape, overshadowed
by the uneasy presence of British rule.

320 pp.   0-14-018352-3 $7.00

Plain Tales from the Hills
*Edited by H. R. Woudhuysen with an
Introduction and Notes by David Trotter*

Originally intended for a provincial readership familiar with colonial life, these stories
of "heat and bewilderment and wasted

effort and broken faith" re-create the sights
and smells of India.

288 pp.   0-14-018312-4 $10.95

See The Penguin Book of First World War
Poetry.

HEINRICH VON KLEIST
1777 – 1811, Prussian

The Marquise of O— and Other Stories
*Translated with an Introduction by
David Luke and Nigel Reeves*

Between 1799, when he left the Prussian
Army, and his suicide in 1811, Kleist developed into a writer of unprecedented and
tragically isolated genius. This collection
of works from the last period of his life
also includes "The Earthquake in Chile,"
"Michael Kohlhaas," "The Beggarwoman
of Locarno," "St. Cecilia or The Power of
Music," "The Betrothal in Santo Domingo,"
"The Foundling," and "The Duel."

320 pp.   0-14-044359-2 $13.00

CHODERLOS DE LACLOS
1741 – 1803, French

Les Liaisons Dangereuses
*Translated with an Introduction by
P. W. K. Stone*

One of the most notorious novels of all time,
this eighteenth-century work describes the
intrigues of a depraved pair of aristocrats
plotting the seduction of a young convent girl.

400 pp.   0-14-044116-6 $9.95

MADAME DE LAFAYETTE
1634 – 1693, French

The Princesse de Clèves
Translated with an Introduction and Notes by Robin Buss

This romance about a woman's dangerous but platonic liaison is one of the first feminist novels and a precursor to the psychological realism of Proust.

192 pp.   **0-14-044587-0**   **$10.95**

JULES LAFORGUE
1860 – 1887, French

Laforgue: Selected Poems
With a Plain Prose Translation, and an Introduction by Graham Dunstan Martin

This extensive, bilingual edition of one of the originators of modern free verse illuminates Laforgue's unique voice and vision. Deeply nihilistic yet full of yearning, tender yet savagely self-mocking, his poems are presented here in the original French with running prose translations.

352 pp.   **0-14-043626-X**   **$12.95**

WILLIAM LANGLAND
c. 1330 – c. 1400, English

Piers the Ploughman
Translated with an Introduction by J. F. Goodridge

Written by a fourteenth-century cleric, this spiritual allegory explores man in relation to his ultimate destiny against the background of teeming, colorful medieval life.

320 pp.   **0-14-044087-9**   **$12.00**

AEMILIA LANYER
1569 – 1645, British

See Renaissance Women Poets.

LAO TZU
c. 6th cent. B.C., Chinese

Tao Te Ching
Translated with an Introduction and Notes by D. C. Lau

The principal classic in the thought of Taoism is a treatise on both personal conduct and government that advances a philosophy of meekness as the surest path to survival.

192 pp.   **0-14-044131-X**   **$7.95**

See The Portable World Bible.

RING LARDNER
1885 – 1933, American

Selected Stories
Edited with an Introduction by Jonathan Yardley

This collection brings together twenty-one of Lardner's best pieces, including the six Jack Keefe stories that comprise *You Know Me, Al*, as well as such familiar favorites as "Alibi Ike," "Some Like Them Cold," and "Guillible's Travels."

400 pp.   **0-14-118018-8**   **$15.00**

FRANÇOIS DE LA ROCHEFOUCAULD
1613 – 1680, French

Maxims
Translated with an Introduction by Leonard W. Tancock

The philosophy of La Rochefoucauld, which influenced French intellectuals as diverse as Voltaire and the Jansenists, is captured here in more than 600 penetrating and pithy aphorisms.

128 pp.   0-14-044095-X $12.95

NELLA LARSEN
1891 – 1964, American

Passing
Edited with an Introduction and Notes by Thadious M. Davis

First published in 1929, this landmark novel by the Harlem Renaissance's premier woman writer candidly explores the destabilization of racial and sexual boundaries.

160 pp.   0-14-243727-1 $10.00
(Available February 2003)

See The Portable Harlem Renaissance Reader.

Quicksand
Edited with an Introduction and Notes by Thadious M. Davis

The compelling story of a black woman's struggle to find acceptance and community evocatively portrays the racial and gender restrictions that can mark a life.

256 pp.   0-14-118127-3 $10.00

"Fine, thoughtful, and courageous It is . . . the best piece of fiction that Negro America has produced since the heyday of [Charles] Chesnutt."

—W. E. B. DU BOIS

BARTOLOMÉ DE LAS CASAS
1484 – 1576, Spanish

A Short Account of the Destruction of the Indies
Translated by Nigel Griffin with an Introduction by Anthony Pagden

No work is a stronger, more exacting, heartbreaking record of the Spanish atrocities in the genocidal enterprise of colonization in the Americas. This account provides an eyewitness's history of the process in the territory of Columbus.

192 pp.   0-14-044562-5 $11.95

LE COMTE DE LAUTRÉAMONT
1846 – 1870, French

Maldoror and Poems
Translated with an Introduction by Paul Knight

One of the earliest and most astonishing examples of surrealist writing, the hallucinatory tale *Maldoror* was hailed as a work of genius by Gide, Breton, Modigliani, and Verlaine. This edition includes a translation of the epigrammatic *Poésies*.

288 pp.   0-14-044342-8 $13.00

MARY LAVIN
1912 – 1996, Irish (b. America)

In a Café
Selected Stories

*Edited by Elizabeth Walsh Peavoy,
with a Foreword by Thomas Kilroy*

Compiled by her daughter, *In a Café* presents some of the masterworks of Mary Lavin, one of the twentieth century's most gifted and influential practitioners of the short story. Among the sixteen stories here are "In the Middle of the Fields," "A Family Likeness," and the title piece.

336 pp.   0-14-118040-4 $13.95

"Mary Lavin's stories have always given me a feeling of wonder and security... she is, after all, so original and astonishing."

—ALICE MUNRO

D. H. LAWRENCE
1885 – 1930, British

"The greatest writer of imaginative literature in the twentieth century."

—E. M. FORSTER

Apocalypse

Edited with an Introduction and Notes by Mara Kalnins

Apocalypse interweaves Lawrence's thoughts on psychology, science, politics, art, God, and man in a radical critique of the foundations of Western civilization—including a fierce attack on Christianity.

240 pp.   0-14-018781-2 $13.00

Complete Poems

Collected and Edited with an Introduction and Notes by Vivian de Sola Pinto and F. Warren Roberts

This definitive collection of Lawrence's poems, with appendices containing juvenilia, variants, and early drafts, and Lawrence's own critical introductions to his poems, also includes full textual and explanatory notes, a glossary, and an index for the work of one of the greatest poets of the twentieth century.

1,088 pp.   0-14-018657-3 $24.95

D. H. LAWRENCE

The son of a miner, the prolific novelist, poet, and travel writer David Herbert Lawrence was born in Eastwood, Nottinghamshire, in 1885. He attended Nottingham University and found employment as a schoolteacher. His first novel, *The White Peacock*, was published in 1911, the same year his beloved mother died and he quit teaching after contracting pneumonia. The next year Lawrence published *Sons and Lovers* and ran off to Germany with Frieda Weekley, his former tutor's wife. His masterpieces *The Rainbow* and *Women in Love* were completed in quick succession, but the first was suppressed as indecent and the second was not published until 1920. Lawrence's lyrical writings challenged convention, promoting a return to an ideal of nature where sex is seen as a sacrament. In 1925 Lawrence's final novel, *Lady Chatterley's Lover*, was banned in England and the United States for indecency. He died of tuberculosis in 1930 in Venice.

D. H. Lawrence and Italy
Twilight in Italy/Sea and Sardinia/ Etruscan Places
Introduction by Anthony Burgess

Taken together, these masterful, often rhapsodic impressions of the Italian countryside constitute "an indispensable guide to the sensibility of one of the most astonishing writers of our century" (Anthony Burgess).

512 pp.   0-14-110030-7 $17.00

The Fox/The Captain's Doll/ The Ladybird
Edited by Dieter Mehl with an Introduction and Notes by David Ellis

Set during and after the First World War, these three short novels feature struggles between men and women, a theme common to much of Lawrence's work.

272 pp.   0-14-018779-0 $15.00

Lady Chatterley's Lover
Edited with an Introduction and Notes by Michael Squires

This restored text of Lawrence's most famous work explicitly chronicles the affair between Constance Chatterley and the gamekeeper Mellors and includes the author's "Á Propos of Lady Chatterley's Lover," his final thoughts on the male-female relationship in the modern world.

400 pp.   0-14-018786-3 $12.00

Mr. Noon
Edited with Notes by Lindeth Vasey and an Introduction by Peter Preston

This edition of *Mr. Noon* brings to paperback readers the first authoritative, annotated version of an autobiographical novel that is, as David Lodge wrote in the *New York Review of Books*, a "vivid illumination on the early days of Lawrence's union with Frieda Weekley."

368 pp.   0-14-018973-4 $21.00

The Prussian Officer and Other Stories
Edited by John Worthen with an Introduction and Notes by Brian Finney

Written between 1907 and 1914, these twelve stories illuminate Lawrence's increasing interest in the conflict between immediate human experience and the eternal, impersonal forces that operate at the level of the unconscious.

304 pp.   0-14-018780-4 $20.00

The Rainbow
Edited by Mark Kinkead-Weekes with an Introduction and Notes by Anne Fernihough

Set in the rural midlands of England, *The Rainbow* revolves around three generations of the Brangwens. When Tom Brangwen marries a Polish widow, Lydia Lensky, and adopts her daughter, Anna, as his own, he is unprepared for the conflict and passion that erupts between them. This edition reproduces the Cambridge text, which is based on Lawrence's original manuscript.

528 pp.   0-14-018813-4 $10.00

Sea and Sardinia
Edited by Mara Kalnins with an Introduction and Notes by Jill Franks

In January 1921, D. H. Lawrence and his wife, Frieda, visited Sardinia. Although the trip lasted only nine days, his intriguing account of Sicilian life not only evokes the place, people, local customs, and wildlife but is also deeply revealing about the writer himself. This edition restores censored passages for the first time and corrects corrupt textual readings.

256 pp.   0-14-118076-5 $13.95

Sketches of Etruscan Places
And Other Italian Essays

Edited with an Introduction by Simonetta de Filippis

For Lawrence, Italy was the place of spiritual rejuvenation to which he frequently visited to escape the bourgeois conventions and grim materialism of his native England. These eight, highly personal short essays include sketches of Tuscany, Florence, and the Etruscan lifestyle.

384 pp.   **0-14-118105-2**   **$14.95**

Sons and Lovers

Edited with an Introduction and Notes by Helen Baron and Carl Baron

Presented in paperback for the first time in its complete form, including the restoration of eighty pages missing from previous editions, *Sons and Lovers* examines the tensions in the Morel family as the world around them moves from the agricultural past to the industrial future and their own dreams and illusions change.

544 pp.   **0-14-018832-0**   **$10.95**

Studies in Classic American Literature

Lawrence expounds on Franklin's *Autobiography*, Cooper's *Leatherstocking* novels, Poe's tales, *The Scarlet Letter, Moby-Dick, Leaves of Grass,* and other works.

192 pp.   **0-14-018377-9**   **$12.95**

Twilight in Italy and Other Essays

Edited by Paul Eggert with an Introduction and Notes by Stefania Michelucci

In 1912, Lawrence left England for the first time, visiting Germany, the Alps, and Italy. Although *Twilight in Italy*, about his experiences on his voyage, was his first travel book, as Anaïs Nin said "it cannot be read as an ordinary travel book, for his voyage is a philosophic, as well as a symbolic and sensuous one."

288 pp.   **0-14-018994-7**   **$12.95**

Women in Love

Edited by David Farmer, Lindeth Vasey, and John Worthen with an Introduction and Notes by Mark Kinkhead-Weekes

Considered by many critics to be Lawrence's masterpiece, *Women in Love* is a powerful, sexually explicit depiction of the destructiveness of human relations.

592 pp.   **0-14-018816-9**   **$10.95**

JOSEPH SHERIDAN LE FANU
1814 – 1873, Irish

Uncle Silas

Edited with an Introduction by Victor Sage

The orphaned Maud Ruthyn is sent to live with her father's mysterious brother, a man with a scandalous and even murderous past. Shunning the conventions of traditional horror, *Uncle Silas* is a chilling psychological thriller.

528 pp.   **0-14-043746-0**   **$11.00**

The State and Revolution

Translated with an Introduction and Glossary by Robert Service

In this seminal work of Soviet literature and Bolshevism, Lenin calls for the destruction of the bourgeoisie and capitalism and the establishment of a new postrevolutionary order.

192 pp.   0-14-018435-X $13.00

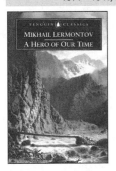

*A Hero of Our Time

Translated with an Introduction by Paul Foote

Lermontov's portrait of a cynical, flamboyant man influenced Tolstoy, Dostoyevsky, Chekhov, and other nineteenth-century masters.

208 pp.   0-14-044795-4 $12.00

See The Portable Nineteenth-Century Russian Reader.

If Not Now, When?

Translated by William Weaver with an Introduction by Irving Howe

Based on a true story and set in the final days of World War II, this powerful novel chronicles the adventures of a band of Jewish partisans making their way from Russia to Italy and waging a personal war of revenge against the Nazis.

360 pp.   0-14-018893-2 $13.95

Moments of Reprieve

Translated by Ruth Feldman

Against the terrifying, tragic background of Auschwitz, Levi preserves for future generations the tales of his friends, companions, and even adversaries who shared his hell during the Holocaust.

176 pp.   0-14-018895-9 $11.95

The Monkey's Wrench

Translated by William Weaver

This exuberant and funny novel, an enchanting collection of tales told between a self-educated construction worker and a writer-chemist, celebrates the joys of work and the art of storytelling.

176 pp.   0-14-018892-4 $12.95

PRIMO LEVI

Born in Turin, Italy, in 1919, Primo Levi was trained as a chemist. Arrested as a member of the anti-Fascist resistance, he was deported to Auschwitz in 1944. His experience in the death camp is the subject of his two classic memoirs, *Survival in Auschwitz* and *The Reawakening,* and of the recently published and acclaimed *The Periodic Table.* Dr. Levi retired from his position as manager of a Turin chemical factory in 1977 to devote himself full time to writing. He died in 1987.

The Monk

*Edited with an Introduction by
Christopher MacLachlan*

Savaged by critics for its blasphemy and
obscenity, *The Monk* shows the diabolical
decline of Ambrosio, a worthy Capuchin
superior who is tempted by Matilda—a
young girl who has entered his monastery
disguised as a boy—and eventually suc-
cumbs to magic, murder, incest, and torture.

416 pp.   0-14-043603-0 $9.95

The Journals of Lewis and Clark

*Edited and with an Introduction by
Frank Bergon*

Meriwether Lewis and William Clark's
remarkable chronicle of their Voyage of
Discovery across the pristine, uncharted
wilderness of the American West occupies
a unique place in American history, recording a natural world never seen by white
men: Edenic landscapes, mysterious native
people, and the first descriptions of
hundreds of plants and animals.

504 pp.   0-14-025217-7 $14.95

Babbitt

*Introduction and Notes by
James M. Hutchisson*

Babbitt captures the flavor of the United
States during the economic boom years of
the 1920s, and its protagonist has become
the symbol of middle-class mediocrity, his
name an enduring part of the American
lexicon.

320 pp.   0-14-018902-5 $9.95

Main Street

*Introduction and Notes by
Martin Bucco*

Main Street, Sinclair Lewis's portrait of
Gopher Prairie, Minnesota, shattered the
myth of the Midwest as God's country and
became a symbol of the cultural narrow-
mindedness and smug complacency of
small towns everywhere.

448 pp.   0-14-018901-7 $11.00

Poems

*Selected and Translated with an
Introduction and Notes by
Arthur Cooper*

More than forty selections from two
eighth-century poets of China cover the
whole spectrum of human life and feeling.

256 pp.   0-14-044272-3 $11.95

ABRAHAM LINCOLN
1809 – 1865, American

The Portable Abraham Lincoln
Edited by Andrew Delbanco

The essential Lincoln, including all of the great public speeches, along with less familiar letters and memoranda that chart Lincoln's political career. With an indispensable introduction, headnotes, and a chronology of Lincoln's life.

384 pp.   0-14-017031-6 $13.95

TITUS LIVY
59 B.C. – A.D. 17, Roman

*The Early History of Rome
Translated by Aubrey de Sélincourt with a Preface by Stephen Oakley and Introduction by Robert Ogilvie

The first five books of Livy's monumental *History of Rome* trace the foundation of Rome through the Gallic invasion of the fourth century B.C.

464 pp.   0-14-044809-8 $14.00

Rome and Italy
Translated and Annotated by Betty Radice with an Introduction by R. M. Ogilvie

Books VI to X span a dramatic century—from Rome's apparent collapse after defeat by the Gauls in 386 B.C. to its emergence as the premier power in Italy in 293 B.C.

400 pp.   0-14-044388-6 $14.00

Rome and the Mediterranean
Translated by Henry Bettenson with an Introduction by A. H. McDonald

Books XXXI to XLV cover the years from 201 B.C. to 167 B.C., when Rome emerged as ruler of the Mediterranean.

704 pp.   0-14-044318-5 $15.00

The War with Hannibal
Edited with an Introduction by Betty Radice and Translated by Aubrey de Sélincourt

Books XXI to XXX cover the declaration of the Second Punic War in 218 B.C. to the battle in 202 B.C. at Zama in Africa, where Hannibal was finally defeated.

712 pp.   0-14-044145-X $16.00

See The Portable Roman Reader.

JOHN LOCKE
1632 – 1704, English

An Essay Concerning Human Understanding
Edited with an Introduction and Notes by Roger Woolhouse

Locke's pioneering investigation into the origins, certainty, and extent of human knowledge set the groundwork for modern philosophy and influenced psychology, literature, political theory, and other areas of human thought and expression. Unabridged.

816 pp.   0-14-043482-8 $14.95

See The Portable Enlightenment Reader.

JACK LONDON
1876 – 1916, American

The Portable Jack London
Edited by Earle Labor

This essential collection includes the complete novel *Call of the Wild*, as well as a selection of London's famous stories, journalism, political writings, literary criticism, and selected letters.

704 pp.   0-14-017969-0 $15.95

The Assassination Bureau, Ltd.
Introduction by Donald Pease

London's suspense thriller focuses on the fine distinction between state-justified murder and criminal violence in the Assassination Bureau—an organization whose mandate is to rid the state of all its enemies.

208 pp.   0-14-018677-8 $14.00

The Call of the Wild, White Fang, and Other Stories

Edited by Andrew Sinclair with an Introduction by James Dickey

This volume contains the best of London's famed adventure stories of the North, including the mythic *Call of the Wild*, a vivid tale of a dog's fight for survival in the Yukon wilderness, and *White Fang*, the story of a wild dog's acclimation to the world of men.

416 pp.   0-14-018651-4 $7.95

Martin Eden

Introduction by Andrew Sinclair

This semi-autobiographical work depicts a young seaman's struggle for education and literary fame, and his eventual disillusionment with success.

480 pp.   0-14-018772-3 $14.00

Northland Stories

Edited with an Introduction and Notes by Jonathan Auerbach

Drawing on his own experiences during the Klondike Gold Rush of 1897, Jack London's stories, originally published in three volumes between 1900 and 1902, bring to life the harrowing hardships of life in the lawless wilderness.

400 pp.   0-14-018996-3 $10.95

The Sea-Wolf and Other Stories

Selected with an Introduction by Andrew Sinclair

In the title story, London writes of an old sea captain who attempts to put the theories of Spencer and Nietzsche into practice. Also included here are "The Sea-Farmer" and "Samuel."

320 pp.   0-14-018357-4 $9.95

Tales of the Pacific

Introduction and Afterword by Andrew Sinclair

At once rugged and deeply philosophical, these stories depict man's struggle for survival, battling not only the elements and the dangers of the great ocean but also the stark cruelty that is bondage, disease, hypocrisy, and secret sin.

240 pp.   0-14-018358-2 $10.95

See The Portable American Realism Reader *and* The Portable Western Reader.

HENRY WADSWORTH LONGFELLOW
1807 – 1882, American

Selected Poems

Edited with an Introduction and Notes by Lawrence Buell

Longfellow was the most popular poet of his day. This selection includes generous samplings from his longer works—*Evangeline, The Courtship of Miles Standish*, and *Hiawatha*—as well as his shorter lyrics and less familiar narrative poems.

240 pp.   0-14-039064-2 $14.00

See Nineteenth-Century American Poetry.

LONGUS
c. 2nd or 3rd cent. A.D., Greek

Daphnis and Chloe

Translated with an Introduction and Notes by Paul Turner

At the heart of much romantic literature of the modern era, this physically explicit and emotionally charged early novel holds an important place in the classical/European canon.

128 pp.   **0-14-044059-3**   **$11.95**

ANITA LOOS
1893 – 1981, American

Gentlemen Prefer Blondes and But Gentlemen Marry Brunettes

Introduction by Regina Barreca with Illustrations by Ralph Barton

This edition combines two brilliant satires of the Jazz Age and American sexual mores, featuring Lorelei Lee—the not-so-dumb blonde flapper from Little Rock. Lorelei's hilarious diaries record her adventures in search of champagne, diamonds, and marriageable millionaires. Intimately illustrated by the inimitable Ralph Barton.

352 pp.   **0-14-118069-2**   **$12.95**

H. P. LOVECRAFT
1890 – 1937, American

"I think it is beyond doubt that H.P. Lovecraft has yet to be surpassed as the twentieth century's greatest practitioner of the classic horror tale."

—STEPHEN KING

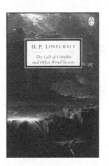

The Call of Cthulhu and Other Weird Stories

Edited with an Introduction and Notes by S. T. Joshi

An original selection of eighteen of Lovecraft's mesmerizing tales, including "Rats in the Walls," "The Colour out of Space," and "The Shadow over Innsmouth."

304 pp.   **0-14-118234-2**   **$12.95**

H. P. LOVECRAFT

H. P. Lovecraft was born in 1890 in Providence, Rhode Island. Frequent illnesses in his youth disrupted his schooling, but Lovecraft gained a wide knowledge of many subjects through independent reading and study. He wrote many essays and poems early in his career, but gradually focused on the writing of horror stories, after the advent in 1923 of the pulp magazine *Weird Tales*, to which he contributed most of his fiction. His relatively small corpus of fiction—three short novels and about sixty short stories—has nevertheless exercised a wide influence on subsequent work in the field, and he is regarded as the leading twentieth-century American author of supernatural fiction. Lovecraft died in Providence in 1937.

The Thing on the Doorstep and Other Weird Stories

Edited with an Introduction and Notes by S.T. Joshi

In these twelve chilling tales from the unrivaled master of the fantastic and macabre, Lovecraft melds together traditional supernaturalism with science fiction to create a dozen stories that will twist and turn readers' imaginations. Included here are "Under the Pyramids," "The Music of Erich Zann," and *At the Mountains of Madness*.

384 pp.   **0-14-218003-3**   **$13.00**

LUCRETIUS
c. 100 – c. 55 B.C., Roman

On the Nature of the Universe

Translated with an Introduction by R. E. Latham and Revised with an Introduction and Notes by John Godwin

This edition of the classic poem and seminal text of Epicurean science and philosophy—which shaped human understanding of the world for centuries—brings new textual research and additional context to Lucretius's explorations of spirit, mind, and soul.

320 pp.   **0-14-044610-9**   **$13.95**

See The Portable Roman Reader.

SIR CHARLES LYELL
1797 – 1875, British (b. Scotland)

Principles of Geology

Edited with an Introduction by James A. Secord

A hugely ambitious attempt to forge links between observable causes—earthquakes, tides, and storms—and the current state of the earth, this work proved crucial in the long-running dispute between science and Scripture. Its clarity, broad sweep, and sheer intellectual passion caught the imagination of Melville, Emerson, and countless readers worldwide.

528 pp.   **30 line drawings**
0-14-043528-X   **$15.95**

LORD THOMAS BABINGTON MACAULAY
1800 – 1859, British

The History of England

Edited and Abridged with an Introduction by Hugh Trevor-Roper

Macaulay's monumental *History* covers the period from the accession of James II through the 1688 revolution and up to the death of William III in 1702.

576 pp.   **0-14-043133-0**   **$14.95**

The Complete Fairy Tales

Edited with an Introduction and Notes by U. C. Knoepflmacher

Admired by his contemporaries including Lewis Carroll and an inspiration for twentieth-century writers such as C. S. Lewis and J. R. R. Tolkien, MacDonald's fairy tales allude to familiar tales but— employing paradox, play, and nonsense— are profoundly experimental and delightfully subversive. This edition brings together all eleven of MacDonald's fairy stories, including "The Light Princess" and "The Golden Key" as well as his essay "The Fantastic Imagination."

352 pp.   0-14-043737-1 $13.95

"One of the most remarkable writers of the nineteenth century."

—W. H. AUDEN

The Portable Machiavelli

Edited by Peter Bondanella and Mark Musa

This essential collection of Machiavelli's writings brings together the complete texts of *The Prince*, *Belfagor*, and *Castruccio Castracani*, as well as an abridged version of *The Discourses*, private letters, and selections from his *The Art of War*.

576 pp.   0-14-015092-7 $15.95

The Discourses

Edited with an Introduction by Bernard Crick with Revisions by Brian Richardson and Translated by Leslie J. Walker

Machiavelli examines the glorious republican past of Rome. In contrast with *The Prince*, this unfinished work upholds the Republic as the best and most enduring style of government.

544 pp.   0-14-044428-9 $12.00

The Prince

Revised Translation by George Bull with an Introduction by Anthony Grafton

Machiavelli's famous portrait of the prince still "retains its power to fascinate, frighten and to instruct." Rejecting the traditional values of political theory, Machiavelli drew upon his own experiences of office under the turbulent Florentine republic when he wrote his celebrated treatise on statecraft. The tough realities of Machiavelli's Italian are well preserved in the clear, unambiguous English of George Bull's translation.

144 pp.   0-14-044915-9 $6.00
(Available February 2003)

Great Books Foundation Readers Guide Available

See The Portable Renaissance Reader.

JAMES MADISON
1751 – 1836, American

ALEXANDER HAMILTON
1755 – 1804, American

JOHN JAY
1745 – 1829, American

The Federalist Papers

Edited with an Introduction by
Isaac Kramnick

The definitive exposition of the American Constitution, *The Federalist Papers* were considered by Thomas Jefferson to be the best commentary on the principle of government ever written. This collection of all eighty-five papers contains the complete first-edition text of the collected essays published from 1787 to 1788 in New York by J. and A. McLean. Includes the U.S. Constitution.

528 pp.   0-14-044495-5 $13.95

BERNARD MALAMUD
1914 – 1986, American

The Fixer

Based on the actual case of a Jewish Russian worker accused of murder in Kiev, *The Fixer* probes into themes common in Malamud's acclaimed work: the solitude of man ostracized by society and the conflicted legacies of the Jewish people.

304 pp.   0-14-018515-1 $14.00

SIR THOMAS MALORY
c. 15th cent., English

Le Morte D'Arthur

Edited with Notes by Janet Cowen and an
Introduction by John Lawlor

One of the most readable and moving accounts of the Knights of the Round Table, this version of the Arthurian legend was edited and first published by William Caxton in 1485.

Vol. 1   496 pp.   0-14-043043-1 $13.00
Vol. 2   560 pp.   0-14-043044-X $13.00

THOMAS ROBERT MALTHUS
1766 – 1834, British

An Essay on the Principle of Population

Edited with an Introduction by
Antony Flew

In a thesis that explores the disparity between the potential rates of population growth and the means of subsistence, Malthus presents the ultimate demographic choice: starvation or restraint.

304 pp.   0-14-043206-X $18.00

OSIP MANDELSTAM
1891 – 1938, Russian

Selected Poems

Selected and Translated by James Greene
with an Introduction by Donald Rayfield
and Forewords by Nadezhda Mandelstam
and Donald Davie

James Greene's acclaimed translations of the poetry of Osip Mandelstam are now in an extensively revised and augmented edition.

144 pp.   0-14-018474-0 $14.00

See The Portable Twentieth-Century Russian Reader.

The Travels of Sir John Mandeville

Translated with an Introduction by
C. W. R. D. Moseley

Though it is still disputed if, and how far, Mandeville actually traveled, his travelogue was consulted for hard geographical information by Leonardo da Vinci and Columbus and stands today as an informative portrait of fourteenth-century Europe.

208 pp.   **0-14-044435-1**   **$12.95**

Mephisto

Translated by Robyn Smyth

Mephisto is the story of an actor who, obsessed with fame and power, renounces his Communist past and deserts his wife and mistress to continue performing in Nazi Germany. The moral consequences of his betrayals eventually haunt him, turning his dream world into a nightmare.

272 pp.   **0-14-018918-1**   **$13.95**

Death in Venice and Other Tales

Translated with a Preface by
Joachim Neugroschel

In an acclaimed new translation that restores the controversial passages censored from the original English version, "Death in Venice" recounts a ruinous quest for love and beauty. Also included are eleven other stories, among them "Tonio Kröger" and "The Blood of the Walsungs."

384 pp.   **0-14-118173-7**   **$9.95**

The Garden Party and Other Stories

In deceptively simple language, Mansfield illuminates complicated relationships and profound, often troubling, ideas. The fifteen stories in this collection range from "At the Bay," an impressionistic evocation of family life set in her native New Zealand, to the title story, an ironic vignette about a society woman briefly touched by the real world at the funeral of her working-class neighbor.

192 pp.   **0-14-018880-0**   **$12.00**

The Betrothed
(I promessi sposi)

Translated with an Introduction by
Bruce Penman

Manzoni chronicles the perils of two lovers caught in the turbulence of seventeenth-century Italy.

720 pp.   **0-14-044274-X**   **$16.00**

MARCUS AURELIUS
121 – 180, Roman

Meditations
Translated with an Introduction by
Maxwell Staniforth

These musings, maxims, and thoughts on life and death reflect the Roman emperor's profound understanding and expression of Stoic philosophy.

192 pp. **0-14-044140-9** **$9.95**

MARGUERITE DE NAVARRE
1492 – 1549, Basque

The Heptameron
Translated with an Introduction by
P. A. Chilton

Inspired by a royal project to produce a French *Decameron*, these seventy stories mirroring Renaissance France's version of the battle of the sexes are attributed to Rabelais's patron, the sister of Francis I.

544 pp. **0-14-044355-X** **$16.00**

MARIE DE FRANCE
c. 12th cent., French

The Lais of Marie de France
Translated with an Introduction by
Glyn S. Burgess and Keith Busby

Twelve short story-poems, based on Breton tales of love in crisis, are presented in plain prose translations as close to the twelfth-century original as possible. The volume includes the Old French text of *Laüstic*.

144 pp. **0-14-0444759-8** **$10.95**

CHRISTOPHER MARLOWE
1564 – 1593, English

The Complete Plays
Edited with an Introduction by J. B. Steane

Reflecting the remarkable range of this Elizabethan dramatist's interests, this volume contains *Dido, Queen of Carthage, Tamburlaine the Great, Doctor Faustus, The Jew of Malta, Edward the Second*, and *The Massacre at Paris*.

608 pp. **0-14-043037-7** **$14.95**

JOSÉ MARTÍ
1853 – 1895, Cuban

Selected Writings
Translated and Edited by Esther Allen with an Introduction by Roberto González Echevarría

In this volume, José Martí, the most renowned political and literary figure in the history of Cuba, demonstrates his versatility as poet, essayist, orator, statesman, abolitionist, and the martyred revolutionary leader of Cuba's fight for independence from Spain.

400 pp. **0-14-243704-2** **$15.00**

"A revelation . . . Martí finally comes to vivid life through Esther Allen's exquisite translations." —CRISTINA GARCIA

ANDREW MARVELL
1621 – 1678, English

The Complete Poems
Edited by Elizabeth Story Donno

Based on recent studies of existing manuscripts, this collection of works by the seventeenth-century poet much admired by T. S. Eliot includes modern translations of Marvell's Greek and Latin poems, as well as his works in English.

320 pp.   **0-14-042213-7**   **$12.95**

KARL MARX
1818 – 1883, Prussian

The Portable Karl Marx
Edited by Eugene Kamenka

This is the ideal introduction to the work of Karl Marx, representing his most important writings, with the complete *Communist Manifesto* and substantial selections from his philosophical and political works, as well as documents, letters, and reminiscences.

720 pp.   **0-14-015096-X**   **$15.95**

Capital
Volume 1
Translated by Ben Fowkes

This 1867 study—one of the most influential documents of modern times—looks at the relationship between labor and value, the role of money, and the conflict between the classes.

1,152 pp.   **0-14-044568-4**   **$16.95**

Capital
Volume 2
Translated by David Fernbach with an Introduction by Ernest Mandel

The "forgotten" second volume of *Capital*, Marx's world-shaking analysis of economics, politics, and history, contains the vital discussion of commodity, the cornerstone to Marx's theories.

624 pp.   **0-14-044569-2**   **$15.95**

Capital
Volume 3
Translated by David Fernbach with an Introduction by Ernest Mandel

The third volume of the book that changed the course of world history, *Capital*'s final chapters were Marx's most controversial writings on the subject, and were never completed.

1,088 pp.   **0-14-044570-6**   **$17.00**

Early Writings
Translated by Gregor Benton and Rodney Livingstone

In this rich body of early work the foundations of Marxism can be seen in essays on alienation, the state, democracy, and human nature.

464 pp.   **0-14-044574-9**   **$15.95**

Grundrisse
Foundations of the Critique of Political Economy
Translated with a Foreword by Martin Nickolaus

Written between *The Communist Manifesto* (1848) and the first volume of *Capital* (1867), *Grundrisse*—essential to the understanding of Marx's ideas—provides the only outline of his full political-economic theories.

912 pp.   **0-14-044575-7**   **$20.00**

KARL MARX
1818 – 1883, Prussian

FRIEDRICH ENGELS
1820 – 1895, Prussian

*The Communist Manifesto

*Edited with an Introduction by
Gareth Stedman Jones*

The most influential piece of political
propaganda ever written is a condensed
and incisive account of the worldview Marx
and Engels developed during their hectic
intellectual and political collaboration. This
edition, with an introduction by a foremost
expert on Marx and Marxism, demonstrates
not only the historical importance of the
text, but also its place in the world today.

160 pp.   0-14-044757-1 $7.00

*Great Books Foundation Readers Guide
Available*

See Friedrich Engels.

A. E. W. MASON
1865 – 1948, British

The Four Feathers

With an Introduction by Gary Hoppenstand

In this classic British tale of one man's
struggle to erase the brand "coward" from
his name, A. E. W. Mason introduces Harry
Feversham, the guardsman who quits his
regiment just before deployment to war.
His friends and fiancée denounce him, and
to disprove his dishonor, he must use a
reinvented bravery to win back their love
and respect.

304 pp.   0-14-218001-7 $12.00

PETER MATTHIESSEN
b. 1927, American

Blue Meridian
The Search for the Great White Shark

Blue Meridian chronicles the search over
thousands of miles of ocean for the most
dangerous predator on earth: the legendary
Great White Shark. Filled with acute observations of natural history in exotic areas
around the world, this harrowing account
is one of the great adventures of our time.

204 pp.   0-14-026513-9 $12.95

The Cloud Forest

Filled with observations and descriptions
of the people and the fading wildlife of the
vast world of South America, *The Cloud
Forest* is Matthiessen's incisive, wry report
of his expedition into some of the last and
most exotic wild terrains in the world.

280 pp.   0-14-025507-9 $13.95

The Snow Leopard

In 1973 Peter Matthiessen and the field
biologist George Schaller went to Nepal
to study the Himalayan blue sheep and,
possibly, to glimpse the rare and beautiful
snow leopard. This National Book Award
winner is the account of their five-week
trek, unfolding and revealing the narrator
and his world.

336 pp.   0-14-025508-7 $15.00

"A beautiful, magnificent book... one of
the most wonderful accounts I know of
journeying in our time."

—W. S. MERWIN

The Tree Where Man Was Born

Skillfully and magically portraying the
sights, scenes, and people he observed
firsthand in several trips over the course of
a dozen years, Peter Matthiessen exquisitely
combines nature and travel writing to bring
East Africa to vivid life.

432 pp.   0-14-023934-0 $16.00

Under the Mountain Wall
A Chronicle of Two Seasons in Stone Age New Guinea

Drawing on his great skills as a naturalist and novelist, Peter Matthiessen offers a remarkable firsthand view of the Kurelu, a Stone Age tribe that survived into the twentieth-century in all its simplicity and violence—on the brink of incalculable change.

272 pp.   0-14-025270-3 $19.00

CHARLES ROBERT MATURIN
1782 – 1824, Irish

Melmoth the Wanderer

Edited with an Introduction and Notes by Victor Sage

Melmoth's satanic pact for immortality condemns him to wander the earth, a tormented outsider. This Gothic masterpiece —first published in 1820—follows in the tradition of both the classics of its genre and the works of Cervantes, Swift, and Sterne.

704 pp.   0-14-044761-X $12.00

W. SOMERSET MAUGHAM
1874 – 1965, British

"Maugham has given infinite pleasure and left us a splendor of writing."
—DIRK BOGARDE

Collected Short Stories
Volume 1

These thirty stories, including the piece "Rain," are set in the Pacific Islands, England, France, and Spain.

448 pp.   0-14-018589-5 $15.00

Collected Short Stories
Volume 2

The stories collected here, including "The Alien Corn," "Flotsam and Jetsam," and "The Vessel of Wrath," reconfirm Maugham's stature as one of the masters of the short story.

256 pp.   0-14-018590-9 $15.00

Collected Short Stories
Volume 3

Maugham learned his craft from Maupassant, and these stories, featuring his alter-ego Ashenden, display the unique and remarkable talent that made him an unsurpassed storyteller.

256 pp.   0-14-018591-7 $15.00

Collected Short Stories
Volume 4

These thirty stories—most set in the colonies at a time when the Empire was still assured, in a world in which men and women were caught between their own essentially European values and the richness and ambiguity of their unfamiliar surroundings—show a master of the genre at the peak of his power.

464 pp.   0-14-018592-5 $14.95

Liza of Lambeth

Maugham's first novel is about the gloomy, poverty-stricken world of South London in the 1890s and how it affects one young girl who tries to escape from it.

128 pp.   0-14-018593-3 $10.95

W. SOMERSET MAUGHAM
The Magician

The Magician

The Magician is one of Maugham's most complex and perceptive novels. Running through it is the theme of evil, deftly woven into a story as memorable for its action as for its astonishingly vivid characters.

208 pp.   0-14-018595-X $12.95

The Moon and Sixpence

Charles Strickland, a dull bourgeois city gent, is driven to abandon his home, wife, and children to devote himself slavishly to painting. In a tiny studio in Paris, he fills canvas after canvas, refusing to sell his works. He drifts to Marseilles and, finally, to Tahiti, where, even after being blinded by leprosy, he produces some of his most passionate and mysterious works of art.

216 pp.   0-14-018597-6 $9.95

Mrs. Craddock

In this penetrating study of an unequal marriage, Maugham explores the nature of love and happiness and finds that the two rarely coincide.

256 pp.   0-14-018594-1 $13.00

The Narrow Corner

First published in 1932, this volume recalls many of Maugham's best short stories, featuring a story of love, money, and mutiny.

224 pp.   0-14-018598-4 $13.95

Of Human Bondage

Introduction by Robert Calder

An obsessive love affair provides the pivot of this powerful evocation of a young man's progress to maturity in the years before the First World War.

608 pp.   0-14-018522-4 $11.95

The Painted Veil

Set in Hong Kong during the heart of a cholera epidemic, this novel portrays a young woman as she learns the true meaning of love—but her discovery comes too late.

256 pp.   0-14-018599-2 $14.00

The Razor's Edge

Introduction by Anthony Curtis

Intimate acquaintances, who are less than friends, meet and part in postwar London and Paris, in this story that encompasses the pain, passion, and poignancy of life itself.

320 pp.   0-14-018523-2 $14.00

The Summing Up

Written to give some account of how Maugham learned his craft and why he became such an acute observer of human beings, *The Summing Up* is like an intimate conversation with one of the great cultured minds of the century.

208 pp.   0-14-018600-X $12.95

GUY DE MAUPASSANT
1850 – 1893, French

Bel-Ami

Translated with an Introduction by Douglas Parmée

In this analysis of power and its corrupting influence, Maupassant captures the sleaziness, manipulation, and mediocrity prevalent in the elegant salons of Paris during the belle epoque.

416 pp.   0-14-044315-0 $13.00

Pierre and Jean

Translated with an Introduction by Leonard Tancock

An intensely personal story of suspicion, jealousy, and family love, this novel shows the influence of such masters as Zola and Flaubert on Maupassant's writings.

176 pp.   0-14-044358-4 $10.95

Selected Short Stories

Translated by Roger Colet with an Introduction by Ernest Mandelby

These thirty stories, including "Boule de Suif," "Madame Tellier's Establishment," "The Jewels," "The Mask," "A Duel," and "Mother Savage," range in subject from murder, adultery, and war, to the simple pleasures of eating and drinking.

368 pp.   0-14-044243-X $13.00

FRANÇOIS MAURIAC
1885 – 1970, French
Nobel Prize winner

Thérèse

Translated by Gerard Hopkins

In four stories set in Bordeaux and Paris and in a world bound by conventional morality, Mauriac charts the tortured life of Thérèse Desqueyroux, who dares to act on longings buried deep in her heart and whose refusal to bow to convention condemns her to solitude.

400 pp.   0-14-018153-9 $12.95

GAVIN MAXWELL
1914 – 1962, Scottish

Ring of Bright Water

Gavin Maxwell's account of his life in the Western Highlands of Scotland is a deeply moving portrait of a land and its inhabitants, including his two remarkable pet otters, Mijbil and Edal.

224 pp.   0-14-024972-9 $13.00

HERMAN MELVILLE
1819 – 1891, American

Billy Budd and Other Stories

Selected with an Introduction by Frederick Busch

"Billy Budd, Sailor," a classic confrontation between good and evil, is the story of an innocent young man unable to defend himself from wrongful accusations. Other selections include "Bartleby," "The Piazza," "The Encantadas," "The Bell-Tower," "Benito Cereno," "The Paradise of Bachelors," and "The Tartarus of Maids."

416 pp.   0-14-039053-7 $7.95

The Confidence-Man

Edited with an Introduction and Notes by Stephen Matterson

Part satire, part allegory, part hoax, *The Confidence-Man* is a slippery metaphysical comedy set on April Fool's Day aboard the Mississippi steamer *Fidèle*.

400 pp.   0-14-044547-1 $12.00

HERMAN MELVILLE

Herman Melville was born in New York, the son of a merchant, and largely self-educated. He started writing after having first sailed to Liverpool in 1839, where he joined the whaler *Acushnet* bound for the Pacific. Deserting ship the following year in the Marquesas, he made his way to Tahiti and Honolulu, returning as an ordinary seaman to Boston, where he was discharged in October 1844. Books based on these adventures, which include his masterpiece *Moby-Dick*, won him immediate success. However, this literary renown soon faded; his complexity increasingly alienated readers. Melville died virtually forgotten, and it was not until the 1920s that his reputation underwent the revision that has made him a key figure in American literature.

Moby-Dick
Or, The Whale
Edited with an Introduction by
Andrew Delbanco and Explanatory
Commentary by Tom Quirk

The story of an eerily compelling madman pursuing an unholy war against a creature as vast and dangerous and unknowable as the sea itself, Melville's masterpiece is also a profound inquiry into character, faith, and the nature of perception.

720 pp.   0-14-243724-7 $12.00
(Available January 2003)
Penguin Readers Guide Available
Great Books Foundation Readers Guide
Available

Moby-Dick, or, The Whale
150th Anniversary Edition
Foreword by Nathaniel Philbrick

This deluxe edition features a new Foreword by Nathaniel Philbrick, bestselling author of *In the Heart of the Sea.*

672 pp.   0-14-200008-6 $14.00

Pierre
Or, The Ambiguities
Introduction and Notes by
William C. Spengemann

A domestic tragedy and a land-based story, both subject and setting represent striking departures for Melville. But this spiritual autobiography in the guise of a Gothic novel, which describes the literary career of its idealistic hero, is now recognized as Melville's advance into the arena of the modern novel.

400 pp.   0-14-043484-4 $13.95

Redburn
Edited with an Introduction and Notes by
Harold Beaver

Based on his own experiences on a ship sailing between New York and Liverpool, Melville tells a powerful story of pastoral innocence transformed to disenchantment and disillusionment.

448 pp.   0-14-043105-5 $14.95

Typee
Introduction and Explanatory
Commentary by John Bryant

Typee is a fast-moving adventure tale, an autobiographical account of the author's Polynesian stay, an examination of the nature of good and evil, and a frank exploration of sensuality and exotic ritual.

320 pp.   0-14-043488-7 $12.95

See Nineteenth-Century American Poetry.

MENANDER
341 – 290 B.C., Greek

Plays and Fragments
Translated with an Introduction by
Norma Miller

The most innovative dramatist of the Greek New Comedy period, Menander concentrated on his characters' daily lives and colloquial speech in these comedies of manners. This selection contains all but two of Menander's surviving plays, passages attributed to him, and textual notes.

272 pp.   0-14-044501-3 $12.95

Mencius

*Translated with an Introduction by
D.C. Lau*

The fullest of the four great Confucian texts, Mencius draws out the implications of the master's moral principles stressing the importance of individual conscience and the necessity for morality in personal and public life.

288 pp.   0-14-044228-6 $12.95

See The Portable World Bible.

The Ordeal of Richard Feverel

*Edited with an Introduction by
Edward Mendelson*

Meredith's 1859 first novel concerns Sir Austin Feverel's misconceived attempts to educate his son, Richard, according to a system based on theories of sexual restraint. This wonderfully ironic and impassioned novel of war between the sexes and the generations shocked Victorian readers but gained a cult following.

560 pp.   0-14-043483-6 $11.95

Fourteen Byzantine Rulers

*Translated with an Introduction by
E. R. A. Sewter*

This chronicle of the Byzantine Empire, beginning in 1025, shows a profound understanding of the power politics that characterized the empire and led to its decline.

400 pp.   0-14-044169-7 $14.95

Five Plays

*Edited with an Introduction by
Bryan Loughrey and Neil Taylor*

Ranging from ingenious comedy to powerful tragedy, five plays—*A Trick to Catch the Old One, The Revenger's Tragedy, A Chaste Maid in Cheapside, Women Beware Women,* and *The Changeling*—portray the corruptive effects of politics and love in Elizabethan London.

464 pp.   0-14-043219-1 $14.00

Autobiography

*Edited with an Introduction by
John M. Robson*

This 1873 work by the founder of Britain's Utilitarian Society and the author of *System of Logic* and *Principles of Political Economy* describes Mill's intellectual and moral development from his earliest years to maturity.

240 pp.   0-14-043316-3 $13.00

On Liberty

*Edited with an Introduction by
Gertrude Himmelfarb*

Dedicated to the principle of the personal sovereignty of the individual, Mill's most famous work still stands as an essential treatise on the subject of human liberty.

192 pp.   0-14-043207-8 $9.95

JOHN STUART MILL
1806 – 1873, British

JEREMY BENTHAM
1748 – 1832, British

Utilitarianism and Other Essays
*Edited with an Introduction by
Alan Ryan*

Bentham's and Mill's influential socio-political ideas are set forth in essays and selections from larger works, enhanced by Alan Ryan's extensive Introduction analyzing the origins, development, and historical context of these ideas.

352 pp.   0-14-043272-8 $11.95

EDNA ST. VINCENT MILLAY
1892 – 1950, American

Early Poems
*Edited and with an Introduction and Notes
by Holly Peppe*

Millay's first three books of lyrics and sonnets are collected here: *Renascence, Second April,* and *A Few Figs from Thistles.* With a balanced and appreciative introduction and useful annotations, this volume presents some of the Pulitzer Prize–winning poet's best work in which she weaves intellect, emotion, and irony.

320 pp.   0-14-118054-4 $12.95

ARTHUR MILLER
b. 1915, American

The Portable Arthur Miller
*Edited by Christopher Bigsby with an
Introductory Essay by Harold Clurman*

This rich cross-section includes six complete plays spanning Miller's career: *The Golden Years, Death of a Salesman, The Crucible, After the Fall, The American Clock, The Last Yankee,* and *Broken Glass.*

608 pp.   0-14-024709-2 $16.95

All My Sons
Introduction by Christopher Bigsby

Winner of the Drama Critics Circle Award for Best New Play in 1947, Miller's first major play established him as a leading voice in American theater. In it he introduced themes that would thread their way through his oeuvre: the relationships between fathers and sons and the conflict between business and personal ethics.

96 pp.   0-14-118546-5 $9.00

ARTHUR MILLER

Arthur Miller was born in New York City in 1915. After attending the University of Michigan, he returned to New York where he began his remarkable career in playwriting after publishing the novel Focus in 1945. His first successful play, *All My Sons*, was soon followed by *Death of a Salesman*, which received a Pulitzer Prize in 1949 and established Miller as a preeminent American playwright. Written in 1953, *The Crucible*, a play about the Salem witch trials, is considered by many to be an allegory for the McCarthy hearings, which Miller attended. He wrote the screenplay for the 1961 film *The Misfits* for his second wife, Marilyn Monroe. *A View from the Bridge* garnered Miller his second Pulitzer Prize and the New York Drama Critics Circle Award in 1955. Miller broke ground in contemporary playwriting by portraying the dreams and despair of American working people.

The Crucible

Introduction by Christopher Bigsby

Based on historical people and real events, Miller's play about the witch-hunts and trials in Salem, Massachusetts, is a searing portrait of a community engulfed by hysteria. *The Crucible* is not only a play of extraordinary dramatic intensity, but a provocative reminder of the dangers of imposed moralities and "correct thinking."

176 pp.   **0-14-243733-6**   **$10.00**
(Available April 2003)

Death of a Salesman
Certain Private Conversations in Two Acts and a Requiem

Introduction by Christopher Bigsby

Hailed as the first great play to lay bare the emptiness of America's relentless drive for material success, *Death of a Salesman* is

Miller's classic portrait of an ordinary man's struggle to leave his mark on the world.

144 pp.   **0-14-118097-8**   **$10.00**

JOHN MILTON
1608 – 1674, English

The Complete Poems

Edited with a Preface and Notes by John Leonard

John Milton was a master of almost every verse style—from the pastoral, devotional, and tenderly lyrical to the supreme grandeur of his epic, *Paradise Lost*. This comprehensive, fully annotated edition of his poetry includes *Paradise Lost* along with his complete English, Latin, and Greek poems.

1,024 pp.   **0-14-043363-5**   **$15.95**

Paradise Lost

Edited with an Introduction and Notes by John Leonard

Long regarded as one of the most powerful and influential poems in the English language, Milton's epic work continues to inspire intense debate. Leonard's Introduction reflects on its controversies and contains full notes on language and the many allusions to other works.

512 pp.   **0-14-042439-3**   **$10.00**

JOHN MILTON

John Milton was educated at Cambridge, before being expelled from the university in 1632 for starting a fistfight with his tutor. Upon leaving the school, he abandoned his plan to become a priest. Instead, he took up writing, producing *A Masque* and "Lycidas." A Puritan supporter during the English Civil War, he wrote many political pamphlets and the famous prose piece in defense of freedom of the press, *Areopagitica*. He lost his sight in 1651, but it only proved to stimulate his desire to compose poetry. His great poems were published later in his life, including a ten-book version of *Paradise Lost, Paradise Regained, Samson Agonistes*, and, later, a twelve-book version of *Paradise Lost*. In 1674, Milton was struck with gout and died, and was buried next to his father in St. Giles, Cripplegate.

MOLIÈRE
1622 – 1673, French

The Misanthrope and Other Plays
A New Selection

*Translated by John Wood and
David Coward with an Introduction and
Notes by David Coward*

The Misanthrope, Molière's richly sophisticated comic drama with its dangerously
deluded and obsessive hero is accompanied
in this volume by *The Would-be Gentleman,
Tartuffe, Such Foolish Affected Ladies,
Those Learned Ladies*, and *The Doctor
Despite Himself*.

352pp.   **0-14-044730-X**   **$8.95**

The Miser and Other Plays
A New Selection

*Translated by John Wood and David Coward
with an Introduction and Notes
by John Wood*

This selection of Molière's scandalous,
shrewd, and witty commentaries includes
*The Miser, The School for Wives, The School
for Wives Criticized, Don Juan,* and *The
Hypochondriac*.

336 pp.   **0-14-044728-8**   **$10.00**

LADY MARY WORTLEY MONTAGU
1689 – 1762, British

Selected Letters

*Edited with an Introduction by
Isobel Grundy*

Lady Mary Wortley Montagu recorded
almost every aspect of her intriguing
existence in letters about love, politics,
science, gossip, and literature.

560 pp.   **0-14-043490-9**   **$16.00**

MICHEL DE MONTAIGNE
1533 – 1592, French

An Apology for Raymond Sebond

*Translated and Edited with an
Introduction and Notes by M. A. Screech*

A masterpiece of Counter-Reformation
and Renaissance argument, Montaigne's
Apology is a witty defense of natural
theology and an eloquent expression of
Christian skepticism.

240 pp.   **0-14-044493-9**   **$13.00**

The Complete Essays

*Translated and Edited with an
Introduction and Notes by M. A. Screech*

Montaigne, a great sage of Western thought,
set out to discover himself in his eclectic
collection of essays. What he discovered
instead was the nature of the human race,
poised at the beginning of the Renaissance.
This celebrated translation, in plain contemporary English, is true to his frank style.

1,344 pp.   **0-14-044604-4**   **$23.95**

Essays
A Selection

*Translated with an Introduction and Notes
by M. A. Screech*

Reflections by the creator of the essay form
display the humane, skeptical, humorous,
and honest views of Montaigne, revealing
his thoughts on sexuality, religion, cannibals,
intellectuals, and other unexpected themes.

480 pp.   **0-14-044602-8**   **$12.95**

"Screech is the master of Montaigne."
—ROY PORTER

See The Portable Renaissance Reader.

CHARLES DE MONTESQUIEU
1689 – 1755, French

Persian Letters
Translated with an Introduction by
C. J. Betts

In the form of letters between two Persian travelers in eighteenth-century Europe, this novel was written to show that France was moving from benevolent monarchy to royal tyranny.

352 pp.   0-14-044281-2 $13.00

See The Portable Enlightenment Reader.

MARIANNE MOORE
1887 – 1972, American

Complete Poems
This definitive edition contains sixty years of Marianne Moore's poems, incorporating her text revisions and her own entertaining notes that reveal the inspiration for complete poems and individual lines.

320 pp.   0-14-018851-7 $14.95

Selected Letters
Edited with an Introduction by
Bonnie Costello

Including correspondence with Eliot, Pound, and Elizabeth Bishop, this collection shows the gradual development of an authoritative woman of letters while documenting the first two-thirds of our century.

624 pp.   0-14-118120-6 $15.95

SIR THOMAS MORE
1478 – 1535, English

Utopia
Translated with an Introduction by
Paul Turner

Utopia revolutionized Plato's classic blueprint for the perfect republic—later seen as a source of Anabaptism, Mormonism, and even Communism.

160 pp.   0-14-044910-8 $7.95

WILLIAM MORRIS
1834 – 1896, British

News from Nowhere and Other Writings
Edited with an Introduction and Notes by
Clive Wilmer

Contained within one volume are the brilliant utopian novel *News from Nowhere* (1891) and essays by the socialist, pioneering environmentalist, designer-craftsman William Morris, whose antipathy toward the dehumanization of the Industrial Revolution was well known.

480 pp.   0-14-043330-9 $14.00

JOHN MUIR
1838 – 1914, American (b. Scotland)

The Mountains of California
With an Introduction by Edward Hoagland

This rhapsodic record of John Muir's time in the Sierras has become an American classic—both as an account of his life in the mountains and as a call for the preservation of America's forests and the establishment of national parks and reservations.

264 pp.   0-14-026661-5 $11.00

My First Summer in the Sierra
With an Introduction by Gretel Ehrlich

In a rapturous tribute to the place he loved most, John Muir tells the story of his first contact with the awe-inspiring mountains he dubbed "The Range of Light." This edition includes more than twenty of Muir's original sketches.

264 pp.   0-14-025570-2 $9.95

Travels in Alaska
With an Introduction by Richard Nelson

The three rigorous, exhilarating trips John Muir took through Alaska between 1879 and 1890 are recorded here in all their incomprehensible beauty.

248 pp.   0-14-026832-4 $10.95

Max Havelaar
Or, The Coffee Auctions of the Dutch Trading Company

Translated with Notes by Roy Edwards and an Introduction by R. P. Meijer

Based on the author's actual experiences, *Max Havelaar* is one of the most forceful indictments of colonialism ever written. Its portrayal of colonial cruelty in Indonesia is rendered in prose that ranges from colloquial informality to cadences of biblical resonance, and the sophistication of its satire led D. H. Lawrence to compare it to the works of Swift, Gogol, and Twain.

352 pp.   0-14-044516-1 $13.95

The Diary of Lady Murasaki

Translated with an Introduction and Notes by Richard Bowring

Witty portraits of ladies-in-waiting and courtiers, delightful anecdotes about intrigues both political and romantic, and intimate musings are interwoven with detailed accounts of official court events in Lady Murasaki's magnificent record of her life as a member of Empress Akiko's entourage during the years 1005 to 1010.

160 pp.   0-14-043576-X $12.00

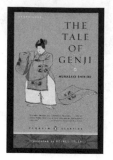

The Tale of Genji

Translated with an Introduction and Notes by Royall Tyler

This exquisite portrait of courtly life in medieval Japan is widely celebrated as the world's first novel. This deluxe edition of Royall Tyler's majestic new translation—the first into English since 1976—captures Genji's passionate nature as well as the family circumstances, love affairs, alliances, and shifting political fortunes that form the core of this ancient epic.

1,216 pp.   0-14-243714-X $28.00

"Superbly written and genuinely engaging . . . one of those works that can be read and reread throughout one's life"

—LIZA DALBY, *LOS ANGELES TIMES BOOK REVIEW*

MURASAKI SHIKIBU

Murasaki Shikibu was born in Japan c. 973, during the Heian period (794–1192), when the head of the major faction of the Fujiwara clan, Michinaga, held sway over the imperial court. Apart from what she reveals in her diary, we know little of her life. She married around the turn of the century, had one daughter, and was widowed soon after. During the next four or five years Murasaki seems to have begun writing *The Tale of Genji*, the astonishingly complex and sophisticated work of fiction that was to bring her fame and eventually be recognized as one of the masterpieces of Japanese literature. It is probable that chapters were read at court and came to the notice of Michinaga, who decided that she would be an excellent addition to the entourage of his daughter Shōshi (or Akiko), the young emperor's young consort. Murasaki entered the service of Shōshi in 1006 and probably died sometime between 1014 and 1025.

IRIS MURDOCH
1919 – 1999, British (b. Dublin)

The Bell

With an Introduction by A. S. Byatt

Murdoch's highly regarded novel of the terrible accidents of human frailty is a funny, sad, and moving exploration of religion, sex, and the fight between good and evil.

336 pp.   **0-14-18669-0**   **$15.00**

The Black Prince

With an Introduction by Martha C. Nussbaum

In this riveting and ingenious tale of love and intellectual intrigue, Murdoch gives us a story with ever-mounting action including seduction, suicide, abduction, romantic idylls, murder, and due process of law.

432 pp.   **0-14-218011-4**   **$14.00**
(Available April 2003)

A Fairly Honourable Defeat

Introduction by Peter Reed

A dark comedy of errors, this novel portrays the mischief wrought by Julius, a cynical intellectual who decides to demonstrate through a Machiavellian experiment how easily loving couples, caring friends, and devoted siblings can be induced to betray their loyalties.

464 pp.   **0-14-118617-8**   **$15.00**

The Good Apprentice

One of Murdoch's most popular and influential novels, *The Good Apprentice* is a supremely sophisticated and entertaining inquiry into the spiritual crises that afflict the modern world.

528 pp.   **0-14-118668-2**   **$15.00**

Nuns and Soldiers

With an Introduction by Karen Armstrong

With a most colorful cast of characters, set in Londuthern, France, Murdoch's most compelling novel is a tragic and funny story of love, honor, and reviving passion.

528 pp.   **0-14-218009-2**   **$15.00**

The Sea, the Sea

Introduction by Mary Kinzie

A celebrated actor, director, and playwright retires from the theater to write his memoir but it becomes, instead, a chronicle of strange events and unexpected visitors—some real, some spectral—that disrupt his world and shake his oversized ego to its very core.

528 pp.   **0-14-118616-X**   **$15.00**

Penguin Readers Guide Available

The Confusions of Young Törless

Translated by Shaun Whiteside with an Introduction by J. M. Coetzee

Musil's devastating parable about the abuse of power that lies beneath the calm surface of bourgeois life takes a dark journey through the irrational undercurrents of humanity and its often depraved psychology.

176 pp.   0-14-218000-9 $12.00

North of South
An African Journey

Based on Naipaul's travels through Kenya, Tanzania, and Zambia in search of answers, this is a travel narrative in the classic tradition—and a scathing, comic, and poignant portrait of the reality behind the rhetoric of liberation.

352 pp.   0-14-018826-6 $15.00

The Guide

Raju was India's most corrupt tourist guide until a peasant mistakes him for a holy man. Gradually he begins to play the part —so well, in fact, that God himself intervenes to put Raju's new holiness to the test.

224 pp.   0-14-018547-X $14.00

Malgudi Days

In this marvelous collection of stories, all kinds of people—simple and not so simple —are drawn in full color and endearing domestic detail as the author creates the imaginary city of Malgudi.

256 pp.   0-14-018543-7 $12.95

R. K. NARAYAN

R. K. Narayan was born in Madras, South India, in 1906, and educated there and at Maharaja's College in Mysore. His first novel, *Swami and Friends* and its successor, *The Bachelor of Arts,* are both set in the enchanting fictional territory of Malgudi and are only two out of the twelve novels he based there. In 1958 Narayan's work *The Guide* won him the National Prize of the Indian Literary Academy, his country's highest literary honor. In addition to his novels, Narayan has authored five collections of short stories, including *A Horse and Two Goats, Malgudi Days*, and *Under the Banyan Tree,* two travel books, two volumes of essays, a volume of memoirs, and the re-told legends *Gods, Demons and Others, The Ramayana*, and *The Mahabharata.* In 1980 he was awarded the A. C. Benson Medal by the Royal Society of Literature and in 1982 he was made an Honorary Member of the American Academy and Institute of Arts and Letters. Narayan died in 2001.

The Man-Eater of Malgudi

Narayan slyly and sometimes wickedly weaves a story of comedic and vastly human conflict in the enchanted city of Malgudi when an entangling dispute errupts between the local owner of a small printing press and his tenant, Vasu, a pugnacious taxidermist in search of an elephant for his stuffed collection.

176 pp.   **0-14-018548-8**   **$12.00**

The Painter of Signs

In this wry, funny, bittersweet story, love gets in the way of progress when Raman, a sign painter, meets the thrillingly independent Daisy, who wishes to bring birth control to the city of Malgudi.

144 pp.   **0-14-018549-6**   **$14.00**

The Ramayana

This shortened modern prose version of the Indian epic—parts of which date from 500 B.C.—was composed by one of today's supreme storytellers.

192 pp.   **0-14-018700-6**   **11.00**

A Tiger for Malgudi

A comic view of human absurdities told from the point of view of a tiger named Raja, and one of Narayan's beloved Malgudi novels, this work is infused with Hindu mysticism and delightful humor.

160 pp.   **0-14-018545-3**   **$13.00**

THOMAS NASHE
1567 – c. 1601, English

The Unfortunate Traveller and Other Works

Edited with an Introduction by J. B. Steane

Elizabethan manners, morality, and mirth are captured in this selection from the works of Thomas Nashe—pamphleteer, poet, satirist, scholar, moralist, and jester.

512 pp.   **0-14-043067-9**   **$15.00**

PABLO NERUDA
1904 – 1973, Chilean
Nobel Prize winner

Twenty Love Poems and a Song of Despair

Translated by W. S. Merwin

This edition of Neruda's most enduring and popular work—love poems of daring symbolism and sensuality—contains the original Spanish text with the English translation on facing pages.

88 pp.   **0-14-018648-4**   **$9.95**

GÉRARD DE NERVAL
1808 – 1855, French

Selected Writings

Translated with Introductions by Richard Sieburth

This selection provides the most inclusive and comprehensive overview in English of the brilliant and eccentric poet, belletrist, short-story writer, and autobiographer admired by Baudelaire, Proust, Breton, and Artaud. Including "Aurélia," "Sylvie," the sonnets of "The Chimeras," the *Doppelgänger* tales, correspondence, and more, this volume won the PEN/Book-of-the-Month Club Translation Prize.

448 pp.   **0-14-044601-X**   **$13.95**

"The most gorgeous lines in the French language." —MARCEL PROUST

JOHN HENRY NEWMAN
1801 – 1890, British

Apologia pro Vita Sua
Edited with an Introduction by Ian Ker

This spiritual autobiography of great power was written in response to personal attacks and conceived as a justification of his own actions when Newman's conversion to Roman Catholicism rocked the Church of England and escalated the spread of anti-Catholicism in Victorian England.

608 pp.   0-14-043374-0 $15.95

THOMAS NICKERSON
1805 – 1883, American

OWEN CHASE
1796 – 1869, American

The Loss of the Ship *Essex*, Sunk by a Whale
First Person Accounts
Edited by Thomas Philbrick with an Introduction by Nathaniel Philbrick

In 1820, the Nantucket whaleship *Essex* was rammed and sunk by an angry sperm whale. The incident was the *Titanic* story of its day and provided the inspiration for Melville's *Moby-Dick*. This edition combines the only extant first-person narratives of the doomed voyage with every relevant contemporary account.

256 pp.   0-14-043796-7 $12.95

FRIEDRICH NIETZSCHE
1844 – 1900, German

The Portable Nietzsche
Edited and Translated by Walter Kaufmann

This essential collection includes the definitive translations of *Twilight of the Idols, The Antichrist, Nietzsche Contra Wagner,* and *Thus Spoke Zarathustra,* as well as selections from his other books, notes, and letters.

704 pp.   0-14-015062-5 $17.00

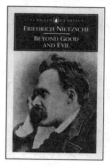

Beyond Good and Evil
Translated by R. J. Hollingdale with a New Introduction by Michael Tanner

Nietzsche discusses how cultures lose their creative drives and become decadent, offering a wealth of fresh insights into such themes as the self-destructive urge of Christianity, the prevalence of "slave moralities," and the dangers of the pursuit of philosophical or scientific truth.

240 pp.   0-14-044923-X $11.95

FRIEDRICH NIETZSCHE

The philosopher Friedrich Nietzsche was born in Prussia in 1844. After the death of his father, a Lutheran minister, Nietzsche was raised from the age of five by his mother in a household of women. In 1869 he was appointed Professor of Classical Philology at the University of Basel, where he taught until 1879 when poor health forced him to retire. He never recovered from a nervous breakdown in 1889 and died eleven years later. Known for saying that "god is dead," Nietzsche propounded his metaphysical construct of the superiority of the disciplined individual (superman) living in the present over traditional values derived from Christianity and its emphasis on heavenly rewards. His ideas were appropriated by the Fascists, who turned his theories into social realities that he had never intended.

The Birth of Tragedy

Edited with an Introduction by
Michael Tanner and Translated by
Shaun Whiteside

Nietzsche's first book, published in 1871 and now a seminal work of Western culture, is filled with passionate energy and argument probing the relationship between our experiences of suffering in life and in art, myths, and legends.

160 pp.   0 14 043330 2 $0.06

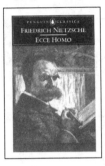

Ecce Homo

Translated by R. J. Hollingdale with an
Introduction by Michael Tanner

This strange and moving autobiography of Nietzsche was begun in late 1888, weeks before his final psychological breakdown.

144 pp.   0-14-044515-3 $12.00

A Nietzsche Reader

Selected and Translated with an
Introduction by R. J. Hollingdale

Designed to give an overview of Nietzsche's thought, of his approach to the conventional problems of Western philosophy, and of his own philosophy of "the will to power," this anthology includes 240 thematically arranged passages from his major philosophical works.

288 pp.   0-14-044329-0 $14.00

Thus Spake Zarathustra

Translated with an Introduction by
R. J. Hollingdale

Nietzsche's most accessible work, this spiritual odyssey through the modern world influenced such writers as Shaw, Lawrence, Mann, and Sartre.

352 pp.   0-14-044118-2 $14.00

Twilight of the Idols and The Anti-Christ

Translated by R. J. Hollingdale with a
New Introduction by Michael Tanner

Written in 1888, before he succumbed to insanity, *Twilight of the Idols* is a fascinating summation of Nietzsche's rejection of the prevalent ideas of his time; *The Anti-Christ* is his passionate challenge to institutional Christianity.

208 pp.   0-14-044514-5 $10.95

FRANK NORRIS
1870 – 1902, American

McTeague
A Story of San Francisco

Introduction by Kevin Starr

Set against the harsh California landscape, this novel by one of America's foremost literary realists preserves, in almost obsessive detail, the darker side of a still-young San Francisco.

496 pp.   0-14-018769-3 $10.95

The Octopus
A Story of California

Introduction by Kevin Starr

Based on an actual violent dispute in California's Great Central Valley, *The Octopus* (1901) depicts the clash between classic opposing interests of the Progressive Era— the farmers and the land-hungry railroads that distributed their wheat.

496 pp.   0-14-018770-7 $14.95

The Pit
A Story of Chicago
Introduction and Notes by Joseph A. McElrath, Jr. and Gwendolyn Jones

This classic literary critique of turn-of-the-century capitalism in the United States reveals Norris's powerful story of an obsessed trader intent on cornering the wheat market and the consequences of his unchecked greed.

496 pp.   **0-14-018758-8**   **$15.00**

NOTKER THE STAMMERER

See Einhard.

SEAN O'CASEY

See J. M. Synge.

MARGARET OLIPHANT
1828 – 1897, Scottish

Miss Marjoribanks
Edited with an Introduction and Notes by Elizabeth Jay

The esteemed English critic Q. D. Leavis declared Oliphant's heroine, Lucilla, to be the "missing link" in nineteenth-century literature between Jane Austen's Emma and George Eliot's Dorothea Brooke, and "more entertaining, more impressive, and more likeable than either."

512 pp.   **0-14-043630-8**   **$15.00**

SIGURD OLSON
1900 – 1982, American

Songs of the North
Edited with an Introduction by Howard Frank Mosher

In these simple, eloquent essays, Sigurd Olson brings briskly to life the primitive and lovely land of deep icy lakes, unmapped streams, and the thick forests of the Quetico-Superior country of northern Minnesota and Ontario.

268 pp.   **0-14-025218-5**   **$17.00**

OMAR KHAYYÁM
c. 1048 – c. 1122, Persian

The Rubaiyat of Omar Khayyám
Selected and Translated with an Introduction by Peter Avery and John Heath-Stubbs

This contemporary edition of Khayyám has been selected and translated by Persian scholar Peter Avery and poet John Heath-Stubbs.

120 pp.   **0-14-044384-3**   **$9.95**

EUGENE O'NEILL
1888 – 1953, American
Nobel Prize winner

Early Plays

*Edited with an Introduction by
Jeffrey H. Richards*

This volume brings together the early works of one of the most significant and influential figures in the history of American theater. Included here are seven one-act plays, and five full-length plays including *The Emperor Jones* and *The Hairy Ape*.

368 pp.   **0-14-118670-4**   **$12.00**

See The Portable Harlem Renaissance Reader.

OVID
43 B.C. – c. A.D. 17, Roman

The Erotic Poems

Translated with an Introduction and Notes by Peter Green

These works by the foremost erotic poet of the Augustan period—*The Art of Love, The Amores, Cures for Love,* and *On Facial Treatment for Ladies*—give testament to the whole spectrum of sexual behavior.

464 pp.   **0-14-044360-6**   **$14.00**

Fasti

Translated and Edited with an Introduction, Notes, and Glossary by A. J. Boyle and R. D. Woodward

The *Fasti* is both a poem on the Roman religious calendar and a witty sequence of stories that contain uncomfortable political echoes. Ovid's final poem playfully subverts the values of the emperor who sent him into exile.

432 pp.   **0-14-044690-7**   **$14.00**

Heroides

Translated with an Introduction and Notes by Harold Isbell

Dramatic monologues in the form of love letters written between mythological lovers demonstrate Ovid's gift for psychological insight.

288 pp.   **0-14-042355-9**   **$13.95**

Metamorphoses

Translated with an Introduction by Mary M. Innes

Culled from Greek poems and myths, Latin folklore, and tales from Babylon and the East, Ovid's *Metamorphoses* is examined in historical and literary context in Mary Innes's Introduction.

368 pp.   **0-14-044058-5**   **$11.00**

See The Portable Roman Reader.

THOMAS PAINE
1737 – 1809, American (b. England)

Common Sense

Edited with an Introduction by Isaac Kramnick

Published anonymously in 1776, *Common Sense* was instrumental in initiating the movement that established the independence of the United States. Drawn from Paine's experience of revolutionary politics, this treatise formulates the principles of fundamental human rights later expounded in his *Rights of Man*.

128 pp.   **0-14-039016-2**   **$7.95**

Rights of Man

Edited with an Introduction by Eric Foner and Notes by Henry Collins

Written in reply to Burke's *Reflections on the Revolution in France*, Paine's *Rights of Man* enshrines the radical democratic attitude in its purest form.

288 pp.   **0-14-039015-4**   **$9.95**

The Thomas Paine Reader

Edited with an Introduction by Michael Foot and Isaac Kramnick

This collection focuses on Paine as the political theorist who was an inspiration to Americans in their struggle for independence, a great defender of individual rights, and the most incendiary of radical writers.

544 pp.   **0-14-044496-3**   **$13.95**

See The Portable Enlightenment Reader.

DOROTHY PARKER
1893 – 1967, American

The Portable Dorothy Parker
Introduction by Brendan Gill

This collection of Parker's most celebrated poems and stories includes reviews, articles, and the complete *Constant Reader*, her collected *New Yorker* book reviews.

640 pp.   **0-14-015074-9**   **$14.95**

Complete Poems
Introduction by Colleen Breese

The first complete edition of Parker's poetry brings together all of the poems published in *Enough Rope, Sunset Gun,* and *Death and Taxes* along with a hundred other previously uncollected works.

320 pp.   **0-14-118022-6**   **$15.00**

Complete Stories
Edited by Colleen Breese with an Introduction by Regina Barreca

Parker's talents extended far beyond brash one-liners and clever rhymes. Her stories lay bare the uncertainties and disappointments of ordinary people living ordinary lives. Included are her best-known stories, thirteen stories never previously collected, and a selection of sardonic sketches.

480 pp.   **0-14-243721-2**   **$15.00**
(Available January 2003)

FRANCIS PARKMAN, JR.
1823 – 1893, American

The Oregon Trail
Edited with an Introduction by David Levin

On April 28, 1846, Francis Parkman left Saint Louis on his first expedition west. *The Oregon Trail* documents his adventures in the wilderness, sheds light on America's westward expansion, and celebrates the American spirit.

504 pp.   **0-14-039042-1**   **$13.00**

BLAISE PASCAL
1623 – 1662, French

Pensées
Translated with a Revised Introduction by A. J. Krailsheimer

This collection of short writings ponders the contrast between man in his fallen state and in a state of grace. It is a work of extraordinary power; a lucid, eloquent, and often satirical look at human illusions, self-deceptions, and follies.

368 pp.   **0-14-044645-1**   **$11.00**

PAUSANIAS
c. 143 – c. 176, Greek

Guide to Greece
Translated with an Introduction by Peter Levi

Pausanias's classic account of every Greek city and sanctuary includes historical introductions and a record of local customs and beliefs. Volume 1 covers central Greece, the country around Athens, Delphi, and Mycenae; Volume 2 describes southern Greece, including Olympia, Sparta, Arcadia, and Bassae.

| Vol. 1 | 592 pp. | 0-14-044225-1 | $16.00 |
| Vol. 2 | 544 pp. | 0-14-044226-X | $16.00 |

THOMAS LOVE PEACOCK
1785 – 1866, British

Nightmare Abbey/Crotchet Castle
*Edited with an Introduction by
Raymond Wright*

Two of Peacock's wittiest works, parodies of
the Gothic novel's excesses, are included
here in one volume.

288 pp.   0-14-043045-8 $17.00

GEORGES PEREC
1936 – 1982, French

Species of Spaces and Other Pieces
*Edited and Translated with an
Introduction by John Sturrock*

This volume features ingenious contempla-
tions on the ways in which we occupy urban
and domestic space; engrossing accounts of
Perec's experience with psychoanalysis;
depictions of the Paris of his childhood; and
thought-provoking examinations of the
"infra ordinary" and of how the commonplace items of our lives elude our attention.

304 pp.   0-14-018986-6 $16.00

PERSIUS

See Horace.

FERNANDO PESSOA
1888 – 1935, Portuguese

The Book of Disquiet
*Edited and Translated with an Introduction
by Richard Zenith*

Winner of the Calouste Gulbenkian Prize for
Portuguese Translation

Part intimate diary, part prose poetry, part
descriptive narrative, *The Book of Disquiet*
is one of the greatest works of the twentieth
century.

544 pp.   0-14-118304-7 $15.00
(Available January 2003)

**"This superb edition of *The Book of
Disquiet* is . . . a masterpiece."**

—JOHN LANCHESTER

FERNANDO PESSOA

Fernando Pessoa was born in Lisbon in 1888 and was brought up in Durban,
South Africa. In 1905 he returned to Lisbon to enroll at the university, but soon
dropped out, preferring to study on his own. He made a modest living translating
the foreign correspondence of various commercial firms, and wrote obsessively—
in English, Portuguese, and French. Pessoa attributed his work to dozens of literary
alter egos that he called "heteronyms"—including Alberto Caeiro, Alvaro de
Campos, Ricardo Reis, and the fictional author of *The Book of Disquiet*, the assistant
bookkeeper Bernardo Soares—whose fully fleshed biographies he invented, giving
them different writing styles and points of view. Although Pessoa was acknowledged
as an intellectual and a poet, his literary genius went largely unrecognized until
after his death in 1935.

PETRONIUS
d. a.d. 66, Roman

SENECA
c. 4 b.c. – a.d. 65, Roman

The Satyricon/The Apocolocyntosis

Translated with an Introduction and Notes by J. P. Sullivan

In *The Satyricon*, the racy adventures of the impotent Encolpius and his friends and lovers provide the definitive portrait of the age of Nero. *The Apocolocyntosis* is a malicious skit on the "deification of Claudius the Clod," designed by Seneca to ingratiate himself with Claudius's successor, Nero.

256 pp.   0-14-044489-0 $11.95

See Lucius Annaeus Seneca and The Portable Roman Reader.

PINDAR
c. 518 – c. 438 B.C., Greek

The Odes

Translated with an Introduction by C. M. Bowra

The entire spectrum of Greek moral order, from earthly competition to fate and mythology, is covered in Pindar's *Epinicia* —choral songs extolling victories in the games at Olympia, Delphi, Nemea, and Corinth.

256 pp.   0-14-044209-X $16.00

See The Portable Greek Reader.

LUIGI PIRANDELLO
1867 – 1936, Italian
Nobel Prize winner

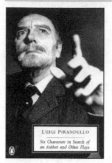

Six Characters in Search of an Author and Other Plays

Translated by Mark Musa

Inverting the conventions of theater and "real" life, Pirandello suggested that people are simply characters acting out the drama of their lives, for which theater provides an absurd, yet strangely logical, mirror. Besides *Six Characters in Search of an Author*, his best-known work, this volume also includes *Henry IV* and *So It Is (If You Think So)*.

224 pp.   0-14-018922-X $11.95

CHRISTINE DE PISAN
1364 – c. 1430, French

The Book of the City of Ladies

Translated with an Introduction by Rosalind Brown-Grant

In this sequel to *The Treasure of the City of Ladies*, de Pisan, with the help of Reason, Rectitude, and Justice, constructs an allegorical city in which to defend womankind and confront the misogyny of fourteenth-century Europe.

336 pp.   0-14-044689-3 $12.95

The Treasure of the City of the Ladies
Or, The Book of Three Virtues
Translated with an Introduction by
Sarah Lawson

A valuable counterbalance to chronicles of medieval life written by men, this 1405 "survival manual" addresses all women, from those at the royal court to prostitutes, and portrays their lives in fine and often wry detail.

192 pp.   0-14-044453-X $11.95

See The Portable Medieval Reader.

PLATO
c. 427 – c. 347 B.C., Greek

The Portable Plato
Edited by Scott Buchanan

This collection brings together Plato's most important dialogues and monumental works of philosophy, including *Protagoras, Symposium, Phaedo,* and *The Republic.*

704 pp.   0-14-015040-4 $17.00

Early Socratic Dialogues
Edited with a General Introduction by
Trevor J. Saunders and Translated with
Introductions by Trevor J. Saunders,
Iain Lane, Donald Watt, and
Robin Waterfield

Rich in drama and humor, seven dialogues provide a definitive portrait of Socrates's thought and times. The selection includes *Ion, Laches, Lysis, Charmides, Hippias Major, Hippias Minor,* and *Euthydemus.*

400 pp.   0-14-044447-5 $14.00

Gorgias
Translated with an Introduction by
Walter Hamilton

Though Gorgias was a teacher of oratory, this dialogue is more concerned with ethics than with the art of public speaking.

160 pp.   0-14-044094-1 $8.95

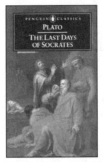

The Last Days of Socrates
Euthyphro/The Apology/Crito/Phaedo
Translated by Hugh Tredennick and Harold
Tarrant with an Introduction and Notes by
Harold Tarrant

The four superb Platonic dialogues that form the classic account of the trial and death of

---

PLATO

Plato was born into a noble Athenian family that was engaged in politics. Disturbed by the endemic political violence and corruption in Athens, and by the execution of his mentor, Socrates, on charges of impiety and corruption of youth in 399 B.C., Plato turned from the life of politics to philosophy. Plato wrote his famous dialogues, including *The Republic*, to interpret Socratic philosophy, using the character of Socrates to espouse his own views. Plato held that abstract concepts such as "good" are absolute and must be understood in order to be experienced. He returned to Athens around 387 B.C. and founded the Academy in Athens—the prototypical Western university, featuring philosophy, mathematics, astronomy, and natural history—in order to train "philosopher-kings." Aristotle was one of his students. Lasting for almost one thousand years, the Academy was suppressed by the Emperor Justinian in A.D. 529.

Socrates—presented in this volume in a revised translation with extensive notes—have almost as central a place in Western consciousness as the trial and death of Jesus.

256 pp.   0-14-044928-0 $11.95

Great Books Foundation Readers Guide Available

The Laws

Translated with an Introduction by Trevor J. Saunders

In his last and longest work, Plato sets forth a detailed code of immutable laws for the ideal state that contrasts sharply with the notion of the philosopher-king developed in *The Republic*. This edition includes a list of crimes and punishments and an appendix of Plato's letters.

560 pp.   0-14-044222-7 $14.00

Phaedrus and Letters VII and VIII

Translated with an Introduction by Walter Hamilton

Phaedrus, chiefly valued for its idyllic setting and magnificent myth, is concerned with establishing the principles of rhetoric based on the knowledge of truth inspired by love. The seventh and eighth letters reflect Plato's involvement in Sicilian politics and reveal fascinating glimpses into the contemporary power struggle.

160 pp.   0-14-044275-8 $9.95

Protagoras and Meno

Translated with an Introduction by W. K. C. Guthrie

These two dialogues explore the question of virtue, the first concluding that all virtues are united by knowledge, the second arguing that virtue is teachable.

160 pp.   0-14-044068-2 $9.95

The Republic

Translated with an Introduction by Desmond Lee

The first great piece of utopian writing, Plato's treatise on an ideal state applies philosophical principles to political affairs.

464 pp.   0-14-044914-0 $9.00
(Available March 2003)

The Symposium

Translated with an Introduction and Notes by Christopher Gill

This magnificent modern translation of Plato's dialogue on the power of love conveys all of the drama, humor, and sharply drawn characters of the original. Perhaps no other single work from antiquity retains such direct and immediate relevance for readers today.

144 pp.   0-14-0449272 $8.95

Theaetetus

Translated with a Critical Essay by Robin Waterfield

Plato examines the idea of knowledge, putting forth and criticizing opposing definitions in this pioneering work in epistemology.

256 pp.   0-14-044450-5 $12.00

Timaeus and Critias
Translated with an Introduction by Desmond Lee

The earliest Greek account of a divine creation, *Timaeus is* concerned with cosmology and anthropology. The unfinished *Critias*, Plato's only work on the natural sciences, tells the story of the lost civilization of Atlantis.

176 pp.   **0-14-044261-8**   **$11.00**

See Classical Literary Criticism *and* The Portable Greek Reader.

PLAUTUS
c. 254 – 184 B.C., Roman

The Pot of Gold and Other Plays
Translated by E. F. Watling

Plautus's broad humor, reflecting Roman manners and contemporary life, is revealed in these five plays: *The Pot of Gold* (Aulularia), *The Prisoners* (Captivi), *The Brothers Menaechmus* (Menaechmi), *The Swaggering Soldier* (Miles Gloriosus), and *Pseudolus*.

272 pp.   **0-14-044149-2**   **$12.00**

The Rope and Other Plays
Translated with an Introduction by E. F. Watling

This modern translation presents, in a form suitable for the modern stage, *The Ghost (Mostellaria)*, *The Rope (Rudens)*, *A Three-Dollar Day (Trinummus)*, and *Amphitruo*.

288 pp.   **0-14-044136-0**   **$10.95**

See The Portable Roman Reader.

PLINY THE ELDER
23 – 79, Roman

Natural History
A Selection
Translated with an Introduction and Notes by John F. Healey

This encyclopedic account of the state of science, art, and technology in the first century A.D. also provides a substantial volume of evidence about Pliny's character, temperament, and attitude toward life. Including more than 20,000 facts—from agriculture, astronomy, botany, and chemistry to geography, pharmacy, and zoology —this work is the major source of ancient beliefs about every form of useful knowledge.

448 pp.   **0-14-044413-0**   **$15.00**

PLINY THE YOUNGER
c. 61 – c. 113, Roman

The Letters of the Younger Pliny
Translated with an Introduction by Betty Radice

This modern translation of the ten books of Pliny's *Letters* provides a wealth of information on the social and political history of Rome at the turn of the first century, including Pliny's famous account of the destruction of Pompeii and his celebrated correspondence with the Emperor Trajan about the early Christians.

320 pp.   **0-14-044127-1**   **$13.00**

The Enneads

*Translated by Stephen MacKenna and
Abridged with an Introduction and
Notes by John Dillon*

Here is a highly original synthesis of
Platonism, mystic passion, ideas from
Greek philosophy, and variants of the
Trinity and other central tenets of Christian
doctrine by the brilliant thinker who has
had an immense influence on mystics and
religious writers.

688 pp.   **0-14-044520-X**   **$16.00**

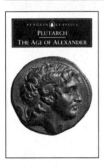

The Age of Alexander

*Translated and Annotated by
Ian Scott-Kilvert with an Introduction by
G. T. Griffith*

Taken from *The Parallel Lives*, this history
of nine great Greek statesmen—Agesilaus,
Pelopidas, Dion, Timoleon, Demosthenes,
Phocion, Alexander, Demetrius, and
Pyrrhus—traces a crucial phase of ancient
history, from the fall of Athens to the rise
of Macedonia.

448 pp.   **0-14-044286-3**   **$13.95**

Essays

*Edited with an Introduction and Notes by
Ian Kidd and Translated by Robin Waterfield*

Whether he is offering abstract specula-
tions or practical ethics, reflections on the
benefits of military versus intellectual
glory, or the reasoning powers of animals,
Plutarch's encyclopedic writings form a
treasure trove of ancient wisdom.

448 pp.   **0-14-044564-1**   **$13.95**

The Fall of the Roman Republic

*Translated by Rex Warner with an
Introduction and Notes by Robin Seager*

Selections on Gaius, Marius, Sulla, Crassus,
Pompey, Caesar, and Cicero are taken from
The Parallel Lives. Plutarch records, simply
and dramatically, the long and bloody
period of foreign and civil war that marked
the collapse of the Roman Republic and
ushered in the Empire.

368 pp.   **0-14-044084-4**   **$13.95**

Makers of Rome

*Translated with an Introduction by
Ian Scott-Kilvert*

Nine of Plutarch's *Roman Lives*—
Coriolanus, Fabius Maximus, Marcellus,
Cato the Elder, Tiberius Gracchus, Gaius
Gracchus, Sertorius, Brutus, and Mark
Antony—illustrate the courage and
tenacity of the Romans in war and their
genius for political compromise, from
the earliest years of the Republic to the
establishment of the Empire.

368 pp.   **0-14-044158-1**   **$14.00**

Plutarch on Sparta

*Translated with an Introduction and Notes
by Richard J. A. Talbert*

Rich in anecdote and personal idiosyncrasy,
Plutarch's writings are a literary, philosophical, and social exploration of this extraordinary Greek city.

224 pp.   **0-14-044463-7**   **$13.00**

The Rise and Fall of Athens
Nine Greek Lives

*Translated with an Introduction by
Ian Scott-Kilvert*

Nine Greek biographies illustrate the rise
and fall of Athens, from the legendary days
of Theseus, the city's founder, through
Solon, Themistocles, Aristides, Cimon,
Pericles, Nicias, and Alcibiades, to the
razing of its walls by Lysander.

320 pp.   0-14-044102-6 $12.95

EDGAR ALLAN POE
1809 – 1849, American

The Portable Poe

Edited by Philip Van Doren Stern

This collection of Poe's stories, letters, articles,
and poetry contains a selection of his most
compelling writings on terror, death, murder,
fantasy, and revenge.

704 pp.   0-14-015012-9 $15.95

The Fall of the House of Usher and Other Writings

*Edited with an Introduction and Notes by
David Galloway*

This selection includes seventeen poems,
among them "The Raven," "Annabel Lee,"
and "The Bells"; nineteen tales, including
"The Fall of the House of Usher," "The
Murders in the Rue Morgue," "The Tell-Tale
Heart," "The Masque of the Red Death,"
and "The Pit and the Pendulum"; and
sixteen essays and reviews.

544 pp.   0-14-143981-5 $9.95

The Narrative of Arthur Gordon Pym of Nantucket

*Edited with an Introduction and Notes by
Richard Kopley*

A stowaway aboard the whaling ship
Grampus, Pym finds himself bound
for the high southern latitudes on an
extraordinary voyage.

320 pp.   0-14-043748-7 $10.00

The Science Fiction of Edgar Allan Poe

*Edited with an Introduction and
Commentary by Harold Beaver*

The sixteen stories in this collection,
including the celebrated "Eureka," reveal
Poe as both an apocalyptic prophet and a
pioneer of science fiction.

432 pp.   0-14-043106-3 $12.95

See Nineteenth-Century American Poetry.

MARCO POLO
1254 – 1324, Venetian

The Travels

*Translated with an Introduction by
Ronald Latham*

Despite piracy, shipwreck, brigandage,
and wild beasts, Polo moved in a world of
highly organized commerce. This chronicle
of his travels through Asia, whether read
as fact or fiction, is alive with adventures,
geographical information, and descriptions
of natural phenomena.

384 pp.   0-14-044057-7 $13.95

POLYBIUS
c. 200 – c. 118 B.C., Greek

The Rise of the Roman Empire

*Translated by Ian Scott-Kilvert with an
Introduction by F. W. Walbank*

The forty books of Polybius's *Universal
History*, covering events in the third and
second centuries B.C. that led to the
supremacy of Rome, present the first

panoramic view of history.

576 pp.   0-14-044362-2 $14.95

See The Portable Greek Historians.

The Manuscript Found in Saragossa

*Translated with an Introduction by
Ian MacLean*

A rich and wondrous mélange of literary
styles and narrative voices, full of philosophical insights, highly charged erotica,
and side-splitting humor. "One of the great
masterpieces of European literature…this
new translation offers us the work as a
whole in English for the first time, in the
dizzyingly elaborate form envisioned by
the author's extraordinary imagination."
—*The New York Times Book Review*

656 pp.   0-14-044580-3 $14.95

**"A Polish classic….It reads like the
most brilliant modern novel."**

—SALMAN RUSHDIE

The Exploration of the Colorado River and Its Canyons

With an Introduction by Wallace Stegner

In May 1869, a Civil War veteran and nine
men descended with four boats in a branch
of the Colorado River for an excursion
through the last uncharted territory of the
United States. Three months and one thousand miles later, six emaciated men in two
boats emerged from the open water. Their
story, recounted by John Wesley Powell in
his journals, remains as fresh and exciting
today as it did when it first appeared in 1874.

400 pp.   0-14-025569-9 $10.95

Manon Lescaut

*Translated by Leonard Tancock with a
New Introduction and Notes by Jean Sgard*

Young Chevalier des Grieux's account dis-
closes his love affair with Manon, a femme
fatale who makes his life a torment—and
without whom it is meaningless.

192 pp.   0-14-044559-5 $10.95

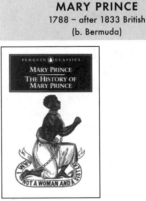

The History of Mary Prince

*Edited with an Introduction and Notes by
Sara Salih*

The first account of the life of a black
woman ever published in Britain, this
moving, painstakingly detailed record of
slavery was an instant bestseller that set
off immense public controversy and
became an instrumental document in the
anti-slavery movement's campaign. This
edition includes supplementary primary
material on enslavement and the case of
Mary Prince.

160 pp.   0-14-043749-5 $12.00

PROCOPIUS
c. 6th cent., Byzantine

The Secret History
Translated with an Introduction by
G. A. Williamson

The other side of sixth-century Byzantium
is revealed as Procopius exposes the
vicious, scheming nature of the splendid
empire and its rulers.

208 pp.   0-14-044182-4 $14.00

MARCEL PROUST
1871 – 1922, French

Swann's Way
Translated by C. K. Scott-Moncrieff

The themes introduced in *Swann's Way*—
the destructive force of obsessive love, the
allure and the consequences of transgressive
sex, and the selective eye that shapes memories—form the threads that unite all the
volumes of *Remembrance of Things Past*.

224 pp.   0-14-118058-7 $12.95

ALEXANDER PUSHKIN
1799 – 1837, Russian

Eugene Onegin
Translated by Charles Johnston with an
Introduction by John Bayley

Hailed by critics as the finest English-
language rendering ever achieved, Charles
Johnston's verse translation of *Eugene
Onegin* captures the lyric intensity and
gusto of Pushkin's incomparable poem.

240 pp.   0-14-044803-9 $9.95

The Queen of Spades and Other Stories
Translated with an Introduction by
Rosemary Edmonds

Known as Russia's greatest poet, Pushkin
was equally at ease working in other literary
forms. The prose collected here includes
"The Captain's Daughter," which chronicles
the Pugachev Rebellion of 1770, "The
Negro of Peter the Great," and "Dubrovsky."

320 pp.   0-14-044119-0 $14.00

Tales of Belkin and Other Prose Writings
Translated by Ronald Wilks with an
Introduction by John Bayley

These stories are wonderful in their purity
of form, humor, and understatement.
This collection also contains a selection
of other Pushkin writings, including the
fragment *Roslavlev, Egyptian Nights*, and
the autobiographical *Journey to Arzrum*.

224 pp.   0-14-044675-3 $10.95

See The Portable Nineteenth-Century
Russian Reader.

THOMAS PYNCHON
b. 1937, American

Gravity's Rainbow
A few months after the Germans' secret
V-2 rocket bombs begin falling on London,
British Intelligence discovers that a map of
the city pinpointing the sexual conquests of
one Lieutenant Tyrone Slothrop, U.S. Army,
corresponds identically to a map showing
V-2 impact sites. The implications of this
discovery launch Slothrop on a wildly
comic extravaganza.

528 pp.   0-14-018859-2 $16.95

"The most profound and accomplished
American novel since the end of
World War II."
—EDWARD MENDELSON

Vineland

Pynchon freely combines disparate elements from American pop culture—spy thrillers, Ninja potboilers, TV soap operas, sci-fi fantasies—in this story of sixties survivors.

400 pp.   **0-14-118063-3**   **$15.00**

EÇA DE QUEIRÓS
1845 – 1900, Portuguese

The Maias

Translated by Patricia McGowan Pinheiro and Ann Stevens with an Introduction by Nigel Griffin

A masterpiece of Portuguese literature, this portrait of a decadent landowning family and their declining fortunes over three generations is at once a damning critique of Portugal and a supreme work of humor and irony.

656 pp.   **0-14-044694-X**   **$15.95**

RAYMOND QUENEAU
1903 – 1976, French

Zazie in the Metro

Translated by Barbara Wright with an Introduction by Gilbert Adair

A metro strike sends impish, foul-mouthed country-girl Zazie on a crazy Parisian adventure in this comic cult classic.

176 pp.   **0-14-218004-1**   **$12.00**

FRANCISCO DE QUEVEDO
1580 – 1645, Spanish

Two Spanish Picaresque Novels

Translated by Michael Alpert

A vigorous and earthy humor animates these sixteenth- and seventeenth-century novels, Quevedo's *El Buscón* (The Swindler) and *Lazarillo de Tormes*, author unknown, in which a slightly disreputable hero who lives by his wits replaces the romantic hero of earlier writings.

216 pp.   **0-14-044211-1**   **$14.00**

FRANÇOIS RABELAIS
c. 1483 – 1553, French

Gargantua and Pantagruel

Translated with an Introduction by J. M. Cohen

Written by a Franciscan monk who was at the center of the sixteenth-century humanist movement, this robust epic parodies everyone from classic authors to Rabelais's own contemporaries.

720 pp.   **0-14-044047-X**   **$15.00**

See The Portable Renaissance Reader.

JEAN RACINE
1639 – 1699, French

Iphigenia/Phaedra/Athaliah

Translated by John Cairncross

Themes of ruthless and unrelenting tragedy are at the heart of these plays. The first two are based on Greek legend, while *Athaliah* depicts the vengeance and the power of the Old Testament Jehovah.

320 pp.   **0-14-044122-0**   **$10.95**

Phèdre

Translated with a Foreword by Margaret Rawlings

A favorite among modern readers, students, amateur companies, and repertory theaters alike, Racine's *Phèdre* is the supreme achievement of French neoclassic tragedy. This edition provides both the English and French texts.

192 pp.   **0-14-044591-9**   **$11.95**

ANN RADCLIFFE
1764 – 1823, British

The Italian
Edited by Robert Miles

Set in the mid-eighteenth century against a dramatic, lush backdrop of the Bay of Naples, *The Italian* is a tale of passion, deceit, abduction, and the horrors of the Inquisition and one of the most powerful Gothic tales ever written. Its villain, the scheming monk Schedoni, has become an archetype of Romantic literature.

544 pp.   **0-14-043754-1**   **$10.00**

The Mysteries of Udolpho
Edited with an Introduction by Jacqueline Howard

The most popular novel of its time, this haunting tale raised the Gothic romance to a new level and inspired a long line of imitators. The orphan Emily St. Aubert is torn from the man she loves and confined in the medieval castle of her aunt's husband. There she encounters threats, terrors, and wild imaginings that may overwhelm her.

704 pp.   **0-14-043759-2**   **$13.00**

JOHN REED
1887 – 1920, American

Ten Days That Shook the World
Introductions by A. J. P. Taylor and V. I. Lenin

Reed's classic eyewitness account of the events in Petrograd in November of 1917 "rises above every other contemporary record" (George F. Kennan).

368 pp.   **0-14-018293-4**   **$11.95**

SAMUEL RICHARDSON
1689 – 1761, British

Clarissa
Edited with an Introduction by Angus Ross

This tale of attracted lovers—one a virtuous young woman, the other a charming and wicked young man—is, like *Pamela*, a novel told in psychologically revealing letters.

1,536 pp.   **0-14-043215-9**   **$24.95**

Pamela
Edited by Peter Sabor with an Introduction by Margaret A. Doody

Told in a series of letters, this story of a maid pursued by her dead mistress's son features the first British heroine to work for a living and deals with such matters as the perversion of sex into power, a radical theme in 1740.

544 pp.   **0-14-043140-3**   **$9.00**

JACOB A. RIIS
1849 – 1914, American (b. Denmark)

How the Other Half Lives
Introduction and Notes by Luc Sante

Published in 1890, Jacob Riis's remarkable study of the horrendous living conditions of the poor in New York City had an immediate and extraordinary impact on society, inspiring reforms that affected the lives of millions of people. Riis brings life to the various ethnic groups who lived in the slums of the Lower East Side, relying on such specific hard facts as the weapons of social criticism. His photographs (included in this edition) made this book a landmark in photojournalism.

224 pp.   **photos throughout**
0-14-043679-0   **$12.00**

ARTHUR RIMBAUD
1854 – 1891, French

Collected Poems
Translated with an Introduction by Oliver Bernard

All the symbolist poet's well-known poems are included in this volume, along with a selection of Rimbaud's letters. Both letters and poems are presented in English prose translations as well as the original French.

384 pp. 0-14-042064-9 **$13.95**

EDWIN ARLINGTON ROBINSON
1869 – 1935, American

Selected Poems
Edited with an Introduction by Robert Faggen

Edwin Arlington Robinson's finely crafted, formal rhythms mirror the tension the poet sees between life's immutable circumstances and humanity's often tragic attempts to exert control. At once dramatic and witty, his poems lay bare the loneliness and despair of life in small genteel towns, the tyranny of love, and unspoken, unnoticed suffering.

288 pp. 0-14-018988-2 **$15.00**

PIERRE DE RONSARD
1524 – 1585, French

Selected Poems
Edited and Translated by Malcolm Quainton and Elizabeth Vinestock

This dual-language, parallel-text collection of wide-ranging verse by France's most influential Renaissance poet embraces a variety of themes from politics, science, and philosophy to bawdy and risqué material that outraged religious reformers.

384 pp. 0-14-042424-5 **$16.00**

See The Portable Renaissance Reader.

CHRISTINA ROSSETTI
1830 – 1894, British

The Complete Poems
Edited by R. W. Crump with an Introduction and Notes by Betty S. Flowers

Christina Rossetti was the Pre-Raphaelite movement's foremost female poet. This definitive edition brings together her fantasy poems, terrifyingly vivid verses for children, love lyrics, sonnets, hymns, and ballads, as well as her vast body of devotional poetry, in one volume that startles the imagination with its truth, beauty, and intensity.

1,312 pp. 0-14-042366-4 **$17.00**

JEAN-JACQUES ROUSSEAU
1712 – 1778, Swiss-French

The Confessions
Translated with an Introduction by J. M. Cohen

The posthumously published *Confessions*, which describes the first fifty-three years of the author's life with a refreshing frankness, has left an indelible imprint on the thought of successive generations, influencing, among others, Proust, Goethe, and Tolstoy.

608 pp. 0-14-044033-X **$13.00**

A Discourse on Inequality

*Translated and Annotated with an
Introduction and Notes by
Maurice Cranston*

The most influential of Rousseau's writings,
the "Second Discourse" set forth a theory
of human evolution that prefigured the discoveries of Darwin, revolutionized the study
of anthropology and linguistics, and made
a seminal contribution to political and
social thought—leading to both the French
Revolution and the birth of social science.

208 pp.   0-14-044439-4 $9.95

Reveries of the Solitary Walker

*Translated with an Introduction and a
Brief Chronology by Peter France*

Ten meditations written in the two years
before Rousseau's death in 1778 provide
an excellent introduction to the thinker's
complex world, expressing in its full force
the agony of isolation and alienation.

160 pp.   0-14-044363-0 $11.00

The Social Contract

*Translated with an Introduction by
Maurice Cranston*

The Social Contract describes the basic
principles of democratic government,
stressing that law is derived from the
will of the people.

192 pp.   0-14-044201-4 $9.00

See The Portable Enlightenment Reader.

SUSANNA ROWSON
1762 – 1828, American (b. England)

Charlotte Temple and Lucy Temple

Edited with an Introduction by Ann Douglas

Rowson's tale of a young girl who elopes to
the United States only to be abandoned by
her fiancé was once the bestselling novel in
American literary history. This edition also
includes *Lucy Temple*, the fascinating story
of Charlotte's orphaned daughter.

320 pp.   0-14-039080-4 $12.95

JOHN RUSKIN
1819 – 1900, British

Unto This Last and Other Writings

*Edited with an Introduction,
Commentary, and Notes by Clive Wilmer*

The complete text of *Unto This Last*,
Ruskin's influential critique of the science
of political economy and the doctrine of
unhindered industrialization, is presented
with selections from *Modern Painters*,
The Stones of Venice, and *Fors Clavigera*.

368 pp.   0-14-043211-6 $14.00

RAFAEL SABATINI
1875 – 1950, British (b. Italy)

Captain Blood

Introduction by Gary Hoppenstand

This classic swashbuckling adventure on
the high seas is alive with color, romance,
excitement and also smoothly comments
on the social injustices of slavery, the
dangers of intolerance, the power of love,
the role of fate, and how oppression can
drive men to desperate measures.

304 pp.   0-14-218010-6 $13.00
(Available January 2003)

**"Glorious . . . I never enjoyed a novel
more than *Captain Blood*."**

—NORMAN MAILER

NICOLA SACCO
1891 – 1927, American (b. Italy)

BARTOLOMEO VANZETTI
1888 – 1927, American (b. Italy)

The Letters of Sacco and Vanzetti

*Edited by Gardner Jackson and
Marion D. Frankfurter with an
Introduction by Richard Polenberg*

First published in 1928, *The Letters of Sacco
and Vanzetti* represents one of the great
personal documents of the twentieth century: a volume of primary source material as
famous for the splendor of its impassioned
prose as for the brilliant light it sheds on the
characters of the two dedicated anarchists
—executed for the holdup murder of two
guards—who became the focus of worldwide attention.

320 pp.   **0-14-118026-9**   **$19.00**

LEOPOLD VON SACHER-MASOCH
1836 – 1895, Galician

Venus in Furs

*Translated with Notes by Joachim Neugroschel
with an Introduction by Larry Wolff*

First published in 1870, *Venus in Furs*
earned its author a degree of immortality
when the word "masochism"—derived
from his name—entered the psychiatric
lexicon. The term remains a classic literary
statement on sexual submission and control.

144 pp.   **0-14-044781-4**   **$10.00**

SAKI
1870 – 1916, Scottish (b. Burma)

"In all literature, he was the first to
employ successfully a wildly outrageous
premise in order to make a serious
point. I love that. And today the best of
his stories are still better than the best
of just about every other writer around."
—ROALD DAHL

The Complete Saki

More than 140 short stories, novels, and
plays make up this complete collection of
Saki's work, and display the brilliant wit
and biting sophistication of a master of
social satire.

960 pp.   **0-14-118078-1**   **$17.00**

SALLUST
c. 86 – 35 B.C., Roman

The Jugurthine War and The Conspiracy of Catiline

*Translated with an Introduction by
S. A. Hanford*

These are the only surviving works by a
man who held various public offices in
Rome and was a friend of Caesar and an
opponent of Cicero.

240 pp.   **0-14-044132-8**   **$14.00**

IGNATIUS SANCHO
1729 – 1780, Afro-Briton

Letters of the Late Ignatius Sancho, an African

*Edited with an Introduction and Notes by
Vincent Carretta*

Born in 1729 on a slave ship bound for the
West Indies, Ignatius Sancho became the
most celebrated Afro-Briton of his time.
His letters reveal a man of sensitivity,
intellect, and charm, and present his
thoughts on race and politics.

352 pp.   **0-14-043637-5**   **$11.95**

LADY SARASHINA
c. 2nd cent. A.D., Japanese

As I Crossed a Bridge of Dreams
Recollections of a Woman in Eleventh-Century Japan

Translated with an Introduction by Ivan Morris

Born at the height of the Heian period, the pseudonymous Lady Sarashina reveals much about the Japanese literary tradition in this haunting self-portrait.

176 pp.   0-14-044282-0 $13.00

DOMINGO F. SARMIENTO
1811 – 1888, Argentinian

Facundo
Or, Civilization and Barbarism

Translated by Mary Peabody Mann with an Introduction by Ilan Stavans

Written in political exile by one of Argentina's greatest statesmen, *Facundo* is ostensibly a biography of the gaucho barbarian Juan Facundo Quiroga. But it is also a complex, passionate work of history, sociology, and political commentary, and Latin America's most important essay of the nineteenth century.

320 pp.   0-14-043677-4 $12.95

> "The single most influential literary work of modern Spanish American culture."
> —EDWIN WILLIAMSON

FRIEDRICH SCHILLER
1759 – 1805, German (b. Württemberg)

Mary Stuart

Translated with an Introduction and Notes by F. J. Lamport

This masterful and vivid drama of the legendary conflict—and fictitious confrontation—between England's Queen Elizabeth I and Mary, Queen of Scots, demonstrates a perfect balance between the classical, the Shakespearean, and the romantic elements of Schiller's genius.

144 pp.   0-14-044711-3 $12.00

The Robbers and Wallenstein

Translated with an Introduction by F. J. Lamport

The foremost dramatist of German classicism wrote *The Robbers*, his first play, in 1781; in the trilogy *Wallenstein*, written nineteen years later, Schiller attempted to combine the strengths of Sophocles, Shakespeare, and French classical drama.

480 pp.   0-14-044368-1 $15.00

ARTHUR SCHOPENHAUER
1788 – 1860, German (b. Danzig)

Essays and Aphorisms

Selected and Translated with an Introduction by R. J. Hollingdale

This selection of thoughts on religion, ethics, politics, women, suicide, books, and much more is taken from Schopenhauer's last work, *Parerga and Paralipomena*, published in 1851.

240 pp.   0-14-044227-8 $14.00

OLIVE SCHREINER
1855 – 1920, South African

The Story of an African Farm
Introduction by Dan Jacobson

Written by an avid feminist and political activist and first published in 1883, this masterful novel reveals much about colonial history as it tells the story of two orphaned sisters growing up on a lonely farm in a Bible-dominated area of South Africa during the 1860s.

304 pp. **0-14-043184-5** **$11.95**

BRUNO SCHULZ
1892 – 1942, Polish

"Schulz wrote sometimes like Kafka, sometimes like Proust, and at times succeeded in reaching depths that neither of them reached."
—ISAAC BASHEVIS SINGER

The Street of Crocodiles
Translated by Celina Wieniewski with an Introduction by Jerzy Ficowski

In the Polish city of Drogobych is a street of memories and dreams where recollections of Schulz's boyhood are evoked in a startling blend of the real and the fantastic.

160 pp. **0-14-018625-5** **$13.00**

WALTER SCOTT
1771 – 1832, Scottish

The Penguin Classics texts are based on the acclaimed Edinburgh Editions of the Waverley novels

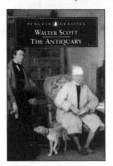

The Antiquary
Edited by David Hewitt with an Introduction by David Punter

The third novel in Scott's Waverley series and his personal favorite, *The Antiquary* centers on a young man who, without wealth or title, wins the daughter of a titled landowner through an extraordinary act of courage.

512 pp. **0-14-043652-9** **$15.00**

The Bride of Lammermoor
Edited by J. H. Alexander with an Introduction by Kathryn Sutherland

Less sprawling than most of Scott's novels but still boasting Scott's characteristic humor and wisdom, *The Bride of Lammermoor* brings to vivid life a historical incident from his own family lore and from Scotland's turbulent past.

400 pp. **0-14-043656-1** **$11.00**

WALTER SCOTT

Sir Walter Scott was born and educated in Edinburgh, but his family roots were in the Borders and he began to collect ballads and tales of that region. His many Romantic narrative poems set in the Border country were a financial success, and though Scott began the Waverley novels in 1805, he abandoned them twice for more marketable work. These novels were published anonymously and followed by many others including *Ivanhoe*, *The Tale of Old Mortality*, and *Rob Roy*. Scott also issued, under his own editorship at a publishing business he financed with the Ballantyne brothers, a great deal of dramatic work and wrote numerous historical, literary, and antiquarian books. He was made a baronet in 1820.

The Heart of Midlothian

Edited with an Introduction and Notes by Tony Inglis

The inventor and master of the historical novel tells the story of a determined heroine's dramatic confrontation with the justice system in a trial for infanticide, mixing historical fact with folklore from the uneasy, changing world of 1730s Scotland.

848 pp.   **0-14-043129-2**   **$12.95**

Ivanhoe

Edited with an Introduction and Notes by Graham Tulloch

A stirring and exciting recreation of the age of chivalry, alive with such legends as Richard-the-Lion-Hearted and Robin Hood, this is Scott's most popular novel.

544 pp.   **0-14-043658-8**   **$9.00**

Kenilworth

Edited with an Introduction by J. H. Alexander

Scott magnificently recreates the drama and the strange mixture of assurance and unease of the Elizabethan Age through the story of Amy Robsart, whose husband, one of the queen's favorites, must keep his marriage secret or incur royal displeasure.

528 pp.   **1 line drawing**   **2 maps**
0-14-043654-5   **$13.95**

Redgauntlet

Edited by G. A. M. Wood and David Hewitt with an Introduction by David Hewitt

Set in the mid-eighteenth century, during the fictitious third Jacobite rebellion, *Redgauntlet* tells of Darsie Latimer, a student of law who becomes embroiled in a plot to put Prince Charles Edward (a.k.a. Bonnie Prince Charlie) on the British throne. The events of *Redgauntlet* form the culmination of Scott's series of Jacobite novels.

544 pp.   **0-14-043655-3**   **$11.00**

Rob Roy

An adventure tale filled with brave deeds and cowardly conspiracies, noble heroes and despicable traitors, *Rob Roy* sweeps readers into the turmoil that erupted in England and Scotland after the death of Queen Anne. Based on the real-life Rob Roy MacGregor, it explores a common theme in Scott's work: the disappearance of the heroic values of chivalry as society became more ordered and prosperous.

512 pp.   **0-14-043554-9**   **$10.00**

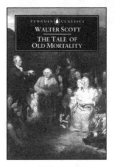

The Tale of Old Mortality

Edited with an Introduction by Douglas S. Mack

The story of two sets of "cruel and bloody bigots" at war in the late seventeenth-century, this is a fast-paced chronicle of a rebellious religious movement and its impact on peasant and nobleman alike.

496 pp.   **0-14-043653-7**   **$13.95**

Waverley

Edited with an Introduction by Andrew Hook

This highly readable story of a young man involved in the Jacobite Rebellion of 1754 blends realism and romance in a classic example of Scott's "invention"— the historical novel.

608 pp.   **0-14-043071-7**   **$10.95**

CATHARINE MARIA SEDGWICK
1789 – 1869, American

Hope Leslie
Or, Early Times in the Massachusetts
Edited with an Introduction and Notes by Carolyn L. Karcher

Set in seventeenth-century New England in the aftermath of the Pequot War, *Hope Leslie* not only chronicles the role of women in building the republic but also refocuses the emergent national literature on the lives, domestic mores, and values of American women.

464 pp.   **0-14-043676-6**   **$13.95**

LUCIUS ANNAEUS SENECA
c. 4 B.C. – A.D. 65, Roman (b. Cordoba)

Dialogues and Letters
Translated with an Introduction by C. D. N. Costa

Included in this volume are the dialogues *On the Shortness of Life* and *On Tranquility of Mind*, which are eloquent classic statements of Stoic ideals of fortitude and self-reliance. This selection also features extracts from *Natural Questions* and the *Consolation of Helvia*.

160 pp.   **0-14-044679-6**   **$12.95**

Four Tragedies and Octavia
Translated with an Introduction by E. F. Watling

Although their themes are borrowed from Greek drama, these exuberant and often macabre plays focus on action rather than moral concerns and are strikingly different in style from Seneca's prose writing. This collection includes *Phaedra, Oedipus, Thyestes,* and *The Trojan Women*.

320 pp.   **0-14-044174-3**   **$14.00**

Letters from a Stoic
Selected and Translated with an Introduction by Robin Campbell

Ranging from lively epistles to serious essays, these 124 letters selected from *Epistulae Morales* and *Lucilium* espouse the philosophy of Stoicism. This volume includes Tacitus's account of Seneca's death.

256 pp.   **0-14-044210-3**   **$13.00**

See The Portable Roman Reader.

MADAME DE SÉVIGNÉ
1626 – 1696, French

Selected Letters
Edited and Translated with an Introduction by Leonard Tancock

An extraordinarily vivid picture of social, literary, and political life in Louis XIV's France is captured in this selection of letters.

320 pp.   **0-14-044405-X**   **$13.95**

WILLIAM SHAKESPEARE
1564 – 1616, English

The Portable Shakespeare
This indispensable volume contains the brightest gems of the Shakespearean treasury, including seven complete plays, all the sonnets and songs, and a vast index to Shakespearean quotations.

780 pp.   **0-14-015008-0**   **$15.95**

The Pelican Shakespeare

*The Complete Pelican Shakespeare

*General Editors: Stephen Orgel and
A. R. Braunmuller*

The classic one-volume Shakespeare has
now been updated to reflect the complete
revision of all forty volumes of Shakespeare's plays and poems. Features new
introductions and notes by distinguished
scholars; authoritative and meticulously
researched texts; essays on Shakespeare's
life, the theatrical world of his time, and the
selection of texts; photos and drawings
reflecting Shakespeare's theatrical legacy;
and a handsome new design inside and out.

1,808 pp.   0-14-100058-9 $65.00

All's Well That Ends Well
*Edited with an Introduction and Notes by
Claire McEachern*
144 pp.   0-14-071460-X $5.95

Antony and Cleopatra
Edited by A. R. Braunmuller
160 pp.   0-14-071452-9 $4.95

As You Like It
Edited by Frances E. Dolan
128 pp.   0-14-071471-5 $3.95

The Comedy of Errors
Edited by Frances E. Dolan
224 pp.   0-14-071474-X $4.95

Coriolanus
Edited by Jonathan Crewe
208 pp.   0-14-071473-1 $5.95

Cymbeline
Edited by Peter Holland
176 pp.   0-14-071472-3 $5.95

Hamlet
Edited by A. R. Braunmuller
192 pp.   0-14-071454-5 $3.95

Henry IV, Part 1
Edited by Claire McEachern
144 pp.   0-14-071456-1 $3.95

Henry IV, Part 2
Edited by Claire McEachern
144 pp.   0-14-071457-X $4.95

Henry V
*Edited by William Montgomery with an
Introduction by Janis Lull*
304 pp.   0-14-071458-8 $4.95

Henry VI, Part 1
*Edited by William Montgomery with an
Introduction by Janis Lull*
256 pp.   0-14-071465-0 $5.95

Henry VI, Part 2
*Edited by William Montgomery with an
Introduction by Janis Lull*
304 pp.   0-14-071466-9 $5.95

Henry VI, Part 3
*Edited by William Montgomery with an
Introduction by Janis Lull*
304 pp.   0-14-071467-7 $5.95

Henry VIII
*Edited with an Introduction and Notes by
Jonathan Crewe*
160 pp.   0-14-071475-8 $5.95

Julius Caesar
*Edited by William Montgomery with an
Introduction by Douglas Trevor*
144 pp.   0-14-071468-5 $3.95

King John
Edited by Claire McEachern
144 pp.   0-14-071459-6 $5.95

King Lear
(The Quarto and the Folio Texts)
Edited by Stephen Orgel
176 pp.   0-14-071490-1 $4.95

King Lear
Edited by Stephen Orgel
176 pp.   0-14-071476-6 $3.95

Love's Labor's Lost
Edited by Peter Holland
144 pp.   0-14-071477-4 $5.95

Macbeth
Edited by Stephen Orgel
128 pp.   0-14-071478-2 $3.95

Measure for Measure
Edited by A. R. Braunmuller
144 pp.   0-14-071479-0 $4.95

The Merchant of Venice
Edited by A. R. Braunmuller
132 pp.   0-14-071462-6 $3.95

The Merry Wives of Windsor
Edited by Russ McDonald
128 pp.   0-14-071464-2 $5.95

A Midsummer Night's Dream
Edited by Russ McDonald
128 pp.   0-14-071455-3 $3.95

Much Ado about Nothing
Edited by Peter Holland
128 pp.   0-14-071480-4 $3.95

The Narrative Poems
Edited by Jonathan Crewe
192 pp.   0-14-071481-2 $5.95

Othello
Edited with an Introduction and Notes by
Russ McDonald
160 pp.   0-14-071463-4 $3.95

Pericles
Edited with an Introduction and Notes by
Stephen Orgel
208 pp.   0-14-071469-3 $5.95

Richard II
Edited by Frances E. Dolan
144 pp.   0-14-071482-0 $4.95

Richard III
Edited by Peter Holland
192 pp.   0-14-071483-9 $4.95

Romeo and Juliet
Edited by Peter Holland
160 pp.   0-14-071484-7 $3.95

Sonnets
Edited by Stephen Orgel with an
Introduction by John Hollander
208 pp.   0-14-071453-7 $4.95

The Taming of the Shrew
Edited by Stephen Orgel
144 pp.   0-14-071451-0 $3.95

The Tempest
Edited by Peter Holland
144 pp.   0-14-071485-5 $3.95

Timon of Athens
Edited by Frances E. Dolan
144 pp.   0-14-071487-1 $5.95

Titus Andronicus
Edited by Russ McDonald
176 pp.   0-14-071491-X $5.95

Troilus and Cressida
Edited by Jonathan Crewe
160 pp.   0-14-071486-3 $5.95

Twelfth Night
Edited by Jonathan Crewe
128 pp.   0-14-071489-8 $4.95

The Two Gentlemen of Verona
Edited by Mary Beth Rose
224 pp.   0-14-071461-8 $5.95

The Winter's Tale
Edited by Frances E. Dolan
160 pp.   0-14-071488-X $4.95

Four Comedies

*Edited with Introductions and Notes by
G. R. Hibbard, Stanley Wells, H. J. Oliver,
and M. M. Mahood*

This collection—including *The Taming of
the Shrew, A Midsummer Night's Dream,
As You Like It,* and *Twelfth Night* in the New
Penguin Shakespeare text—is engagingly
introduced and skillfully annotated, bringing together four of Shakespeare's most
spirited comedies.

688 pp.   0-14-043454-2 $12.95

Four Histories

*Edited with Introductions and Notes
by Stanley Wells, P. H. Davison, and
A. R. Humphreys*

Shakespeare explores matters of honor,
history, tradition, and change in this cycle of
plays chronicling the turbulent transition of
the British monarchy. Included are *Richard
II; Henry IV, Parts 1 and 2*; and *Henry V*.

576 pp.   0-14-043450-X $12.95

Four Tragedies

*Edited with Introductions and Notes by
T. J. B. Spencer, Anne Barton, Kenneth Muir,
and G. K. Hunter*

These four tragedies—*Hamlet, Othello,
King Lear,* and *Macbeth* in the New
Penguin Shakespeare text—contain
some of Shakespeare's most celebrated protagonists and finest dramatic poetry.

960 pp.   0-14-043458-5 $12.95

The Sonnets and
A Lover's Complaint

*Edited with an Introduction by
John Kerrigan*

This volume of poetry was originally entitled
Shakespeares Sonnets. Neuer before Imprinted
and appeared in 1609 but his inspiration
for these masterpieces of wit and erotic
word-play remain shrouded in mystery.

464 pp.   0-14-043684-7 $7.95

Three Roman Plays

*Edited with Introductions and Notes by
Norman Sanders, Emrys Jones, and
G. R. Hibbard*

Each of these plays, previously published
separately in the New Penguin Shakespeare
series, investigates political action and the
relationship between the personal and the
political. In this volume are *Coriolanus,
Julius Caesar,* and *Antony and Cleopatra*.

672 pp.   0-14-043461-5 $12.95

WILLIAM SHAKESPEARE

William Shakespeare was born in 1564 in Stratford-upon-Avon in the English
Midlands and married Ann Hathaway in 1582. It is clear from a satirical mention
by an envious fellow playwright that by 1592 Shakespeare already had a successful
career in London as an actor, playwright, and poet, and in 1598 he took a ten-
percent share in the new Globe playhouse, making him shareholder in his own
company. In 1605 the historian William Camden referred to Shakespeare as one
of the "most pregnant wits of these our times" and joined him with such contemporary luminaries as Ben Jonson, John Marston, and Edmund Spenser. By 1613,
Shakespeare had retired from London to Stratford-upon-Avon, though he still
participated in theatrical activity. He died in 1616.

Kolyma Tales

Translated with a Foreword by John Glad

Out of his seventeen years in the Siberian labor camps of Kolyma, Shalamov fashioned a fictional recreation of that world and created this powerful collection of stories from the raw cruelty of Soviet history.

544 pp.   0-14-018695-6   **$15.00**

THE BERNARD SHAW LIBRARY

The definitive texts, under the editorial supervision of Dan H. Laurence

Heartbreak House

Introduction by David Hare

Shaw's favorite play, *Heartbreak House* is a comedy of manners that takes a probing look at the conflict between "old-fashioned" idealism and the realities of the modern age.

176 pp.   0-14-043787-8   **$9.00**

Major Barbara

Introduction by Margery Morgan

In this sparkling comedy, Andrew Undershaft, a millionaire armaments dealer, loves money and despises poverty. His energetic daughter Barbara, however, is a devout major in the Salvation Army and sees her father as just another soul to be saved. But when the Salvation Army needs funds, it is Undershaft who saves the day.

176 pp.   0-14-043790-8   **$8.00**

Man and Superman

Introduction by Stanley Weintraub

A wonderfully original twist on the Don Juan myth, this finely tuned combination of intellectual seriousness and popular comedy is a classic exposé of the eternal struggle between the sexes.

288 pp.   0-14-043788-6   **$10.00**

Plays Unpleasant

Introduction by David Edgar

This 1898 collection includes *Widowers' Houses, The Philanderer*, and *Mrs. Warren's Profession*, and challenges audiences' moral complacency in the face of serious social problems.

304 pp.   0-14-043793-2   **$11.00**

BERNARD SHAW

George Bernard Shaw was born in Dublin in 1856. Essentially shy, he created the persona of G.B.S., the showman, satirist, critic, wit, and dramatist. Commentators brought a new adjective into English: Shavian, a term used to embody all his brilliant qualities. After his arrival in London in 1876 he became an active Socialist and platform speaker. He undertook his own education at the British museum and consequently became keenly interested in cultural subjects. He invented the comedy of ideas, expounding on social and political problems with a razor-sharp tongue, yet never sacrificing the comic vitality that ensures regular revivals of his plays. Shaw won the Nobel Prize for literature in 1925 and lived long enough to see a few of his plays made into films. He died in 1950.

Pygmalion

Introduction by Nicholas Grene

Shaw radically reworks Ovid's tale with a feminist twist: while Henry Higgins successfully teaches Eliza Doolittle to speak and act like a duchess, she adamantly refuses to be his creation. This brilliantly witty exposure of the British class system will always entertain—first produced in 1914, it remains one of Shaw's most popular plays.

176 pp.   **0-14-143950-5**   **$8.00**
(Available February 2003)

Saint Joan

Introductions by Imogen Stubbs and Joley Wood

Fascinated by the story of Joan of Arc, but unhappy with "the whitewash which disfigures her beyond recognition," Shaw presents a realistic Joan: proud, intolerant, naïve, foolhardy, and always brave—a rebel who challenged the conventions and values of her day.

176 pp.   **0-14-043791-6**   **$10.00**

Three Plays for Puritans

Introduction by Michael Billington

Comprising *The Devil's Disciple, Caesar and Cleopatra*, and *Captain Brassbound's Conversion*, this volume reveals Shaw's constant delight in turning received wisdom upside down.

368 pp.   **0-14-043792-4**   **$12.00**

MARY SHELLEY
1797 – 1851, British

Frankenstein

Edited with an Introduction by Maurice Hindle

The story of Victor Frankenstein, who creates a new being that later sets out to destroy him, is the world's most famous horror novel—and a devastating exploration of the limits of human creativity.

320 pp.   **0-14-043362-7**   **$7.95**

Great Books Foundation Readers Guide Available

See Three Gothic Novels *and* Mary Wollstonecraft.

SHEN FU
c. 18th cent., Chinese

Six Records of a Floating Life

Translated with an Introduction and Notes by Leonard Pratt and Chiang Su-Hui

This autobiographical novel, published in 1809, contains lively depictions of the powerful role of the courtesan, the arrogance of untrained officials, and the formal and often strained arranged marriages in turn-of-the-century China.

176 pp.   **0-14-044429-7**   **$13.00**

RICHARD BRINSLEY SHERIDAN
1751 – 1816, Irish

The School for Scandal and Other Plays
Edited with an Introduction by Eric S. Rump

Although Sheridan tried his hand at statesmanship, his reputation as a dramatist was enhanced by these three masterpieces of ingenious plotting, eloquent wit, and biting satire. This edition also includes *The Rivals*, his first play, and *The Critic*.

288 pp.   **0-14-043240-X**   **$10.95**

WILLIAM TECUMSEH SHERMAN
1820 – 1891, American

Memoirs
Introduction and Notes by Michael Fellman

Before his spectacular career as General of the Union forces, Sherman drifted between the Old South and New West. His *Memoirs* evoke the uncompromising and deeply complex man as well as the turbulent times that transformed America into a world power.

848 pp.   **0-14-043798-3**   **$16.95**

MARY SIDNEY
1561 – 1621, British

See Renaissance Women Poets.

SIR PHILIP SIDNEY
1554 – 1586, British

The Countess of Pembroke's Arcadia
Edited with an Introduction and Notes by Maurice Evans

As much a work of entertainment and wit as of instruction, *Arcadia* affords the best insight we have into the tastes and standards of the Elizabethans and embodies the highest literary aspirations of the age.

880 pp.   **0-14-043111-X**   **$15.00**

UPTON SINCLAIR
1878 – 1968, American

The Jungle
Introduction by Ronald Gottesman

Perhaps the most influential and harrowing of Sinclair's writings, this savage novel of the Chicago stockyards established its author as one of the major modern American propaganda novelists.

432 pp.   **0-14-039031-6**   **$9.95**

ISAAC BASHEVIS SINGER
1904 – 1991, American (b. Poland)
Nobel Prize winner

The Death of Methuselah and Other Stories

Themes of envy, betrayal, and sexual perversity run through this richly varied collection. Among the twenty stories is "Disguised," a transvestite tale of the yeshiva student whose deserted wife finds him dressed as a woman and married to a man, and "The Jew of Babylon," in which a miracle worker's good works are bitterly resented by the demonic forces of evil.

256 pp.   **0-14-018698-0**   **$16.00**

"All human life is here. . . . An irresistible book."
—SALMAN RUSHDIE

I. J. SINGER
1893 – 1944, American (b. Poland)

The Brothers Ashkenazi
Translated by Joseph Singer with an Introduction by Irving Howe

Yiddish novelist Singer's sweeping family saga set against the rise of capitalism and the Jewish bourgeoisie in Lodz, Poland.

448 pp.   **0-14-018777-4**   **$16.00**

A Texas Cowboy
Or, Fifteen Years on the Hurricane Deck of a Spanish Pony

Edited with an Introduction and Notes by Richard Etulain

Siringo's 1885 chronicle of his life as a cowboy was one of the first classics about the Old West.

256 pp.   **0-14-043751-7**   **$12.00**

Sailing Alone around the World

Introduction and Notes by Thomas Philbrick

Setting off alone from Boston aboard the thirty-six foot wooden sloop *Spray* in April 1895, Captain Slocum began a three-year solo voyage of more than 46,000 miles that remains unmatched in maritime history for courage, skill, and determination. This autobiographical account endures as one of the greatest adventure narratives ever written.

320 pp.   **b/w illustrations throughout**
0-14-043736-3   **$9.00**

"Slocum has become the archetype of the American wanderer: creating himself on the page, he drew a classic hero, as resilient, as full of signification in his own rough-diamond way, as Huckleberry Finn."
—JONATHAN RABAN

The Wealth of Nations
Books I–III

Edited with an Introduction by Andrew Skinner

In this work, which laid the foundations of economic theory in general and of "classical" economics in particular, Smith pinpointed the division of labor as a major explanation of economic growth.

544 pp.   **0-14-043208-6**   **$11.95**

The Wealth of Nations
Books IV-V

Edited with an Introduction and Notes by Andrew Skinner

In these final two books of his landmark treatise, Smith offers his considered response to the French Physiocrats and famously predicted that America "will be one of the foremost nations of the world."

672 pp.   **0-14-043615-4**   **$13.95**

See The Portable Enlightenment Reader.

The Expedition of Humphry Clinker

Edited with an Introduction by Angus Ross

Written toward the end of Smollett's life, this picaresque tour of eighteenth-century British society abounds with eccentric characters and comic adventures.

416 pp.   **0-14-043021-0**   **$10.95**

King Harald's Saga

Translated with an Introduction by Magnus Magnusson and Hermann Pálsson

The biography of one of the most remarkable and memorable of the medieval kings of Norway, this saga culminates in the conflict between Norway and England in 1066.

192 pp.   **0-14-044183-2**   **$10.95**

See Hrafnkel's Saga.

SOPHOCLES
c. 496 – 406 B.C., Greek

Electra and Other Plays
Translated with an Introduction by
E. F. Watling

These verse translations of four plays—
Ajax, Electra, The Women of Trachis, and
Philoctetes— exhibit the structure that set the
standard for most modern dramatic works.

224 pp.   0-14-044028-3 $10.00

The Theban Plays
Translated with an Introduction by
E. F. Watling

Based on the legend of the royal house of
Thebes, *King Oedipus, Oedipus at Colonus,*
and *Antigone* are Sophocles's tragic
masterpieces. This verse translation is supplemented by E. F. Watling's Introduction,
which places Sophocles in historical context, discusses the origins of the art of
drama, and interprets each play in the
Theban legend.

168 pp.   0-14-044003-8 $10.95

The Three Theban Plays
Antigone/Oedipus the King/
Oedipus at Colonus
Translated by Robert Fagles with an
Introduction and Notes by Bernard Knox

Fagles's lucid modern translation captures
the majesty of Sophocles's masterwork and
is enhanced by insightful Introductions to
each play, an essay on the history of the text,
extensive notes, bibliography, and glossary.

432 pp.   0-14-044425-4 $9.95
See The Portable Greek Reader.

EDMUND SPENSER
c. 1552 – 1599, English

The Faerie Queene
Edited by Thomas P. Roche, Jr. with
C. Patrick O'Connell, Jr.

The first English-language epic, Spenser's
masterful extended allegory of knightly
virtue and supreme grace brilliantly unites
medieval romance to Renaissance epic.

1,248 pp.   0-14-042207-2 $18.95

The Shorter Poems
Edited by Richard A. McCabe

Spenser showed his supreme versatility
and skill as a eulogist, satirist, pastoral
poet, and prophet in his shorter poetry.
This edition is a sweeping collection of his
verse that includes *The Shepheardes Calendar,*
Amoretti, and *Mother Hubberd's Tale.*

816 pp.   0-14-043445-3 $19.95

EDDIUS STEPHANUS
c. 8th cent., Anglo-Saxon

See Bede.

WALLACE STEGNER
1909 – 1993, American

Angle of Repose
Introduction by Jackson J. Benson

Stegner's Pulitzer Prize–winning novel
is at once an enthralling portrait of four
generations in the life of an American
family and a fascinating illumination of
the civilization carved into the surface of
America's western frontier.

592 pp.   0-14-118547-3 $15.00

Wolf Willow
A History, a Story, and a
Memory of the Last Plains Frontier
Introduction by Page Stegner

A weave of fiction and nonfiction, history and impressions, childhood remembrance and adult reflections form Stegner's unusual portrait of his childhood on the family homestead in southern Saskatchewan.

320 pp. **0-14-118501-5** **$14.00**

See The Portable Western Reader.

GERTRUDE STEIN
1874 – 1946, American

Three Lives
Introduction by Ann Charters

Redefining the writer's art, *The Good Anna, The Gentle Lena,* and *Melanctha* capture the sensibilities of an author and an age in a way that continues to influence writers of this century.

320 pp. **0-14-018184-9** **$9.95**

JOHN STEINBECK
1902 – 1968, American
Nobel Prize winner

"Steinbeck shaped a geography of conscience."
—DON DELILLO

The Portable Steinbeck
Edited by Pascal Covici, Jr.

This grand sampling of Steinbeck's most important works includes two complete novels, *Of Mice and Men* and *The Red Pony*, as well as excerpts from many of his other books, short stories, and his 1962 Nobel Prize Acceptance Speech.

736 pp. **0-14-015002-1** **$18.00**

Burning Bright

Written as a play in story form, this novel traces the story of a man ignorant of his own sterility, a wife who commits adultery to give her husband a child, the father of that child, and the outsider whose actions affect them all.

128 pp. **0-14-018742-1** **$10.95**

Cannery Row
Introduction by Susan Shillinglaw

Steinbeck's tough but loving portrait evokes the lives of Monterey's vital laboring class and their emotional triumph over the bleak existence of life in Cannery Row.

224 pp. **0-14-018737-5** **$11.00**

JOHN STEINBECK

Born and raised in Salinas, California, John Steinbeck attended Stanford University from 1919 until 1925 without attaining a degree before working at a series of mostly blue-collar jobs and embarking on his literary career. Profoundly committed to social progress, Steinbeck's novels, such as *The Grapes of Wrath, Cannery Row,* and *Tortilla Flat,* raised issues of labor exploitation during the Great Depression. *The Grapes of Wrath* won both the National Book Award and the Pulitzer Prize in 1939. *Travels with Charley,* a travelogue chronicling his tour of the United States with his dog, was published in 1962, the same year he received the Nobel Prize in Literature. In 1964, Steinbeck was presented with the United States Medal of Freedom by President Lyndon B. Johnson. Steinbeck died in New York in 1968.

Cup of Gold

Steinbeck's first novel, and the only historical novel he ever wrote, brings to life the exciting, violent adventures of the infamous pirate Henry Morgan.

272 pp.   **0-14-018743-X**   **$13.00**

East of Eden

Introduction by David Wyatt

The masterpiece of Steinbeck's later years, *East of Eden* is the powerful and vastly ambitious novel that is both family saga and a modern retelling of the book of Genesis.

624 pp.   **0-14-018639-5**   **$14.00**

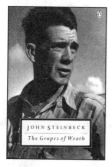

The Grapes of Wrath

Introduction by Robert DeMott

This Pulitzer Prize–winning epic of the Great Depression follows the western movement of one family and a nation in search of work and human dignity.

640 pp.   **0-14-018640-9**   **$14.00**

In Dubious Battle

Introduction and Notes by Warren French

This powerful social novel, set in the California apple country, is a story of labor unrest in the migrant community and the search for identity of its protagonist, young Jim Nolan.

360 pp.   **0-14-018641-7**   **$14.00**

The Log from the *Sea of Cortez*

Introduction by Richard Astro

This exciting day-by-day account of Steinbeck's trip to the Gulf of California with biologist Ed Ricketts, drawn from the longer *Sea of Cortez,* is a wonderful combination of science, philosophy, and high-spirited adventure.

288 pp.   **0-14-018744-8**   **$13.95**

The Long Valley

Introduction by John H. Timmerman

First published in 1938, this collection of stories set in the rich farmland of the Salinas Valley includes the O. Henry Prize–winning story "The Murder," as well as one of Steinbeck's most famous short works, "The Snake."

304 pp.   **0-14-018745-6**   **$14.00**

The Moon Is Down

Introduction by Donald V. Coers

In this masterful tale set in Norway during World War II, Steinbeck explores the effects of invasion on both the conquered and the conquerors. As he delves into the emotions of the German commander and the Norwegian traitor, and depicts the spirited patriotism of the Norwegian underground, Steinbeck uncovers profound, often unsettling truths about war—and about human nature.

192 pp.   **0-14-018746-4**   **$12.00**

Of Mice and Men

Introduction by Susan Shillinglaw

A parable about commitment, loneliness, hope, and loss, *Of Mice and Men* remains one of America's most widely read and beloved novels.

160 pp.   **0-14-018642-5**   **$11.00**

Once There Was a War

Steinbeck's dispatches filed from the front lines during World War II vividly evoke the human side of the war.
256 pp.   0-14-018747-2 $14.00

The Pastures of Heaven

Introduction and Notes by James Nagel

Each of these interconnected tales is devoted to a family living in a fertile valley on the outskirts of Monterey, California, and the effects, either intentional or unwitting, that one family has on all of them.
256 pp.   0-14-018748-0 $13.00

The Pearl

Introduction by Linda Wagner-Martin with Drawings by José Clemente Orozco

The diver Kino believes that his discovery of a beautiful pearl means the promise of a better life for his impoverished family. His fall from innocence is one of Steinbeck's most moving stories about the American dream.
128 pp.   0-14-018738-3 $9.95

The Red Pony

Introduction by John Seelye

This cycle of coming-of-age stories tells of a spirited adolescent boy whose encounters with birth and death teach him about loss and profound emptiness, instead of giving him the more conventional hero's pragmatic "maturity."
128 pp.   0-14-018739-1 $10.00

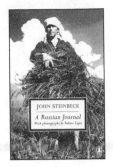

A Russian Journal

With Photographs by Robert Capa
Introduction by Susan Shillinglaw

First published in 1948, *A Russian Journal* is a remarkable memoir and unique historical document that records the writer and acclaimed war photographer's journey through Cold War Russia.
224 pp.   70 pp. b/w photographs
0-14-118019-6 $13.95

The Short Reign of Pippin IV

Steinbeck's only work of political satire turns the French Revolution upside down, creating the hilarious characters of the motley royal court of King Pippin.
176 pp.   0-14-018749-9 $13.00

Sweet Thursday

Returning to the scene of *Cannery Row*— the weedy lot and junk heaps and flophouses of Monterey, California —Steinbeck once more brings to life the denizens of a netherworld of laughter and tears, from Fauna, new headmistress of the local brothel, to Hazel, a bum whose mother must have wanted a daughter.
288 pp.   0-14-018750-2 $13.00

To a God Unknown

Introduction and Notes by Robert DeMott

Set in familiar Steinbeck territory, *To a God Unknown* is a mystical tale, exploring one man's attempt to control the forces of nature and, ultimately, to understand the ways of God.
288 pp.   0-14-018751-0 $12.95

Tortilla Flat

Introduction by Thomas Fensch

Adopting the structure and themes of the Arthurian legend, Steinbeck created a "Camelot" on a shabby hillside above Monterey on the California coast and peopled it with a colorful band of knights. As Steinbeck chronicles their thoughts and emotions, temptations and lusts, he spins a tale as compelling, and ultimately as touched by sorrow, as the famous legends of the Round Table.

192 pp.　　**0-14-018740-5**　　**$10.00**

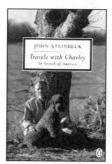

Travels with Charley in Search of America

Introduction by Jay Parini

In September 1960, Steinbeck and his poodle, Charley, embarked on a journey across America. A picaresque tale, this chronicle of their trip meanders along scenic backroads and speeds along anonymous superhighways, moving from small towns to growing cities to glorious wilderness oases.

288 pp.　　**0-14-018741-3**　　**$12.00**

The Wayward Bus

In this imaginative and unsentimental chronicle of a bus traveling California's back roads, Steinbeck creates a vivid assortment of characters, all running away from their shattered dreams but hoping that they are running toward the promise of a future.

304 pp.　　**0-14-018752-9**　　**$13.00**

The Winter of Our Discontent

Ethan Hawley works as a clerk in the grocery store owned by an Italian immigrant. His wife is restless, and his teenaged children are hungry for the tantalizing material comforts he cannot provide. Then one day, in a moment of moral crisis, Ethan decides to take a holiday from his own scrupulous standards.

288 pp.　　**0-14-018753-7**　　**$13.00**

See The Portable Western Reader.

STENDHAL
1783 – 1842, French

The Charterhouse of Parma

Translated with an Introduction by Margaret R. B. Shaw

This fictionalized account explores the intrigues within a small Italian court during the time of Napoleon's final exile.

504 pp.　　**0-14-044061-5**　　**$11.95**

Love

Translated by Gilbert Sale and Suzanne Sale with an Introduction by Jean Stewart and B. C. J. G. Knight

Stendhal draws on history, literature, and his own experiences in this intensely personal yet universal story of unrequited love.

336 pp.　　**0-14-044307-X**　　**$13.00**

*The Red and the Black

Translated with an Introduction by Roger Gard

In the atmosphere of the fearful and greedy drawing-room conformity that followed Waterloo, Julian Sorel rebels against his circumstances and wills himself to make something of his life by adopting a code of hypocrisy and a life of crime.

512 pp.　　**0-14-044764-4**　　**$9.00**

Great Books Foundation Readers Guide Available

LAURENCE STERNE
1713 – 1768, Irish

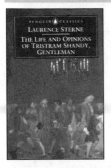

The Life and Opinions of Tristram Shandy
Edited by Melvyn New and Joan New with an Introductory Essay by Christopher Ricks and an Introduction and Notes by Melvyn New

This comic novel about writing a novel is bawdy, profane, irreverent, brazenly illogical, and exceedingly shrewd in its understanding of human behavior and of the infinite possibilities and insurmountable limitations of the art of fiction.

720 pp.   **0-14-143977-7**   **$11.00**

*A Sentimental Journey
Edited with an Introduction and Notes by Paul Goring

Begun as an account of a trip through France and Italy, this novel is a treasury of dramatic sketches, ironic incidents, philosophical musings, reminiscences, and anecdotes, all recorded in Sterne's delightful, meandering style.

160 pp.   **0-14-043779-7**   **$7.00**

ROBERT LOUIS STEVENSON
1850 – 1894, Scottish

"He lighted up one whole side of the globe, and was in himself a whole province of one's imagination."

—HENRY JAMES

The Strange Case of Dr. Jekyll and Mr. Hyde and Other Tales of Terror
Edited with an Introduction and Notes by Robert Mighall

One of the most celebrated works of horror fiction ever, "The Strange Case of Dr. Jekyll and Mr. Hyde" has become synonymous with the idea of a split personality—and humanity's basest capacity for evil. This volume includes two more chilling stories: "The Body Snatcher" and "Olalla."

224 pp.   **0-14-143973-4**   **$8.00**

In the South Seas
Edited with an Introduction by Neil Rennie

Combining personal anecdote and historical account, autobiography and anthropology, Stevenson and the South Sea Island, the English novelist's posthumously published work is a classic of travel writing.

336 pp.   **1 map**   **0-14-043436-4**   **$13.95**

Kidnapped

Edited with an Introduction and Notes by
Donald McFarlan

Set in the aftermath of the Jacobite Rebellion
of 1745, *Kidnapped* is a swashbuckling
adventure tale of family treachery,
abduction, and murder.

272 pp.   0-14-043401-1 $7.95

The Master of Ballantrae

Edited with an Introduction and Notes by
Adrian Poole

In the ancestral home of the Duries, a family divided by the Jacobite risings of 1745,
two brothers, James and Henry, carry out a
fatal rivalry over a wealthy and beautiful
kinswoman who loves one brother but
marries the other.

288 pp.   0-14-043446-1 $10.95

Selected Poems

Edited by Angus Calder

This definitive anthology brings together the
complete *A Child's Garden of Verses* (1885),
substantial extracts from the published collections, and many uncollected poems.

256 pp.   0-14-043548-4 $9.95

Treasure Island

With an Introduction by John Seelye

The quintessential British adventure
story, Stevenson's novel is narrated by
the teenage Jim Hawkins, who outwits a
gang of murderous pirates. This edition
includes Stevenson's own essay about
the composition of *Treasure Island*, written
just before his death.

224 pp.   0-14-043768-1 $5.95

The Morgesons

Edited with an Introduction and Notes by
Lawrence Buell and Sandra A. Zagarell

This 1862 female bildungsroman—which
explores the conflict between a woman's
instinct, passion, and will, and the social
taboos, family allegiances, and traditional
New England restraint that inhibit her—
evoked comparisons during Stoddard's
lifetime with Balzac, Tolstoy, Eliot, the
Brontës, and Hawthorne.

304 pp.   0-14-043651-0 $13.00

Dracula

Edited with an Introduction and Notes by
Maurice Hindle

The first—and most chilling—portrait of
the unbridled lusts and desires of a vampire
is still the ultimate terror myth.

560 pp.   0-14-043406-2 $10.95

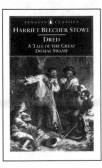

The Minister's Wooing

Edited with an Introduction by Susan K. Harris and Notes by Susan K. Harris and Danielle Conger

In this novel set in eighteenth-century Newport, Rhode Island, Stowe satirizes Calvinism, celebrating its intellectual and moral integrity while critiquing its rigid theology. With colorful characters and an element of romance, *The Minister's Wooing* combines domestic comedy with regional history to show the convergence of daily life, slavery, and religion in post-Revolutionary New England.

480 pp.   0-14-043702-9   **$15.00**

Dred
A Tale of the Great Dismal Swamp

Edited with an Introduction and Notes by Robert S. Levine

Written partly in response to critics of *Uncle Tom's Cabin*, Stowe's compelling second novel brings to life conflicting beliefs about race through the stories of Nina Gorden, the mistress of a slave plantation, and Dred, a black revolutionary. Exploring the political and spiritual goals that fuel Dred's rebellion, Stowe creates a figure far different from the acquiescent Christian martyr Uncle Tom.

656 pp.   0-14-043904-8   **$18.00**

Uncle Tom's Cabin
Or, Life Among the Lowly

Edited with an Introduction by Ann Douglas

Perhaps the most powerful document in the history of American abolitionism, this controversial novel goaded thousands of readers to take a stand on the issue of slavery and played a major political and social role in the Civil War period.

640 pp.   0-14-039003-0   **$8.95**

See The Portable American Realism Reader.

HARRIET BEECHER STOWE

Harriet Beecher Stowe was born in Litchfield, Connecticut, on June 14, 1811, the seventh child of Lyman and Roxanna Foote Beecher. At 13, Stowe was sent away to school in Hartford, rejoining her family in 1832 after their move to Cincinnati, where her father ran the Lane Theological Seminary. Her proximity to Kentucky, a slave state, made her and her family increasingly aware of the horrors of slavery, which they protested vehemently. In 1843 Stowe published her first book, *The Mayflower*, followed in 1852 by her bestselling first novel, *Uncle Tom's Cabin*, the first major work of fiction to criticize the institution of slavery. Her instant success prompted the *Independent* magazine in New York to offer her a position, and she was asked to tour England where she was received by Queen Victoria. She went on to write many more novels, but none are today as well known as her first, which was the bestselling novel of the nineteenth century. She died on July 1, 1896, and was buried in Andover, Massachusetts.

Eminent Victorians
Introduction by Michael Holroyd

Marking an epoch in the art of biography, this volume has been hailed as the "work of a great anarch, a revolutionary textbook on bourgeois society" (Cyril Connolly).

272 pp.   0-14-018350-7 $12.95

Three Plays
Translated with an Introduction by Peter Watts

Combining acute psychological insight and masterful language, Strindberg depicts the war between the sexes in *The Father* and class struggle in *Miss Julie; Easter* is a mystical play, written after Strindberg underwent a religious conversion.

176 pp.   0-14-044082-8 $11.00

The Twelve Caesars
Translated by Robert Graves and Revised with an Introduction by Michael Grant

This fascinating and colorful Latin history vividly records incidents in the lives of the first twelve Caesars: Julius, Augustus, Tiberius, Gaius (Caligula), Claudius, Nero, Galba, Otho, Vitellius, Vespasian, Titus, and Domitian.

320 pp.   0-14-044921-3 $14.00

See Lives of the Later Caesars.

Sunjata
*Translated and Annotated by Gordon Innes
Edited with an Introduction and Additional Notes by Lucy Durán and Graham Furniss*

The stories brought together here are central to the culture of the Mande-speaking peoples. Wars, magic, and the founding of an empire are related through vivid translations of one of the major epic oral traditions in Africa.

160 pp.   1 map   0-14-044736-9 $13.00

*Gulliver's Travels
Edited with an Introduction by Robert DeMaria, Jr.

Swift's account of Gulliver's encounters with the Lilliputians, the Brobdingnagians, the scientists of Laputa, and the Houyhnhnms and Yahoos make this fantastic book supremely relevant in our own age of distortion, hypocrisy, and irony.

336 pp.   0-14-143949-1 $7.00

(Available March 2003)

ALGERNON CHARLES SWINBURNE
1837 – 1909, British

Poems and Ballads and Atalanta in Calydon
Edited by Kenneth Haynes

Collecting Swinburne's passionate, musical verse, this volume brings together *Atalanta in Calydon*, a drama in classical Greek form, and poems that are opulent hymns to sensual love, to the loss of love, and to death.

448 pp.   1 map   0-14-042250-1 $15.00

J. M. SYNGE
1871 – 1909, Irish

The Aran Islands
Edited with an Introduction by Tim Robinson

The dramatic record of Synge's visit to the savagely beautiful Aran Islands at the turn of the century, this work is drenched in the Gaelic soul of Ireland.

208 pp.   0-14-018432-5 $11.95

J. M. SYNGE
1871 – 1909, Irish

W. B. YEATS
1865 – 1939, Irish
Nobel Prize winner

SEAN O'CASEY
1880 – 1964, Irish

The Playboy of the Western World and Two Other Irish Plays
Introduction by W. A. Armstrong

This volume brings together three of the greatest and most controversial plays ever presented at the famed Abbey Theatre: *The Playboy of the Western World, The Countess Cathleen,* and *Cock-a-doodle Dandy*. These plays mark important stages in the rich explosion of Irish drama that began at the turn of the century.

224 pp.   0-14-018878-9 $9.95

See W. B. Yeats.

CORNELIUS TACITUS
c. 56 – c. 120, Roman

The Agricola and The Germania
Translated with an Introduction by H. Mattingly and Revised by S. A. Hanford

The Agricola, Tacitus's eulogistic description of his father-in-law, the governor of Roman Britain, contains the first detailed account of the British Isles. *The Germania*, an ethnographical account of the Germanic tribes, contrasts the primitive virtues of the Germans with the degeneracy of contemporary Rome.

176 pp.   0-14-044241-3 $14.00

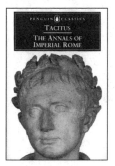

The Annals of Imperial Rome
Translated with an Introduction by Michael Grant

Surviving passages from Tacitus's last and best-known work cover the reigns of Tiberius, Gaius (Caligula), Claudius, and Nero, and detail the Roman Empire at its zenith.

464 pp.   0-14-044060-7 $14.95

The Histories
Translated with an Introduction by Kenneth Wellesley

The surviving books of *The Histories* reconstruct the terrible events of the year of the Four Emperors (A.D. 69), which shook the whole edifice of the Empire.

336 pp.   0-14-044150-6 $12.95

See The Portable Roman Reader.

SIR RABINDRANATH TAGORE
1861 – 1941, Indian
Nobel Prize winner

The Home and the World
Translated by Surendranath Tagore with an Introduction by Anita Desai

Sir Rabindranath Tagore's powerful novel, set on a Bengali noble's estate in 1908, is both a love story and a novel of political awakening. Today, ninety years after the time it describes, the novel remains astonishingly relevant.

208 pp.   0-14-018187-3 $13.00

Selected Poems
Translated with an Introduction by William Radice

Forty-eight selections cover the period 1882 to 1941 and provide a long-overdue reappraisal of the Bengali Nobel laureate's poetry.

224 pp.   0-14-018366-3 $14.00

Selected Short Stories
Translated with an Introduction by William Radice

Tagore was the first romantic poet and the first Bengali to write short stories, a form he adopted from his reading of European short stories. This collection is a representative selection from the span of his career.

336 pp.   0-14-018854-1 $14.00

JOHN TANNER
1780 – unknown, American

The Falcon
Introduction by Louise Erdrich

This is the fascinating autobiography of John Tanner (the Falcon), who is captured by the Shawnee tribe in 1789 at the age of nine and sold to an Ojibwa family with whom he spends the first half of his adult life. His effort to return to white society proves unsuccessful and he returns to his tribe, only to be forced to flee after he is wrongfully accused of murder.

280 pp.   0-14-028871-6 $15.00

ALFRED, LORD TENNYSON
1809 – 1892, British

Idylls of the King
Edited with an Introduction and Notes by J. M. Gray

For Tennyson, the *Idylls* embodied the universal and unending war between sense and soul, and Arthur the highest ideals of manhood and kingship, an attitude in keeping with the moral outlook of his day.

376 pp.   0-14-042253-6 $12.00

Selected Poems
Edited by Aidan Day

From a genius at painting human emotions in rich and sensuous imagery, this volume focuses on *In Memoriam* (1850), a record of spiritual conflict considered to be Tennyson's greatest work.

400 pp.   0-14-044545-5 $12.95

TERENCE
c. 186 – 159 B.C., Roman

The Comedies
Translated with an Introduction by Betty Radice

All six of the Roman dramatist's comedies —from *The Girl from Andros*, the first romantic comedy ever written, to the socially sophisticated *The Brothers* —show why Terence became a model for playwrights from the Renaissance onward. Also included are *The Self-Tormentor, The Eunuch, Phormio,* and *The Mother-in-Law.*

400 pp.   0-14-044324-X $14.00

The Life of St. Teresa of Ávila by Herself
*Translated with an Introduction by
J. M. Cohen*

This story of how a willful and unbalanced woman was transformed by profound religious experiences delves into the nature of exalted states. After *Don Quixote*, it is the most widely read prose classic of Spain.

320 pp.   0-14-044073-9 $10.95

WILLIAM MAKEPEACE THACKERAY
1811 – 1863, British

*Vanity Fair
*Edited with an Introduction and Notes by
John Carey*

Becky Sharp, one of the most resourceful, engaging, and amoral women in literature, is the heroine of this sparkling satirical panorama of British society during the Napoleonic Wars.

912 pp.   0-14-143983-1 $8.00

THEOGNIS

See Hesiod.

THOMAS À KEMPIS
c. 1379 – 1471, German (b. Cologne)

The Imitation of Christ
*Translated with an Introduction by
Leo Sherley-Price*

One of the most read and influential of Christian classics, this is a seminal work of the Devotio Moderna, the late-medieval reform movement that returned to the original Apostolic zeal and simplicity of Christianity.

232 pp.   0-14-044027-5 $10.95

See The Portable Renaissance Reader.

HENRY DAVID THOREAU
1817 – 1862, American

The Portable Thoreau
Edited by Carl Bode

This collection comprises the complete texts *Walden, A Week on the Concord and Merrimack Rivers*, and "Civil Disobedience" as well as eighteen poems and selections from Thoreau's other writings, including "Walking" and "The Last Days of John Brown."

704 pp.   0-14-015031-5 $15.95

HENRY DAVID THOREAU

Henry David Thoreau was born in Concord, Massachusetts, in 1817. He graduated from Harvard in 1837, the same year he began his lifelong journal. Inspired by Ralph Waldo Emerson, Thoreau became a key member of the Transcendentalist movement. He tested the Transcendentalists' faith in nature between 1845 and 1847, when he lived for twenty-six months in a homemade hut at Walden Pond. There he worked on the only two books published during his lifetime, *Walden* and *A Week on the Concord and Merrimack Rivers*. Several of his other works were published posthumously. Thoreau died in Concord in 1862.

Cape Cod

With an Introduction by Paul Theroux

With his unique perceptions and precise descriptions, *Cape Cod* chronicles Thoreau's journey of discovery along this evocative stretch of Massachusetts coastline.

320 pp.   **0-14-017002-2**   **$12.00**

The Maine Woods

With an Introduction by Edward Hoagland

Over a period of three years, Thoreau made three trips to the largely unexplored woods of Maine. Using the careful notes made during these journeys, Thoreau managed to capture a wilder side of America and revealed his own adventurous spirit.

440 pp.   **0-14-017013-8**   **$15.00**

Walden and Civil Disobedience

Introduction by Michael Meyer

Two classic examinations of individuality in relation to nature, society, and government, *Walden* conveys at once a naturalist's wonder at the commonplace and a Transcendentalist's yearning for spiritual truth and self-reliance. "Civil Disobedience" is perhaps the most famous essay in American literature—and the inspiration for social activists around the world, from Gandhi to Martin Luther King, Jr.

440 pp.   **0-14-039044-8**   **$12.00**

A Week on the Concord and Merrimack Rivers

Edited with an Introduction by H. Daniel Peck

Thoreau's account of his 1839 boat trip is a finely crafted tapestry of travel writing, essays, and lyrical poetry. An invaluable companion to *Walden*, it also stands alone as one of the most remarkable literary achievements of the nineteenth century.

384 pp.   **0-14-043442-9**   **$10.95**

A Year in Thoreau's Journal: 1851

Introduction and Notes by H. Daniel Peck

Thoreau's journal of 1851 reveals profound ideas and observations in the making, including wonderful writing on the natural history of Concord.

464 pp.   **0-14-039085-5**   **$13.95**

See Nineteenth-Century American Poetry.

THUCYDIDES
c. 460 – c. 400 B.C., Greek

The History of the Peloponnesian War
Revised Edition

Translated by Rex Warner with an Introduction and Notes by M. I. Finley

The eight books of Thucydides's account of the clash between two great powers, Athens and Sparta, are contained in Rex Warner's acclaimed modern translation.

656 pp.   **0-14-044039-9**   **$12.95**

See The Portable Greek Historians *and* The Portable Greek Reader.

The Portable Tolstoy

Edited by John Bayley

This masterful anthology includes the complete short novel *The Kreutzer Sonata*; passages from the author's fictional memoirs; short stories; the play "The Power of Darkness"; and selections from Tolstoy's philosophic, social, and critical writings.

896 pp.   0-14-015091-9 $17.95

Anna Karenin

Translated with an Introduction by Rosemary Edmonds

Tolstoy's intense, imaginative insight is brilliantly apparent in this psychological novel and its portraits of the passionate Anna, Count Vronsky, and Levin, who may be seen as a reflection of Tolstoy himself.

872 pp.   0-14-044041-0 $9.95

Penguin Readers Guide Available

Anna Karenina

Translated by Richard Pevear and Larissa Volokhonsky with an Introduction by Richard Pevear

Winner of the PEN/Book-of-the-Month Club Translation Prize

One of the world's greatest novels, *Anna Karenina* is both an immortal drama of personal conflict and social scandal and a vivid, richly textured panorama of nineteenth-century Russia. While previous versions have softened the robust, and sometimes shocking, quality of Tolstoy's writing, Pevear and Volokhonsky have produced a magnificent translation that is true to his powerful voice.

864 pp.   0-14-200027-2 $16.00

Great Books Foundation Readers Guide Available

"Pevear and Volokhonsky are at once scrupulous translators and vivid stylists of English, and their superb rendering allows us, perhaps as never before, to grasp the palpability of Tolstoy's 'characters, acts, situations.' "

—JAMES WOOD, *THE NEW YORKER*

LEO TOLSTOY

Count Leo Nikolayevich Tolstoy was born in 1828 at Yasnaya Polyana in the Tula province of Russia. As a young man, he studied Oriental languages and law at the University of Kazan. After he completed his schooling, Tolstoy fought in the Crimean war while writing *The Sebastopol Stories*, which established his reputation. In 1862, he married Sophie Andreyevna Behrs and the next fifteen years proved to be a period of great happiness; they had thirteen children and Tolstoy managed his vast estates in the Volga Steppes and, in 1868, completed *War and Peace*, following that work with *Anna Karenina* in 1876. *A Confession*, finished in 1882, marked an outward change in his life and works; he became an extreme rationalist and moralist, and in a series of pamphlets he expressed his doctrines such as inner self-perfection, rejection of institutions, indictment of the demands of the flesh, and denunciation of private property. His teaching earned him numerous followers in Russia and abroad, but also much opposition. In 1901, Tolstoy was excommunicated by the Russian holy synod. He died in 1910, in the course of a dramatic flight from home, at the small railway station of Astapovo.

Childhood/Boyhood/Youth

Translated with an Introduction by Rosemary Edmonds

These sketches, a mixture of fact and fiction, provide an expressive self-portrait of the young Tolstoy and hints of the man and writer he would become.

320 pp.   **0-14-044139-5**   **$14.00**

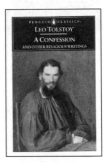

A Confession and Other Religious Writings

Translated with an Introduction by Jane Kentish

Tolstoy's passionate and iconoclastic writings—on issues of faith, immortality, freedom, violence, and morality—reflect his intellectual search for truth and a religion firmly grounded in reality. The selection includes "A Confession," "Religion and Morality," "What Is Religion, and of What Does Its Essence Consist?," and "The Law of Love and the Law of Violence."

240 pp.   **0-14-044473-4**   **$13.00**

The Death of Ivan Ilyich and Other Stories

Translated with an Introduction by Rosemary Edmonds

"The Death of Ivan Ilyich" is a magnificent story of a spiritual awakening; "The Cossacks" tells of a disenchanted nobleman who finds happiness amid the simple people of the Caucasus; and "Happily Ever After" traces the maturing of romantic love into "family attachment."

336 pp.   **0-14-044508-0**   **$9.95**

How Much Land Does a Man Need? and Other Stories

Edited with an Introduction by A. N. Wilson and Translated by Ronald Wilks

These short works, ranging from Tolstoy's earliest tales to the brilliant title story, are rich in the insights and passion that characterize all of his explorations in love, war, courage, and civilization.

240 pp.   **0-14-044506-4**   **$11.95**

The Kreutzer Sonata and Other Stories

Translated with an Introduction by David McDuff

These four tales—the title story plus "The Devil," "The Forged Coupon," and "After the Ball"—embody the moral, religious, and existential themes of Tolstoy's final creative period.

288 pp.   **0-14-044469-6**   **$9.95**

Master and Man and Other Stories

Translated with an Introduction by Paul Foote

Written in the 1890s, both "Master and Man" and "Father Sergius" are preoccupied with material desires—for the flesh in one instance and for money in the other. In *Hadji Murat*, Tolstoy offers a precisely written and memorable portrait of a treacherous soldier.

272 pp.   **0-14-044331-2**   **$13.00**

"One hesitates to value *Hadji Murat* over all of Tolstoy's other achievements in the short novel...[but] it is my personal touchstone for the sublime of prose fiction, to me the best story in the world, or at least the best that I have ever read."

—HAROLD BLOOM

Resurrection

Translated with an Introduction by Rosemary Edmonds

In this story of a fallen man and an emphatically non-Christian "resurrection," Tolstoy writes a compelling tale of the underworld and turns a highly critical eye on the law, the penal system, and the Church.

576 pp.   0-14-044184-0 $11.95

The Sebastopol Sketches

Translated with an Introduction and Notes by David McDuff

These three short stories stem from Tolstoy's military experience during the Crimean War: "Sebastopol in December," "Sebastopol in May," and "Sebastopol in August 1855."

176 pp.   0-14-044468-8 $12.00

War and Peace

Translated with an Introduction by Rosemary Edmonds

This epic presents a complete tableau of Russian society during the great Napoleonic Wars, from 1805 to 1815.

1,456 pp.   0-14-044417-3 $13.95

What Is Art?

Translated by Richard Pevear and Larissa Volokhonsky with a Preface by Richard Pevear

This profound analysis of the nature of art is the culmination of a series of essays and polemics on issues of morality, social justice, and religion. Considering and rejecting the idea that art reveals and reinvents through beauty, Tolstoy perceives the question of the nature of art to be a religious one. Ultimately, he concludes, art must be a force for good, for the progress and improvement of mankind.

240 pp.   0-14-044642-7 $13.00

See The Portable Nineteenth-Century Russian Reader.

ANTHONY TROLLOPE
1815 – 1882, British

Barchester Towers

Edited with an Introduction and Notes by Robin Gilmour and a Preface by I. K. Galbraith

In this second novel of the Barsetshire Chronicles series, Trollope continues the story begun in *The Warden* and explores the conflict between the High and Low Church during the mid-Victorian period.

576 pp.   0-14-043203-5 $8.95

"Anthony Trollope wrote about conscience and conflict, self-deception and love....His people are recognizably real today and if English men and women no longer talk as his people talk, some intuition tells us that their speech was once precisely as Trollope renders it."

—RUTH RENDELL

Can You Forgive Her?

Edited with an Introduction and Notes by Stephen Wail

The first of Trollope's Palliser novels is concerned with a spirited young woman in London who rejects her faultless fiancé to marry an aggressive opportunist, a decision her Victorian society cannot accept.

848 pp.   0-14-043086-5 $11.95

Dr. Wortle's School
Edited with an Introduction by Mick Imlah

Warmhearted schoolmaster Dr. Wortle comes to the rescue when bigamy and blackmail threaten to undo British Mr. Peacocke and his beautiful American wife. *Dr. Wortle's School* is one of the sharpest and most engaging of Trollope's later novels and the only one to have American scenes—in the Wild West.

256 pp.   0-14-043404-6 $10.00

The Eustace Diamonds
Edited by Stephen Gill and John Sutherland

Trollope examines the many guises of "truth" in this taut novel about Lizzie Eustace, a brave, beautiful, and unscrupulous young woman.

760 pp.   0-14-043041-5 $10.00

Framley Parsonage
Edited with an Introduction and Notes by David Skilton and Peter Miles

In the fourth novel of the Barsetshire Chronicles series, a young Victorian clergyman's social ambition leads him to the brink of ruin.

520 pp.   0-14-043213-2 $9.95

He Knew He Was Right
Edited with an Introduction by Frank Kermode

Written at a time of heated controversy about women's emancipation—and published the same year as John Stuart Mill's *The Subjection of Women—He Knew He*

Was Right examines the conflict between male fantasies of total possession and a married woman's right to a measure of independence.

864 pp.   0-14-043391-0 $11.95

The Last Chronicle of Barset
Edited with an Introduction and Notes by Sophie Gilmartin

In the compelling conclusion to his Barsetshire series, Trollope turns his unerring eye for the most intrinsic details of human behavior on the gloomy, brooding, and proud Mr. Crawley, curate of Hogglestock. Trollope's powerful portrait of this complex man achieves tragic dimensions.

864 pp.   0-14-043752-5 $10.00

The Prime Minister
Edited with an Introduction and Notes by David Skilton

In this penultimate book in the Palliser series, Trollope chronicles Plantagenet Palliser's ascent to the highest office in the land and explores how the realities of political life challenge his scrupulously moral hero.

736 pp.   0-14-043349-X $14.00

The Small House at Allington
Edited with an Introduction and Notes by Julian Thompson

This story of Lily Dale and her love for the ambitious, self-seeking, faithless Crosbie offers a vivid portrayal of the social and political changes occurring in the mid–nineteenth century.

752 pp.   0-14-043325-2 $7.95

The Warden
Edited with an Introduction and Notes by Robin Gilmour

The first book in the Barsetshire Chronicles tells the story of an elderly clergyman who resigns his church sinecure when it becomes the center of public controversy.

240 pp.   0-14-043214-0 $10.00

The Way We Live Now

Edited with an Introduction and Notes by Frank Kermode

First published in 1874 and widely regarded as the finest of all Trollope's novels, *The Way We Live Now* satirizes to devastating effect the grip of the monetary ethic on politics, the aristocracy, the literary world, the London scene, and the marriage market.

816 pp.   0-14-043392-9 $12.00

FANNY TROLLOPE
1779 – 1863, British

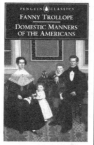

Domestic Manners of the Americans

Edited with an Introduction and Notes by Pamela Neville-Sington

Part satire, part masterpiece of nineteenth-century travel writing, this perceptive and humorous book grew from Fanny Trollope's ill-fated attempt to escape growing debts and the oppressively black moods of her husband by fleeing to the United States. After two miserable years she retreated to England, where she launched her remarkably successful literary career with this timeless and biting commentary on a society torn between high ideals and human frailties.

416 pp.   0-14-043561-1 $12.95

SOJOURNER TRUTH
c. 1797 – 1883, American

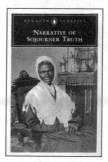

Narrative of Sojourner Truth

Edited with an Introduction and Notes by Nell Irvin Painter

Sojourner Truth's landmark narrative, dictated to a neighbor, chronicles her experiences as a slave in upstate New York and her transformation into a well-known abolitionist, feminist, orator, and preacher. This unique volume is based on the most complete text, the 1884 edition of the *Narrative*.

288 pp.   0-14-043678-2 $9.95

MARINA TSVETAYEVA
1892 – 1941, Russian

Selected Poems

Translated with an Introduction by Elaine Feinstein

An admired contemporary of Rilke, Akhmatova, and Mandelstam, Russian poet Marina Tsvetayeva bore witness to the turmoil and devastation of the Revolution, and chronicled her difficult life in exile, sustained by the inspiration and power of her modern verse.

160 pp.   0-14-018759-6 $15.00

TU FU

See Li Po.

IVAN TURGENEV
1818 – 1883, Russian

Fathers and Sons
Translated by Rosemary Edmonds

This powerful novel resounds with a recognition of the universal clash between generations, in this instance localized in the hostility between the reactionary 1840s and the revolutionary 1860s. Included is the 1970 Romanes Lecture "Fathers and Children" by Isaiah Berlin.

296 pp.   **0-14-044147-6**   **$11.00**

First Love
Translated by Isaiah Berlin with an Introduction by V. S. Pritchett

Isaiah Berlin's translation reproduces in finely wrought English the original story's simplicity, lyricism, and sensitivity.

112 pp.   **0-14-044335-5**   **$8.95**

Home of the Gentry
Translated by Richard Freeborn

Through the story of one man, Turgenev describes a whole generation of Russians who discover the emptiness of European ideas and long for a reconciliation with their homeland.

208 pp.   **0-14-044224-3**   **$14.00**

Rudin
Edited and Translated by Richard Freeborn

Rudin, the hero of Turgenev's first novel, is in part an example of the banality of the Russian intelligentsia of the 1840s, in part a hero with the charms and failings of Don Quixote.

192 pp.   **0-14-044304-5**   **$14.00**

Sketches from a Hunter's Album
Translated with an Introduction and Notes by Richard Freeborn

First published in 1852, Turgenev's impressions of Russian peasant life and the tyranny of serfdom led to his arrest and confinement.

416 pp.   **0-14-044522-6**   **$12.00**

Spring Torrents
Translated with an Introduction, Notes, and a Critical Essay by Leonard Shapiro

This is an exquisitely written, partly autobiographical treatment of one of Turgenev's favorite themes—man's inability to learn about love without first losing his innocence.

240 pp.   **0-14-044369-X**   **$13.00**

See The Portable Nineteenth-Century Russian Reader.

MARK TWAIN
1835 – 1910, American

The Portable Mark Twain
Edited by Bernard DeVoto

This delightful assembly of Twain's most representative writings includes the complete *Huckleberry Finn* and *The Mysterious Stranger*, a selection of his short stories and essays, and substantial excerpts from his other novels.

802 pp.   **0-14-015020-X**   **$15.95**

*The Adventures of Huckleberry Finn
Introduction by John Seelye and Notes by Guy Cardwell

A novel of immeasurable richness, filled with adventures, ironies, and wonderfully drawn characters, all conveyed with Twain's mastery of humor and language, *Huckleberry Finn* is often regarded as the masterpiece of American literature.

368 pp.   **0-14-243717-4**   **$6.00**
(Available January 2003)

"All modern American literature comes from one book by Mark Twain called *Huckleberry Finn*."
—ERNEST HEMINGWAY

The Adventures of Tom Sawyer
Introduction by John Seelye

Evoking life in a small Mississippi River town, *Tom Sawyer* is Twain's hymn to the secure and fantastic world of boyhood and adventure.

256 pp.   **0-14-039083-9**   **$7.00**

A Connecticut Yankee in King Arthur's Court
Edited with an Introduction by Justin Kaplan

This imaginary confrontation of a nineteenth-century American with life in sixth-century England is both a rich, extravagant comedy and an apocalyptic vision of terrifying violence and destruction.

416 pp.   **0-14-043064-4**   **$7.95**

The Innocents Abroad
Introduction by Tom Quirk and Notes by Guy Cardwell

These irreverent writings on travel in Europe are a burlesque of the sentimental travel books popular in the mid-nineteenth century and launched Twain's career. Bringing his fresh and humorous perspective to bear on hallowed European landmarks, Twain ultimately concludes that, for better or worse, "human nature is very much the same all over the world."

560 pp.   **0-14-243708-5**   **$14.00**

Life on the Mississippi
Introduction by James M. Cox

Twain's firsthand portrait of the steamboat age and the science of riverboat piloting recalls the history of the Mississippi River, from its discovery by Europeans to the writer's own time.

464 pp.   **0-14-039050-2**   **$9.95**

The Prince and the Pauper
Introduction by Jerry Griswold

This 1881 novel about a poor boy, Tom Canty, who exchanges identities with Edward Tudor, the prince of England, is at once an adventure story, a fantasy of timeless appeal, and an intriguing example of the author's abiding preoccupation with separating the true from the false, the genuine from the impostor. Included is the story "A Boy's Adventure," written as part of the novel but published separately.

224 pp.   **0-14-043669-3**   **$8.95**

Pudd'nhead Wilson

Edited with an Introduction by
Malcolm Bradbury

While it retains the comic exuberance of
Huckleberry Finn, this is Twain's darker and
more disturbing account of human nature
under slavery.

320 pp.   0-14-043040-7 $10.00

Roughing It

Edited with an Introduction by Hamlin Hill

A fascinating picture of the American
frontier emerges from Twain's fictionalized
recollections of his experiences prospecting
for gold, speculating in timber, and writing
for a succession of small Western newspapers
during the 1860s.

592 pp.   0-14-039010-3 $12.95

Tales, Speeches, Essays, and Sketches

Edited with an Introduction by Tom Quirk

Masterful short fiction and prose pieces
display the variety of Twain's imaginative
invention, his diverse talents, and his
extraordinary emotional range. The
volume includes "Jim Smiley and His
Jumping Frog," "The Man That Corrupted
Hadleyburg," "Fenimore Cooper's Literary
Offenses," and the spectacularly scatalogical
"Date, 1601."

448 pp.   0-14-043417-8 $14.00

A Tramp Abroad

Introduction by Robert Gray Bruce and
Hamlin Hill

Cast in the form of a walking tour through
Germany, Switzerland, France, and Italy,
A Tramp Abroad sparkles with the author's
shrewd observations and highly opinion-
ated comments on Old World culture,
and showcases his unparalleled ability to
integrate humorous sketches, autobiographical tidbit, and historical anecdotes
in consistently entertaining narrative.

640 pp.   0-14-043608-1 $14.95

See The Portable American Realism Reader.

MARK TWAIN
1835 – 1910, American

CHARLES DUDLEY WARNER
1829 – 1900, American

The Gilded Age
A Tale of Today

Introduction and Notes by Louis J. Budd

With his characteristic wit and perception,
Mark Twain and his collaborator, Charles
Dudley Warner, attack the greed, lust,
and naïveté of their own time in a work
that endures as one of America's most
important satirical novels.

528 pp.   0-14-043920-X $15.00

**"Our best political novel . . . To under-
stand America, read Mark Twain."**

—GARY WILLS

WILLIAM TYNDALE
1494 – 1536, English

The Obedience of a Christian Man

Edited with an Introduction and Notes by David Daniell

In this 1528 treatise, which would become one of the most important publications of the first phase of the English Reformation, Tyndale boldly develops the argument that ordinary believers should take their spiritual sustenance direct from Scripture. He was the first to translate the Bible into English, a heretical undertaking that eventually led to his execution.

272 pp.   0-14-043477-1 $13.00

SIGRID UNDSET
1882 – 1949, Norwegian (b. Denmark)
Nobel Prize winner

Gunnar's Daughter

Edited with an Introduction and Notes by Sherrill Harbison and Translated by Arthur G. Chater

Written in 1909, this swift and compelling tale of a female avenger from the Saga Age was Undset's first published novel with a medieval setting. Unlike most of the Viking-inspired art of its period, it is not a historical romance but addresses questions as troublesome in Undset's own time—and in ours—as they were in the Saga Age: rape and revenge, civil and domestic violence.

240 pp.   3 maps   0-14-118020-X $11.95

Kristin Lavransdatter
I: The Wreath

Translated with an Introduction and Notes by Tiina Nunnally

Originally published in 1920 and set in fourteenth-century Norway, the first volume of *Kristin Lavransdatter* chronicles the courtship of a strong-willed and passionate young woman and a dangerously charming man. This new translation—a finalist for the PEN Center USA West Translation Prize—brings Undset's magnificent epic to life with clarity and lyrical beauty.

288 pp.   1 map   0-14-118041-2 $13.00

SIGRID UNDSET

Sigrid Undset was born in Denmark, the eldest daughter of a Norwegian daughter and a Danish mother, and moved with her family to Oslo two years later. She published her first novel in 1907 and *Gunnar's Daughter*, her first work set in the Middle Ages, followed in 1909. In 1920, Undset published the first volume of *Kristin Lavransdatter*, the medieval trilogy that would become her most famous work. In 1928, Sigrid Undset won the Nobel Prize for literature. During the Nazi occupation of Norway, Undset lived as a refugee in New York City. She returned home in 1945 and lived in Lillehammer until her death in 1949.

Kristin Lavransdatter
II: The Wife

Translated with Notes by Tiina Nunnally and an Introduction by Sherrill Harbison

The Wife chronicles Kristin's marriage to Erlend Nikulausson, a man whose single-minded determination to become a powerful social and political figure forces Kristin to manage his estate while raising their seven sons. Tiina Nunnally's beautiful new translation, which restores passages ommitted from the original English-language version, was a finalist for both the PEN Center USA West and the PEN/Book-of-the-Month Club Translation Prizes.

352 pp. 2 maps 0-14-118128-1 $13.00

Kristin Lavransdatter
III: The Cross

Translated with Notes by Tiina Nunnally and an Introduction by Sherrill Harbison

Winner of the PEN/Book-of-the-Month Club Translation Prize

In the most devastating and emotional volume of the trilogy, Kristin returns with her husband and children to her childhood home. *The Cross* exquisitely completes the first new English translation of Undset's masterpiece.

448 pp. 2 maps 0-14-118235-0 $12.95

Penguin Readers Guide Available for Kristin Lavransdatter I–III.

BARTOLOMEO VANZETTI

See Nicola Sacco.

GIORGIO VASARI
1511 – 1574, Italian (b. Arezzo)

Lives of the Artists
Volume 1

Translated and Edited with an Introduction by George Bull

Vasari offers insights into the lives and techniques of twenty artists, from Cimabue, Giotto, and Leonardo to Michelangelo and Titian.

480 pp. 0-14-044500-5 $14.00

Lives of the Artists
Volume 2

Translated and Edited with an Introduction by George Bull and Notes on the Artists by Peter Murray

Vasari's knowledge was based on his own experience as an early Renaissance painter and architect. Volume 2 explores the lives of twenty-five artists, from Perugino to Giovanni Pisano.

376 pp. 0-14-044460-2 $13.00

See The Portable Renaissance Reader.

THORSTEIN VEBLEN
1857 – 1929, American

The Theory of the Leisure Class

Introduction by Robert Lekachman

With exquisite irony, Veblen, the "best critic of America that America has produced" (C. Wright Mills), lays bare the hollowness of our canons of taste and culture.

144 pp. 0-14-018795-2 $12.00

Cavalleria Rusticana and Other Stories

Translated with an Introduction by G. H. McWilliam

Giovanni Verga's brilliant stories of love, adultery, and honor are set against the scorched landscapes of the slopes of Mount Etna and the Plain of Catalan. This edition contains the first major English translations since those of D. H. Lawrence in the 1920s.

272 pp.   0-14-044741-5 $14.00

New Science

Translated by David Marsh with an Introduction by Anthony Grafton

This astonishingly ambitious attempt to provide a comprehensive science of all human society by decoding the history, mythology, and law of the ancient world marked a turning-point in humanist thinking as significant as Newton's contemporary revolution in physics.

560 pp.   0-14-043569-7 $16.00

See The Portable Enlightenment Reader.

"My imagination grows every time I read Vico."

—JAMES JOYCE

Duluth

Spoofing everything from social pretenses, motherhood, law enforcement, marriage, and racism, to literature, television, science fiction, and sex, this wild burlesque tells of two women who die in a snowdrift to be reborn on a popular television show, *Duluth*, and in a romance novel.

224 pp.   0-14-118042-0 $13.95

Kalki

Vidal takes on the unmitigated follies born of the unholy partnership of religion, the media, and a public that longs for a savior.

272 pp.   0-14-118037-4 $16.00

The Messiah

A deft and daring blend of satire and prophecy first published in 1954, *The Messiah* eerily anticipates the excesses of Jim Jones, David Koresh, and "Do," the guru of Heaven's Gate.

256 pp.   0-14-118039-0 $13.95

Myra Breckinridge/Myron

When *Myra Breckinridge* first appeared in 1968, critics were delighted, baffled, and somewhat appalled by this comedy of sex change. Thirty years later, Myra has become literature's most famous transsexual. In the sequel, *Myron* (1974), the Breckinridge saga takes an increasingly bizarre turn. Vidal combines time travel with the ultimate Hollywood fantasy, as Myra attempts to alter cinema history.

432 pp.   0-14-118028-5 $14.95

See Jean de Joinville.

Aeneid

Edited by Frederick M. Keener and Translated by John Dryden

Virgil's epic vividly recounts Aeneas's tortuous journey after the Trojan War and the struggles he faced as he lay the foundations for the greatest continental empire. Rendered into a vigorous and refined English by the most important man of letters of the seventeenth century, this translation of the *Aeneid* "set a new, august standard so influential as to be epochal." For his version, John Dryden drew on his personal experiences during periods of political unrest.

480 pp.   0-14-044627-3 $17.00

The Aeneid

Translated by W. F. Jackson Knight

In this fresh prose translation, W. F. Jackson Knight discusses *The Aeneid*'s impact on Western civilization and provides a list of variations from the Oxford text.

368 pp.   0-14-044051-8 $9.95

The Aeneid
A New Prose Translation

Translated with an Introduction by David West

This prose translation by David West has been widely acclaimed for its directness and clarity.

288 pp.   0-14-044932-9 $10.95

The Eclogues

Translated with an Introduction and Notes by Guy Lee

Written between 42 and 37 B.C., ten pastoral poems believed to be the first authentic work by Virgil are presented with the original Latin on the left-hand page and the translation on the right.

144 pp.   0-14-044419-X $13.00

The Georgics

Translated with an Introduction and Notes by L. P. Wilkinson

A eulogy to Italy as the temperate land of perpetual spring, and a celebration of the values of rustic piety, *The Georgics* is probably the supreme achievement of Latin poetry.

160 pp.   0-14-044414-9 $13.00

See The Portable Roman Reader.

VIRGIL

Generally regarded as ancient Rome's greatest poet, Publius Vergilius Maro was born of peasant stock near Mantua in 70 B.C. He was later sent to Rome to further his education and there came under the influence of Epicureanism. *The Georgics*, a superb expression of agricultural living, was composed during the final period of the civil wars, and was dedicated to Maecenas, an important Roman official and art patron. Virgil devoted the last years of his life to writing *The Aeneid*, the epic story of the foundation of Rome and Virgil's embodiment of Roman ideals. In the last year of his life, 19 B.C., he journeyed to Greece to do research for a revision of his epic.

The Portable Voltaire

Edited by Ben Ray Redman

This encyclopedic anthology acquaints us with Voltaire's vast range of expression in such works as *Candide, Zadig, The English Letters*, and *The Philosophical Dictionary*, as well as many other essays and stories.

576 pp. 0-14-015041-2 $17.00

Candide

Translated and Cast in the Form of a Walking Tour through Germany, Switzerland, France, and Italy by John Butt

Voltaire takes Candide and Dr. Pangloss through a variety of ludicrous adventures and reversals of fortune in this satirical challenge to the empty optimism prevalent in Voltaire's eighteenth-century society.

144 pp. 0-14-044004-6 $6.95

Penguin Readers Guide Available

Letters on England

Translated with an Introduction by Leonard Tancock

Also known as the *Lettres anglaises ou philosophiques*, Voltaire's response to his exile in England offered the French public of 1734 a panoramic view of British culture. Perceiving them as a veiled attack against the *ancien régime*, however, the French government ordered the letters burned and Voltaire persecuted.

160 pp. 0-14-044386-X $9.95

Micromégas and Other Short Fictions

Translated by Theo Cuffe with an Introduction and Notes by Haydn Mason

Somewhere between tales and polemics, these funny, ribald, and inventive pieces show Voltaire doing what he does best: brilliantly challenging received wisdom, religious intolerance, and naïve optimism. Traveling through strange environments, Voltaire's protagonists are educated, often by surprise, into the complexities and contradictions of their world.

192 pp. 0-14-044686-9 $10.00

Philosophical Dictionary

Translated and Edited with an Introduction by Theodore Besterman

Voltaire's irony, scrutiny, and passionate love of reason and justice are fully evident in this deliberately revolutionary series of essays on religion, metaphysics, society, and government.

400 pp. 0-14-044257-X $13.95

Zadig/L'Ingénu

Translated with an Introduction by John Butt

One of Voltaire's earliest tales, *Zadig* is set in the exotic East and is told in the comic spirit of *Candide; L'Ingénu*, written after *Candide*, is a darker tale in which an American Indian records his impressions of France.

192 pp. 0-14-044126-3 $9.95

See The Portable Enlightenment Reader.

JACOBUS DE VORAGINE
c.1229 – 1298, French

The Golden Legend
Selections
*Selected and Translated by Christopher Stace
with an Introduction and Notes by
Richard Hamer*

This single-volume sourcebook of all the
core Christian stories attracted a huge
audience across thirteenth-century Europe,
including Geoffrey Chaucer. The more
than seventy biographies here are essential
reading for anyone who wants to understand medieval imagery, art, and thought.
432 pp.   0-14-044648-6 $15.00

HORACE WALPOLE
1717 – 1797, British

The Castle of Otranto
Edited with an Introduction by Michael Gamer
Set in the time of the Crusades, this tale of
fatal prophecy established the Gothic as a
literary form in England. Blending psychological realism and supernatural terror,
guilty secrets and unlawful desires, it has
influenced a tradition stretching from
Ann Radcliffe and Bram Stoker to
Daphne Du Maurier and Stephen King.
208 pp.   0-14-043767-3 $8.00
See Three Gothic Novels.

"[Walpole] is the father of the first
romance and surely worthy of a higher
place than any living writer."
—LORD BYRON

BOOKER T. WASHINGTON
1856 – 1915, American

Up from Slavery
Introduction by Louis R. Harlan
Washington's autobiography reveals the
conviction he held that the black man's
salvation lay in education, industriousness,
and self-reliance.
336 pp.   0-14-039051-0 $9.95

MAX WEBER
1864 – 1920, German

The Protestant Ethic and the "Spirit" of Capitalism and Other Writings
*Edited, Translated, and with an Introduction
by Peter Baehr and Gordon C. Wells*

In what is arguably the most important
work of twentieth-century sociology, Max
Weber opposes the Marxist concept of
dialectical materialism and relates the rise
of the capitalist economy to the Calvinist
belief in the moral value of hard work and
the fulfillment of one's worldly duties.
Based on the original German 1905 edition.
384 pp.   0-14-043921-8 $16.00

REBECCA WEST
1892 – 1983, British

Black Lamb and Grey Falcon
A Journey through Yugoslavia
A magnificent blend of cultural commentary, travel journal, and historical insight,
this volume—written on the eve of World
War II—probes the troubled history of
the Balkans and their uneasy alliance of
ethnic groups.
1,200 pp.   0-14-018847-9 $23.00

"Surely one of the great books of our
century."
—DIANA TRILLING

The Return of the Soldier

Introduction by Samuel Hynes

Writing her first novel during World War I, West examines the relationship between three women and a soldier suffering from shell-shock. This novel of an enclosed world invaded by public events also embodies in its characters the shifts in England's class structures at the beginning of the twentieth century.

128 pp.   **0-14-118065-X**   **$10.95**

EDITH WHARTON
1862 – 1937, American

The Age of Innocence

Edited with an Introduction by Cynthia Griffin Wolff and Notes by Laura Dluzynski Quinn

Winner of the Pulitzer Prize

Edith Wharton's sharp, ironic wit and Jamesian mastery of form create a disturbingly accurate picture of men and women caught in a society that denies humanity while desperately defending its civilization.

384 pp.   **0-14-018970-X**   **$9.95**

Penguin Readers Guide Available

Great Books Foundation Readers Guide Available

The Custom of the Country

Introduction by Anita Brookner

Wharton blends sharp cultural criticism with a biting indictment of American culture. This is a portrait of a woman advancing herself through matrimony in a world where no business transaction is honest, and no marriage is for love.

352 pp.   **0-14-018190-3**   **$12.00**

Ethan Frome

Introduction by Doris Grumbach and Notes by Sarah Higginson Begley

This classic novel of despair, forbidden emotion, and sexual undercurrents set against an austere New England background is different in both theme and tone from Wharton's other writings.

224 pp.   **0-14-018736-7**   **$7.95**

EDITH WHARTON

Edith Wharton was born into a prosperous social circle that centered in New York, New England, and Europe. In *The House of Mirth* (1905) and *The Age of Innocence* (1920) she brought to life ironic portraits of aristocratic American society and the constraints it placed upon women with its demands and expectations. Her 1911 tale, Ethan Frome, the story of the stifled existence of a snowbound, desolate household, is set in the stark New England landscape that she knew well. After her unhappy marriage had dissolved, Wharton sold "The Mount," her lavish home in western Massachusetts, and moved to France, where she lived independently, and traveled and wrote inexhaustibly, forming friendships with such notables as Henry James and Bernard Berenson.

The House of Mirth

Introduction and Notes by
Cynthia Griffin Wolff

Published in 1905, this daring novel about the shallow, brutal world of Eastern monied society deals with powerful social and feminist themes.

384 pp.   0-14-018729-4 $9.95

Penguin Readers Guide Available

Summer

Introduction and Notes by Elizabeth Ammons

The novel Wharton called her "hot Ethan" is set in the Massachusetts Berkshires and delves into the thwarted dreams and sexual passions of a repressed rural woman.

224 pp.   0-14-018679-4 $9.95

See Four Stories by American Women *and* The Portable American Realism Reader.

PHILLIS WHEATLEY
c. 1753 – 1784, American
(b. western Africa)

Complete Writings

Edited and with an Introduction and Notes by Vincent Carretta

This volume collects the astonishing writings of the eighteenth-century American slave who published her first poem at the age of 14. It includes her letters, poetry, hymns, elegies, translations, tales, and epyllions.

192 pp.   0-14-042430-X $12.00

WALT WHITMAN
1819 – 1892, American

The Portable Walt Whitman

Edited by Mark Van Doren

This impressive collection includes one hundred poems from *Leaves of Grass*, as well as two of Whitman's prose works in their entirety: *Democratic Vistas* and *Specimen Days*.

688 pp.   0-14-015078-1 $16.95

The Complete Poems

Edited with an Introduction by
Francis Murphy

Of the nine editions Whitman prepared of his *Leaves of Grass*, this final "deathbed" edition (1891–92) is printed in accordance with a note of instruction left by the poet to his future editors.

896 pp.   0-14-042222-6 $15.95

Leaves of Grass

Edited with an Introduction by
Malcolm Cowley

This is the original and complete 1855 edition of one of the greatest masterpieces of American literature, including Whitman's own introduction to the work.

192 pp.   0-14-042199-8 $7.95

See Nineteenth-Century American Poetry *and* The Portable Western Reader.

ISABELLA WHITNEY
c. 1550 – ?, British

See Renaissance Women Poets.

OSCAR WILDE
1854 – 1900, Irish

The Portable Oscar Wilde

Edited by Richard Aldington and
Stanley Weintraub

This marvelous anthology includes the complete novel *The Picture of Dorian Gray,* the plays *The Importance of Being Earnest* and *Salomé,* Wilde's prison memoir *De Profundis,* and selections of his other plays, poems, dialogues, letters, and tales.

752 pp.   0-14-015093-5 $15.95

Complete Short Fiction

Edited with an Introduction and Notes by
Ian Small

This volume gathers the short masterpieces that brought Wilde his first fame as a writer of fiction and includes the complete texts of *The Happy Prince and Other Tales, A House* of *Pomegranates, Lord Arthur Savile's Crime and Other Stories,* "Poems in Prose," and "Portrait of Mr. W. H."

336 pp. **0-14-143969-6** **$13.00**

De Profundis and Other Writings

Introduction by Hesketh Pearson

This collection contains many examples of Wilde's humorous and epigrammatic genius that captured the London theater and, by suddenly casting light from an unexpected angle, widened the bounds of truth. Included are "The Soul of Man Under Socialism," "The Decay of Lying," and a selection of poems, including *The Ballad of Reading Gaol,* "Sonnet to Liberty," "Requiescat," and "To My Wife."

256 pp. **0-14-043089-X** **$10.95**

The Importance of Being Earnest and Other Plays

Edited by Richard Allen Cave

This volume collects the essential plays of the brilliant, witty, and enduring playwright: *Lady Windermere's Fan, Salomé, A Woman of No Importance, An Ideal Husband, A Florentine Tragedy,* and *The Importance of Being Earnest*—including an excised scene.

464 pp. **0-14-043606-5** **$10.00**

*The Picture of Dorian Gray

Edited with an Introduction by Robert Mighall and a Preface by Peter Ackroyd

First published to scandal and protest in 1891, this story of a flamboyant hedonist is a sterling example of Wilde's wit and aestheticism.

304 pp. **0-14-143957-2** **$8.00**

(Available February 2003)

OSCAR WILDE

Oscar Wilde was born in Dublin in 1854, the son of an eminent surgeon. He attended Trinity College, Dublin, then Magdalen College, Oxford, where, in the last years of the seventies, he started the cult of "Aetheticism"—of an art of life. He wrote several books, including *The Picture of Dorian Gray* (1891), before he became a successful playwright in both England and France. In 1895 Wilde brought a libel action against the Marquis of Queensberry; he lost the case and was himself sentenced to two years' imprisonment with hard labor for acts of gross indecency. He was released from prison, bankrupt, in 1897 and went to Paris, where he lived until his death in 1900.

The Soul of Man under Socialism and Selected Critical Prose

Edited with an Introduction and Notes by Linda Dowling

Wilde's critical writings reveal a rarely seen side of the famously witty playwright, showing him as a deep and serious reader of literature and philosophy as well as an eloquent thinker about society and art. This illuminating collection includes "The Portrait of Mr. W. H.," "In Defence of *Dorian Gray*," and the essays from *Intentions*.

432 pp.   0-14-043387-2 $13.00

OWEN WISTER
1860 – 1938, American

The Virginian

With an Introduction and Notes by John Seelye

Set in the vast Wyoming territory, Wister's powerful story of the silent stranger who rides into the uncivilized West and defeats the forces of evil embodies one of the most enduring themes in American mythology.

458 pp.   0-14-039065-0 $10.00

MARY WOLLSTONECRAFT
1759 – 1797, British

A Vindication of the Rights of Woman

Edited with an Introduction by Miriam Brody

Published in 1792, this classic treatise applied the egalitarian principles of the French and American revolutions to the social, political, and economic conditions of women.

320 pp.   0-14-043382-1 $10.95

> "As a thinker on social issues, Wollstonecraft was bold and original, and expressed her views through essays, fiction, and travel writing."
>
> —CLAIRE TOMALIN

See The Portable Enlightenment Reader.

MARY WOLLSTONECRAFT
1759 – 1797, British

MARY SHELLEY
1797 – 1851, British

Mary/Maria/Matilda

Edited with an Introduction by Janet Todd

Three short novels written by mother and daughter offer insight into the personal lives of both authors as they illuminate struggles for identity within the early feminist movement.

256 pp.   0-14-043371-6 $14.00

See Mary Shelley.

VIRGINIA WOOLF
1882 – 1941, British

Jacob's Room

Introduction and Notes by Sue Roe

Imparted in a poetic prose style reflecting her experiments with reality, memory, and time, Woolf's third novel signals her bold departure from the traditional methods of the English novel.

192 pp.   0-14-018570-4 $9.95

Night and Day
*Edited with an Introduction and Notes by
Julia Briggs*

A love story and a social comedy in the
tradition of Jane Austen, *Night and Day*
transcends traditional romance to raise
questions about women's intellectual
freedom, marriage, social expectations,
and social reform.

496 pp.   0-14-018568-2 $13.95

The Voyage Out
*Edited with an Introduction and Notes by
Jane Wheare*

Woolf's first novel is the story of an impres-
sionable young British woman sailing to
South America, whose innocence makes
her susceptible to love and ripe for tragedy.

432 pp.   0-14-018563-1 $11.95

WILLIAM WORDSWORTH
1770 – 1850, British

The Prelude
The Four Texts
*Edited with an Introduction by
Jonathan Wordsworth*

This unique edition contains an early draft
of Wordsworth's masterpiece, entitled *Was
It for This*, composed in 1798; *The Prelude*
in two books, composed in 1799; and the
1805 and 1850 versions, presented here in
parallel texts to show the poem's evolution.

736 pp.   0-14-043369-4 $19.95

Selected Poems
Edited by John O. Hayden

This generous selection of Wordsworth's
best poems, freshly edited and chronologically arranged, concentrates on his greater
short works.

624 pp.   0-14-042375-3 $11.95

See English Romantic Verse *and*
The Portable Romantic Poets.

XENOPHON
c. 430 – c. 350 B.C., Greek

Conversations of Socrates
*Edited with an Introduction by
Robin Waterfield and Translated by
Hugh Tredennick and Robin Waterfield*

Xenophon's complete Socratic works—
*Socrates' Defence, Memoirs of Socrates, The
Dinner Party,* and *The Estate-Manager*—
not only portray the character and teach-
ings of the great philosopher but apply
Socratic principles to the daily life of
Greece, giving insight into the religious,
political, and moral views of the Athenians.

384 pp.   0-14-044517-X $12.95

A History of My Times
*Translated by Rex Warner with an
Introduction and Notes by
George Cawkwell*

Continuing the story of the Peloponnesian
War where Thucydides left off, Xenophon
records the politics and battles that brought
about the ultimate decline of Greece.

432 pp.   0-14-044175-1 $13.00

The Persian Expedition
*Translated by Rex Warner with an
Introduction and Notes by
George Cawkwell*

This historical account tells of Xenophon's
march with the Ten Thousand against the
barbarian Persians.

376 pp.   0-14-044007-0 $15.00

See The Portable Greek Historians.

Writings on Irish Folklore, Legend, and Myth

Edited with an Introduction and Notes by Robert Welch

In these ruminations on magic, folklore, and the supernatural, Yeats attempts to discover a specifically Irish imagination and to create a movement in literature enriched by, and rooted in, a vital narrative tradition.

496 pp.   0-14-018001-X $13.00

"Yeats stood for enchantment. . . . He was the real original rationalist who said the fairies stand to reason."

—G. K. CHESTERTON

See J. M. Synge.

Hungry Hearts

Introduction by Blanche H. Gelfant

In stories that draw heavily on her own life, Anzia Yezierska portrays the immigrant's struggle to become a "real" American, in such stories as "Yekl," "Hunger," "The Fat of the Land," and "How I Found America." Set mostly in New York's Lower East Side, the stories brilliantly evoke the oppressive atmosphere of crowded streets and shabby tenements and lay bare the despair of families trapped in unspeakable poverty, working at demeaning jobs, and coping with the barely hidden prejudices of their new land.

288 pp.   0-14-118005-6 $12.00

We

Translated with an Introduction and Notes by Clarence Brown

Orwell's inspiration for *1984*, Zamyatin's masterpiece describes life under the regimented totalitarian society of OneState, ruled over by the all-powerful "Benefactor."

240 pp.   0-14-018585-2 $12.95

See The Portable Twentieth-Century Russian Reader.

"The best single work of science fiction yet written."

—URSULA K. LE GUIN

ZITKALA-ŠA
1876 – 1938, American

ÉMILE ZOLA
1840 – 1902, French

American Indian Stories, Legends, and Other Writings

Edited with an Introduction and Notes by Cathy N. Davidson and Ada Norris

In evocative prose laced with political savvy, the writings of Zitkala-Ša reevaluate the perceptions, assumptions, and customs of both Sioux and white cultures and raise issues of assimilation, identity, and race relations that remain compelling today. This original collection includes her powerful autobiographical stories and retold tales, along with a selection of her poetry and nonfiction writings.

304 pp.   0-14-243709-3 $13.00
(Available March 2003)

See The Portable American Realism Reader *and* American Local Color Writing, 1880–1920.

L'Assommoir (The Dram Shop)

Translated with an Introduction by Robin Buss

Now in a vibrant new translation, this edition of Zola's story of a good-hearted but vulnerable laundress includes Zola's response to critics who denounced the work as immoral. The seventh novel in Les Rougon-Macquart cycle, this dark and gritty exploration of working-class life was a publishing sensation and is widely hailed as Zola's masterpiece.

480 pp.   0-14-044753-9 $11.00

ZITKALA-ŠA

Zitkala-Ša, known also as Gertrude Simmons Bonnin, was born on the Yankton Sioux reservation in South Dakota in 1876. A life-long writer and activist who sometimes took controversial stances that drew criticism from other Native Americans, she is best known for a series of semi-autobiographical stories about her childhood and schooling in eastern boarding schools. Zitkala-Ša was a teacher, a student at the New England Conservatory of Music, coauthor of an opera entitled *The Sun Dance*, secretary-treasurer of the first pan-Indian political organization, The Society of American Indians, and editor of its quarterly magazine, *American Indian Magazine*. She wrote fiction, Sioux legends, manifestos, speeches, poetry, and musical scores and was founder and president of the National Council of American Indians, the Washington-based tribal advocacy group that she led until her death in 1938.

Au Bonheur Des Dames (The Ladies' Delight)

Translated and Edited by Robin Buss

In the original sex-and-shopping novel, Zola charts the beginnings of the capitalist economy and bourgeois society, capturing in lavish detail the obsession with image, fashion, greed, and gratification of nineteenth-century France consumer society.

464 pp.   0-14-044783-0 $12.00

La Bête Humaine

Translated with an Introduction by Leonard Tancock

In this taut thriller of violent passions, crime, and the law, Zola bitterly attacks the politics and corruption of the French judicial system.

368 pp.   0-14-044327-4 $12.00

The Debacle

Translated with an Introduction by Leonard Tancock

Zola's only purely historical work, this realistic, detailed, and accurate account of France's defeat in the Franco-Prussian War is a grim testament to the human horrors of war.

512 pp.   0-14-044280-4 $13.95

The Earth

Translated with an Introduction by Douglas Parmée

With humor and flashes of tenderness, Zola depicts the human cycle of birth, marriage, and death against the natural changes of the agricultural seasons.

512 pp.   0-14-044387-8 $14.95

Germinal

Translated with an Introduction by Leonard Tancock

Written to draw attention to the misery prevailing among the lower class in France during the Second Empire, *Germinal* depicts the grim struggle between capital and labor in a coal field in northern France.

512 pp.   0-14-044045-3 $8.95

Nana

Translated with an Introduction by George Holden

An evocation of the corrupt world of the Second Empire, this story of a prostitute embodies Zola's theory that behavior is predetermined by one's origin.

472 pp.   0-14-044263-4 $9.95

Thérèse Raquin

Translated with an Introduction by Leonard Tancock

This tale of adultery, murder, and revenge, condemned as pornography when it was published in 1867, is one of Zola's earliest novels.

272 pp.   0-14-044120-4 $10.95

ANONYMOUS

Beowulf

Edited with an Introduction, Notes, and Glossary by Michael Alexander

This edition presents Anglo-Saxon verse text on the left-hand page, faced by a page on which almost every word is glossed. Succinct footnotes clarify historical and cultural matters.

272 pp.   0-14-043377-5 $12.95

*Beowulf
A Verse Translation
Translated with an Introduction by Michael Alexander

This acclaimed verse translation of the most important Old English poem, the epic story of the Scandinavian hero Beowulf, slayer of monsters and later king of Geatland, captures a richly allusive narrative that blends history with legend, and resonates with eloquence and tragic reserve. Includes genealogical tables and an index of proper names.

192 pp.   1 map   0-14-044931-0 $10.00

Beowulf
A Prose Translation
Introduction by David Wright

Based on a Norse legend, this prose translation of the epic depicts the Scandinavian warrior and his struggles against monsters.

128 pp.   0-14-044070-4 $8.95

*The Bhagavad Gita
Translated by Juan Mascaró with an Introduction by Simon Brodbeck

The eighteen chapters of The Bhagavad Gita (c. 500 B.C.), the glory of Sanskrit literature, encompass the whole spiritual struggle of a human soul. Its central themes arise from the symphonic vision of God in all things and all things in God.

128 pp.   0-14-044918-3 $10.00
(Available March 2003)

See The Portable World Bible.

The Classic of Mountains and Seas
Translated with an Introduction and Notes by Anne Birrell

Traditionally ascribed to the mythical figure Yü the Great this treasure trove of colorful fiction and eclectic information is a spectacular guided tour of the known world in antiquity and a major source of Chinese mythology. This is the first complete annotated edition of *The Classic of Mountains and Seas* (third century B.C. to second century A.D.).

**336 pp.   9 line drawings
0-14-044719-9 $19.00**

*The Cloud of Unknowing and Other Writings
Translated with an Introduction and Notes by A. C. Spearing

In this new translation of four unique and enigmatic masterpieces of medieval mysticism—*The Cloud of Unknowing, The Mystical Theology of Saint Denis, The Book of Privy Counselling,* and *An Epistle of Prayer*—the unknown author, thought to be a priest or monk, describes an abstract, transcendent God beyond human knowledge and human language.

208 pp.   0-14-044385-1 $13.00

The Death of King Arthur
Translated with an Introduction by James Cable

Set in the twilight of the Arthurian world, this medieval romance tells of Lancelot's adultery with Guinevere, the arrival of the treacherous Mordred, and the deaths of both Arthur and Lancelot.

240 pp.   0-14-044255-3 $12.95

The Dhammapada
Translated with an Introduction by Juan Mascaró

Compiled in the third century B.C., these aphorisms illustrate the Buddhist dhamma, or moral system, pointing out the narrow Path of Perfection that leads toward Nirvana.

96 pp.   0-14-044284-7 $8.95

See The Portable World Bible.

Egil's Saga
*Translated with an Introduction by
Hermann Pálsson and Paul Edwards*

Thought to have been written in 1230, *Egil's
Saga* chronicles the histories of the ruling
clans of Iceland and Norway, giving a
wide-ranging view of the Viking world in
the ninth and tenth centuries.

256 pp.   0-14-044321-5 $14.00

The Epic of Gilgamesh
*Translated with an Introduction
by N.K. Sandars*

Fifteen centuries before Homer, this
Mesopotamian cycle of poems tells of
Gilgamesh, the great King, Uruk, and his
long and arduous journey to the spring of
youth in search of immortality.

128 pp.   0-14-044919-1 $9.95

The Epic of Gilgamesh
A New Translation
*Translated with an Introduction by
Andrew George*

George's gripping new translation brilliantly
brings together all the variant traditions
and transforms a "damaged masterpiece"
into a fluent, coherent narrative.

288 pp.   28 line drawings   1 map
0-14-044721-0 $9.00

Eyrbyggja Saga
*Translated with an Introduction by
Hermann Pálsson and Paul Edwards*

This saga dramatizes a thirteenth-century
view of the past, from the pagan anarchy of
the Viking Age to the settlement of Iceland,
the coming of Christianity, and the beginnings of organized society.

192 pp.   0-14-044530-7 $14.00

The Greek Alexander Romance
*Translated with an Introduction by
Richard Stoneman*

One of the most influential works of late
classical Greek literature, this fast-paced,
wonderfully exuberant entertainment
portrays the fabulous adventures of
Alexander the Great.

208 pp.   0-14-044560-9 $14.00

Hrafnkel's Saga
*Translated with an Introduction by
Hermann Pálsson*

These seven stories, dating from the
thirteenth century, combine pagan
elements and Christian ethics; some are
set in the pastoral society of Iceland, while
others are concerned with the royal courts
of Norway and Denmark.

144 pp.   0-14-044238-3 $13.00

See Snorri Sturluson.

The Koran
*Translated with an Introduction and Notes
by N. J. Dawood*

N. J. Dawood's vivid translation is presented
with opposing-page parallel Arabic text
in the traditional calligraphic style. The
volume includes a comprehensive index.
Oversized format.

1,088 pp.   0-14-044542-0 $23.95

The Koran
Revised Edition
*Translated with an Introduction and Notes
by N. J. Dawood*

This authoritative translation reflects the
characteristic flavor and rhythm of Islam's
most sacred work, following the original
sequence of the Koranic suras.

456 pp.   0-14-044558-7 $11.00

See The Portable World Bible.

The Laws of Manu

*Translated by Wendy Doniger O'Flaherty
with Brian K. Smith*

No understanding of modern India is possible without this extraordinary model of jurisprudence, philosophy, and religion, written from 200 B.C. to A.D. 200.

368 pp.   0-14-044540-4 $13.95

Laxdaela Saga

*Translated with an Introduction by
Magnus Magnusson and Hermann Pálsson*

This dynastic chronicle, composed around 1245, sweeps across 150 years of Iceland's early history.

272 pp.   0-14-044218-9 $12.95

Lives of the Later Caesars

*Translated with an Introduction by
Anthony Birley*

Covering the emperors from Hadrian to Heliogabalus (A.D. 117–222), this edition contains the only true sequel to Suetonius's *The Twelve Caesars.*

336 pp.   0-14-044308-8 $14.00

The Mabinogion

*Translated with an Introduction by
Jeffrey Gantz*

These tales from the Welsh oral tradition were first written down in the thirteenth century and remain an alluring combination of fact and fantasy, myth, history, and folklore.

376 pp.   0-14-044322-3 $11.00

The Nibelungenlied

*Translated with an Introduction by
A. T. Hatto*

This great German epic poem, written during the thirteenth century, is the principal literary source of Richard Wagner's *The Ring.*

416 pp.   0-14-044137-9 $14.00

*Njal's Saga

Edited and Translated by Robert Cook
Taken from *The Complete Sagas of Icelanders*

This newly translated edition of the most powerful and popular of the great Icelandic Family Sagas describes a fifty-year blood feud from its violent beginnings to its tragic end.

384 pp.   0-14-044769-5 $14.00

Orkneyinga Saga
The History of the Earls of Orkney

*Translated with an Introduction by
Hermann Pálsson and Paul Edwards*

Describing the conquest of the Orkney Islands by the Kings of Norway, this is the only medieval Norse chronicle concerned with what is now part of the British Isles.

256 pp.   0-14-044383-5 $13.95

The Poem of the Cid

*Translated by Rita Hamilton and
Janet Perry with an Introduction and Notes
by Ian Michael*

This epic poem, the only one to have survived from medieval Spain, depicts the career of the warlord El Cid in a unique blend of fiction and historical fact. Both English and Spanish texts are provided.

256 pp.   0-14-044446-7 $12.00

The Quest of the Holy Grail

Translated with an Introduction by
P. M. Matarasso

This classic tale of chivalrous adventures was intended as an allegory of man's perilous search for the grace of God.

304 pp.   0-14-044220-0 $12.95

The Rig Veda

Selected, Translated, and Annotated by
Wendy Doniger O'Flaherty

This collection of more than 1,000 Sanskrit hymns from the timeless world of myth and ritual forms a unique insight into early Indian mythology, philosophy, and religion.

512 pp.   0-14-044402-5 $12.95

See The Portable World Bible.

The Saga of King Hrolf Kraki

Translated with an
Introduction by Jesse L. Byock

Written in fourteenth-century Iceland, this extraordinary saga ranks among the masterworks of the Middle Ages.

144 pp.   1 map   0-14-043593-X $11.95

The Saga of the Volsungs

Translated with an Introduction, Notes, and
Glossary by Jesse L. Byock

Based on Viking Age poems and composed in thirteenth-century Iceland, this saga combines mythology, legend, and sheer human drama to relate the heroic deeds of Sigurd the dragon slayer. Yet its setting is a very human world that incorporates oral memories of the fourth and fifth centuries.

160 pp.   2 maps   0-14-044738-5 $13.00

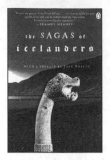

The Sagas of Icelanders
A Selection

Introduction by Robert Kellogg with a
Preface by Jane Smiley

Taken from *The Complete Sagas of Icelanders*

The eleven Sagas and six shorter tales in this volume recount the adventures of the settlers who first came from Norway to Iceland's shores, and how they founded a unique commonwealth of chieftains with no king in this brave new world of towering mountains and lonely fjords. These selections are drawn from the first English translation of the entire corpus of the Icelandic Sagas, together with the forty-nine connected tales—a five-volume set published by Leifur Eiríksson Publishing, Iceland.

848 pp.   0-14-100003-1 $20.00

"Here is the poetry of the Atlantic . . . a testimony to the human spirit's ability not only to endure what fate may send but to be renewed by the experience."

—SEAMUS HEANEY

Sagas of Warrior-Poets

Edited with an Introduction by
Diana Whaley

Taken from *The Complete Sagas of Icelanders*

Lovers, poets, and dragon-slaying heroes populate these five timeless Icelandic sagas of love, honor, and adventure. Set in a time when the old Viking ethos of honor and heroic adventure merged with new ideas of romantic infatuation, these stories continue to fascinate nearly a millennium later. Includes *Kormak's Saga, The Saga of Hallfred Troublesome-Poet, The Saga of Gunnlaug Serpent-Tongue, The Saga of Bjorn,* and *Viglund's Saga.*

400 pp.   0-14-044771-7 $14.00

Sir Gawain and the Green Knight
Edited by J. A. Burrow

Dating from the latter part of the fourteenth century, this subtle and accomplished poem is roughly contemporary with *The Canterbury Tales,* though written in a more provincial dialect. This edition is accessible to modern readers while retaining the integrity of the original.

176 pp.   0-14-042295-1 $9.95

Sir Gawain and the Green Knight
Translated with an Introduction by Brian Stone

This masterpiece of medieval alliterative poetry by an unknown fourteenth-century author is both magical and human, full of drama and descriptive beauty.

176 pp.   0-14-044092-5 $8.95

The Song of Roland
Translated with an Introduction and Notes by Glyn Burgess

Chronicling the massacre in A.D. 778 of Charlemagne's army at Roncesvalles, this age-old French epic transforms a legendary defeat into an allegorical clash between Christianity and paganism.

224 pp.   0-14-044532-3 $10.95

The Song of Roland
Translated by Dorothy Sayers

Nowhere in literature is the medieval code of chivalry more perfectly expressed than in this masterly and exciting poem, translated here by Dorothy Sayers, an expert in medieval literature perhaps best known for her sixteen crime novels.

208 pp.   0-14-044075-5 $11.95

Tales from the Thousand and One Nights
Translated with an Introduction by N. J. Dawood

This volume includes the finest and best known of the *Tales,* representing an expression of the secular imagination in revolt against the religious austerity of other works of medieval Near Eastern literature.

416 pp.   0-14-044289-8 $14.00

The Upanishads
Selected and Translated with an Introduction by Juan Mascaró

First written in Sanskrit between 800 and 400 B.C., these spiritual treatises form the foundation of Hindu beliefs.

144 pp.   0-14-044163-8 $10.00

See The Portable World Bible.

The Vinland Sagas and The Norse Discovery of America
Translated by Magnus Magnusson and Hermann Pálsson

These two Icelandic sagas tell the arresting stories of the discovery of North America five centuries before the arrival of Christopher Columbus.

128 pp.   0-14-044154-9 $12.00

ANTHOLOGIES AND COLLECTIONS

Against Slavery
An Abolitionist Reader
Edited and with an Introduction by Mason Lowance

An original anthology of primary documents from the eighteenth- and nineteenth-century antislavery and abolitionist movements, including speeches, lectures, and essays by Garrison, Douglass, Emerson, and Lydia Maria Child.

384 pp.   0-14-043758-4 $13.95

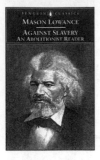

American Local Color Writing, 1880–1920
Edited with an Introduction by Elizabeth Ammons and Valerie Rohy

Organized geographically, *American Local Color Writing* features familiar writers such as Kate Chopin, Hamlin Garland, Joel Chandler Harris, and Sarah Orne Jewett, and introduces lesser-known voices like Abraham Cahan, Sui Sin Far, and Zitkala-Ša. The writing sheds light on varying concepts of the "American identity": the African American experience; shifting notions of gender and sexuality; and racial, class, and ethnic stereotypes.

400 pp.   0-14-043688-X $13.95
See Abraham Cahan, Kate Chopin, Joel Chandler Harris, and Sarah Orne Jewett.

Buddhist Scriptures
Selected and Translated by Edward Conze

This selection of writings from the golden age of Buddhist literature (A.D. 100–400) focuses on texts intended for the layperson rather than for the monk and exhibits the humanity rather than the profundity of the scriptures. Passages from the *Dhammapada*, the *Buddhacarita*, the *Questions of King Milinda*, and the *Tibetan Book of the Dead* are included.

256 pp.   0-14-044088-7 $14.00

A Celtic Miscellany
Selected and Translated with a Preface and Notes by Kenneth Hurlstone Jackson

More than 240 thematically arranged selections of Celtic poetry and prose, translated from the Welsh, Irish, Scottish Gaelic, Cornish, Breton, and Manx languages, provide insight into the Celtic mind from the earliest times to the nineteenth century.

352 pp.   0-14-044247-2 $12.95

The Cistercian World
Monastic Writings of the Twelfth Century
Edited and Translated with an Introduction by Pauline Matarasso

Collected in this volume are letters, sermons, biographies, satires, and stories by the influential abbot St. Bernard of Clairvaux and other monks of the Cistercian Order—a medieval order devoted to strict asceticism and a life of poverty.

336 pp.   0-14-043356-2 $16.00

*Classical Literary Criticism
Translated by Penelope Murray and T. S. Dorsch with an Introduction by Penelope Murray

This anthology brings together core landmark texts for understanding literature—Plato's *Ion* and Chapters 2, 3, and 10 of *The Republic*; Aristotle's *Poetics*; Horace's *The Art of Poetry*; and the treatise *On the Sublime*, generally attributed to Longinus—in accessible and lucid translations.

256 pp.   0-14-044651-6 $12.00
See Aristotle, Horace, and Plato.

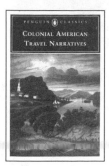

Colonial American Travel Narratives

Edited with an Introduction by
Wendy Martin

Four journeys by early Americans Mary Rowlandson, Sarah Kemble Knight, William Byrd II, and Dr. Alexander Hamilton recount the vivid physical and psychological challenges of colonial life. Essential primary texts in the study of early American cultural life, they are now conveniently collected in a single volume.

336 pp.   0-14-039088-X $13.95

The Earliest English Poems
Third Revised Edition

Translated with an Introduction by
Michael Alexander

This select volume includes translations of heroic poems (including the oldest poem in the English language), a passage from *Beowulf*, "riddles" from *The Exeter Book*, and elegies in Anglo-Saxon meter and alliteration.

176 pp.   0-14-044594-3 $11.95

Early American Drama

Edited with an Introduction and Notes by
Jeffrey H. Richards

This unique volume includes eight early dramas that mirror American literary, social, and cultural history: Royall Tyler's *The Contrast* (1789); William Dunlap's *André* (1798); James Nelson Barker's *The Indian Princess* (1808); Robert Montgomery Bird's *The Gladiator* (1831); William Henry Smith's *The Drunkard* (1844); Anna Cora Mowatt's *Fashion* (1845); George Aiken's *Uncle Tom's Cabin* (1852); and Dion Boucicault's *The Octoroon* (1859).

576 pp.   0-14-043588-3 $15.00

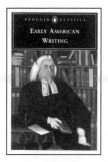

Early American Writing

Edited with an Introduction by
Giles Gunn

Drawing materials from journals and diaries, political documents and religious sermons, prose and poetry, Giles Gunn's anthology provides a panoramic survey of early American life and literature—including voices black and white, male and female, Hispanic, French, and Native American.

720 pp.   0-14-039087-1 $16.00

Early Christian Lives

Translated and Edited by
Carolinne White

Shedding light on the men who were the founding fathers of monasticism in both the eastern and western areas of the Roman Empire, these accounts—Athanasius's *Life of Antony*; St. Jerome's *Life of Paul of Thebes*, *Life of Hilarion*, and *Life of Malchus*; Sulpicius Severus's *Life of Martin of Tours*; and Pope Gregory the Great's *Life of Benedict*—also illuminate the beliefs and values of their celebrated authors.

288 pp.   0-14-043526-3 $15.00

Early Christian Writings
The Apostolic Fathers

*Translated by Maxwell Staniforth with
Revised Translation, Introductions, and
New Editorial Material by Andrew Louth*

These letters and short theological treatises
provide a rich guide to the emerging traditions and organization of the infant Church.

208 pp.   0-14-044475-0 $14.00

*Early Greek Philosophy

*Translated and Edited with an
Introduction by Jonathan Barnes*

The early sages of Western philosophy and
science, the Presocratics, paved the way for
Plato and Aristotle and their successors.
Their writings formed part of a revolution
in human thought that relied on reasoning.
This collection painstakingly brings
together the surviving Presocratic
fragments in their original context.

352 pp.   0-14-044815-2 $14.00

Early Irish Myths and Sagas

*Translated with an Introduction and Notes
by Jeffrey Gantz*

These fourteen myths and tales, probably
first written down around the eighth century A.D., represent the oral tradition of
Iron Age Celts who flourished in Europe
during the seven centuries before Christ.

288 pp.   0-14-044397-5 $14.00

English Romantic Verse

Edited with an Introduction by David Wright

Nearly all the famous and beloved masterworks can be found here—"Intimations of
Immortality," "Rime of the Ancient Mariner,"
and "The Tyger"—as well as some less
familiar poems from such writers as
Christopher Smart, Walter Savage Landor,
John Clare, and Thomas Lovell Beddoes.

384 pp.   0-14-042102-5 $8.95

*See William Blake, Samuel Coleridge, and
William Wordsworth.*

Four Stories by American Women

*Edited with an Introduction by
Cynthia Griffin Wolff*

Representing four prominent American
women writers who flourished in the
period following the Civil War, this
collection comprises "Life in the Iron
Mills," Rebecca Harding Davis; "The Yellow
Wallpaper," Charlotte Perkins Gilman; "The
Country of the Pointed Firs," Sarah Orne
Jewett; and "Souls Belated," Edith Wharton.

240 pp.   0-14-039076-6 $9.95

*See Charlotte Perkins Gilman,
Sarah Orne Jewett, and Edith Wharton.*

German Idealist Philosophy

*Edited with an Introduction by
Rüdiger Bubner*

In this masterful introduction to German
idealism, Rüdiger Bubner brings together
key texts and lesser-known extracts
from works of four powerful intellects—
Immanuel Kant, Johann Fichte, Friederich

Schelling, and George Hegel—with insightful overviews of each philosopher and an account of the movement as a whole.

368 pp.   0-14-044660-5 $20.00

See Georg Wilhelm Friedrich Hegel.

Hindu Myths

Translated by Wendy Doniger O'Flaherty

This selection and translation of seventy-five myths spans a wide range of Indian sources, from the serpent-slaying Indra of the Vedas to the medieval pantheon.

272 pp.   0-14-044306-1 $16.00

Hippocratic Writings

*Edited with an Introduction by
G. E. R. Lloyd and Translated by
J. Chadwick, W. N. Mann, E. T. Withington,
and I. M. Lonie*

The origins of Western medicine and the ideal of ethical practice, as well as the origin of the scientific method are revealed in these writings by Hippocrates and other medical pioneers.

384 pp.   0-14-044451-3 $13.95

Japanese Nō Dramas

*Translated with an Introduction and
Notes by Royall Tyler*

These twenty-four plays of mesmerizing beauty fuse the spiritual and the sensual in the esoteric Nō art form, which combines music, dance, costume, and language. The collection includes full notes and stage directions, as well as new interpretations of the plays that influenced writers such as Yeats, Pound, and Brecht.

384 pp.   0-14-044539-0 $14.95

Medieval English Verse

*Edited and Translated with an
Introduction by Brian Stone*

Short narrative poems, religious and secular lyrics, and moral, political, and comic verses are all included in this comprehensive collection of works from the thirteenth and fourteenth centuries.

256 pp.   0-14-044144-1 $15.00

Medieval Writings on Female Spirituality

*Edited with an Introduction and Notes by
Elizabeth Spearing*

This wide-ranging collection of writings by and about religious women presents some of the most original and compelling literature of the Middle Ages. These selections, among them biographies, poetic compositions, and visionary works, reflect the developments in medieval piety, particularly in the link between female spirituality and the body.

320 pp.   0-14-043925-0 $14.00

*See Hildegard of Bingen, Margery Kempe,
and Julian Norwich.*

The Metaphysical Poets

*Edited with an Introduction by
Helen Gardner*

These select works feature thirty-eight poets, among them Carew, Crashaw, Donne, Herbert, Jonson, Lovelace, Marvell, Suckling, and Vaughan.

332 pp.   0-14-042038-X $9.95

*See John Donne, George Herbert,
Ben Jonson, and Andrew Marvell.*

Nineteenth-Century American Poetry

*Edited with an Introduction and Notes by
William C. Spengemann with
Jessica F. Roberts*

Whitman, Dickinson, and Melville occupy the center of this anthology of nearly three hundred poems, spanning the course of the century, from Joel Barlow to Edwin Arlington Robinson, by way of Bryant, Emerson, Longfellow, Whittier, Poe, Holmes, Jones Very, Thoreau, Lowell, and Lanier.

480 pp.   0-14-043587-5 $14.95

*See Ralph Waldo Emerson, Henry
Wadsworth Longfellow, Herman Melville,
Edgar Allan Poe, Henry David Thoreau,
and Walt Whitman.*

The Penguin Book of First World War Poetry

Edited with an Introduction by Jon Silkin

More than photographs or eyewitness reports of the First World War, it is the poetry written during this devastating conflict that has embedded the horror of that time in our consciousness. Now supplemented with five new poems, the works of thirty-eight British, European, and American writers collected here include some of the most outstanding and poignant poems of this century.

320 pp.   0-14-118009-9 $15.00

See Thomas Hardy and Rudyard Kipling.

The Penguin Book of French Poetry
1820–1950

Edited by William Rees

This anthology offers a broad range of French poetry from writers such as Theophile Gautier, Stephane Mallarmé, Charles Baudelaire, and Guillaume Appollinaire. The French text is accompanied by English prose translations.

856 pp.   0-14-042385-0 $19.95

See Charles Baudelaire.

The Penguin Book of
Modern African Poetry

The Penguin Book of Modern African Poetry
Fourth Edition

Edited with an Introduction by Gerald Moore and Ulli Beier

The definitive one-volume survey of modern African poetry, this edition contains the poetry of ninety-nine from twenty-seven countries and displays the wide-ranging forms of African verse: war songs, satires, political protests, and poems about love, nature, and life's surprises.

480 pp.   0-14-118100-1 $15.95

The Penguin Book of Renaissance Verse
1509–1659

Edited by H. R. Woudhuysen and Selected with an Introduction by David Norbrook

Organized thematically, this superbly edited anthology offers a new view of one of the most fertile periods in the history of English literature. Generous space is devoted to writings of women, works of popular culture, and regional noncourtly poetry.

960 pp.   0-14-042346-X $23.95

The Penguin Book of Victorian Verse

Selected and Edited with an Introduction by Daniel Karlin

Works by almost 150 poets, from late Romantics to high modernists, are included in this rich, far-ranging survey. Cross-references and complete biographical and textual notes make this the ideal anthology for general readers and students alike.

928 pp.   0-14-044578-1 $17.95

Poems of Heaven and Hell from Ancient Mesopotamia

Translated with an Introduction by N. K. Sandars

Five poems from the height of Babylonian civilization reflect the cyclical nature of the lives and beliefs of the Mesopotamian culture. Included are *The Babylonian Creation, The Sumerian Underworld, Inanna's Journey to Hell, Adapa: The Man,* and *A Prayer to the Gods of Night.*

192 pp.   0-14-044249-9 $11.95

The Portable American Realism Reader

Edited and Introduced by James Nagel and Tom Quirk

Bringing together more than forty of the best stories published in the United States between 1865–1918, this reader includes the works of Kate Chopin, Willa Cather, Mark Twain, Edith Wharton, and more.

576 pp.   0-14-026830-8 $14.95

See Willa Cather, Charles W. Chesnutt, Kate Chopin, Stephen Crane, Theodore Dreiser, Joel Chandler Harris, Bret Harte, William Dean Howells, Henry James, Jack London, Harriet Beecher Stowe, Mark Twain, Edith Wharton, and Zitkala-Ša.

The Portable Beat Reader

Edited by Ann Charters

The essential collection of Beat writing, including poetry, fiction, essays, song lyrics, letters, and memoirs by Jack Kerouac, Allen Ginsberg, William Burroughs, Neal Cassady, Bob Dylan, and more.

686 pp.   0-14-015102-8 $17.00

See Jack Kerouac.

"The best introduction to America's liveliest postwar literary movement."
—EDMUND WHITE

The Portable Enlightenment Re

Edited by Isaac Kramnick

This volume brings together the era's clas works from great thinkers such as Kant, Diderot, Voltaire, Newton, Rousseau, Locke, Franklin, Jefferson, and Paine, among others.

704 pp.   0-14-024566-9 $17.00

See Francis Bacon, Pierre-Augustin Caron de Beaumarchais, Edmund Burke, René Descartes, Denis Diderot, Benjamin Franklin, David Hume, Thomas Jefferson, John Locke, Charles de Montesquieu, Thomas Paine, Jean-Jacques Rousseau, Adam Smith, Giambattista Vico, Voltaire, and Mary Wollstonecraft.

The Portable Greek Historians

Edited by M. I. Finley

This essential guide to the Greek historians for modern readers brings to life the greatest works of the pioneering scholars Herodotus, Thucydides, Xenophon, and Polybius.

512 pp.   0-14-015065-X $16.95

See Herodotus, Polybius, Thucydides, and Xenophon.

The Portable Greek Reader

Edited by W. H. Auden

This fundamental guide to ancient Greek writing, ranging across drama, philosophy, fables, science, and poems, includes the work of Aeschylus, Sophocles, Euripides, Plato, Aristotle, Aesop, Pindar, Euclid, Hippocrates, and more.

734 pp.   0-14-015039-0 $17.00

See Aeschylus, Aesop, Aristophanes, Aristotle, Euripides, Hesiod, Homer, Pindar, Plato, Sophocles, and Thucydides.

The Portable Harlem Renaissance Reader

Edited by David Levering Lewis

This essential collection magnificently represents the greatest voices of the Harlem Renaissance with the works of Nella Larsen, Zora Neale Hurston, Langston Hughes, W. E. B. Du Bois, Richard Wright, and many more.

816 pp.   0-14-017036-7 $17.00

See W. E. B. Du Bois, James Weldon Johnson, and Nella Larsen.

"A fresh and brilliant portrait of African American art and culture in the 1920s."

—ARNOLD RAMPERSAD

The Portable Medieval Reader

Edited by James Bruce Ross and Mary Martin McLaughlin

This volume brings together the works of some of the best minds of the Middle Ages, including Chaucer, Petrarch, Aquinas, and Abelard, as well as a host of lesser-known figures.

704 pp.   0-14-015046-3 $16.95

See Peter Abélard, Anna Comnena, Thomas Aquinas, Giovanni Boccaccio, Geoffrey Chaucer, Héloise, Jean de Joinville, Margery Kempe, and Christine de Pisan.

The Portable Nineteenth-Century Russian Reader

Edited by George Gibian

This reader includes selections from Pushkin, Chekhov, Gogol, Tolstoy, Dostoyevsky, Turgenev, and more.

692 pp.   0-14-015103-6 $17.00

See Anton Chekhov, Fyodor Dostoyevsky, Nikolai Gogol, Mikhail Lermontov, Alexander Pushkin, Leo Tolstoy, and Ivan Turgenev.

The Portable North American Indian Reader

Edited by Frederick W. Turner III

This compilation includes myths, poetry, tales, and oratory from the Iroquois, Cherokee, Winnebago, Sioux, Hopi, and many other tribes.

640 pp.   0-14-015077-3 $17.00

The Portable Renaissance Reader

Edited by James Bruce Ross and Mary Martin McLaughlin

Presenting the gorgeous, troubled tapestry of the European Renaissance, this collection contains the writing of monarchs, prelates, ordinary citizens, artists, and such writers as Cervantes, Boccaccio, Bacon, Rabelais, and Copernicus.

768 pp.   0-14-015061-7 $16.95

See Leon Battista Alberti, Ludovico Ariosto, Francis Bacon, Giovanni Boccaccio, Miguel de Cervantes, Michel de Montaigne, Niccolò Machiavelli, François Rabelais, Pierre de Ronsard, Thomas à Kempis, and Giorgio Vasari.

The Portable Roman Reader

Edited by Basil Davenport

This collection includes the finest English translations of the essential Roman writers, such as Julius Caesar, Livy, Cicero, Virgil, Horace, and many more.

672 pp.   0-14-015056-0 $18.00

See Apuleius, Julius Caesar, Catullus, Marcus Tullius Cicero, Horace, Juvenal, Titus Livy, Lucretius, Ovid, Petronius, Plautus, Lucius Annaeus Seneca, Cornelius Tacitus, Terence, and Virgil.

The Portable Romantic Poets

Edited by W. H. Auden and
Norman Holmes Pearson

Including selections from Blake, Wordsworth, Byron, Shelley, Keats, Emerson, and more, this collection features the work of the most important Romantic poets.

576 pp.   0-14-015052-8 $15.95

See William Blake, Lord Byron, Ralph Waldo Emerson, John Keats, and William Wordsworth.

The Portable Sixties Reader

Edited by Ann Charters

From civil rights to free love, JFK to LSD, Woodstock to the Moonwalk, the Sixties was a time of change, political unrest, and radical experiments in the arts, sexuality, and personal identity. This unprecedented literary time capsule from the decade that changed the world is organized into thematic chapters and brings this ebullient time back to life.

672 pp.   0-14-200194-5 $16.00
(Available January 2003)

See Ken Kesey.

The Portable Twentieth-Century Russian Reader

Edited by Clarence Brown

The most resonant voices of twentieth-century Russia are assembled in one volume, including stories by Chekhov, Gorky, Bunin, Zamyatin, Nabokov, and excerpts from the great works of Bulgakov, Pasternak, Olesha, and more.

640 pp.   0-14-015107-9 $15.95

See Anna Akhmatova, Mikhail Bulgakov, Ivan A. Bunin, Anton Chekhov, Maxim Gorky, Osip Mandelstam, and Yevgeny Zamyatin.

The Portable Western Reader

Edited by William Kittredge

This compilation presents stories, poems, essays, and excerpts that transcend the Western myth and explore the vast range of Western experience. Includes writings by Edward Abbey, Sherman Alexie, Raymond Carver, Ivan Doig, Richard Ford, Ernest Hemingway, Larry McMurtry, Norman MacLean, and Wallace Stegner, among others.

592 pp.   0-14-023026-2 $16.00

See Ken Kesey, Jack London, Wallace Stegner, and John Steinbeck.

The Portable World Bible

Edited by Robert O. Ballou

The fundamental tenets of the world's religions are presented in one volume, featuring the sacred writings of Buddhism, Christianity, Hinduism, Islam, Judaism, Taoism, and more.

624 pp.   0-14-015005-6 $15.95

See The Bhagavad Gita, *Confucius,* The Dhammapada, The Koran, *Lao Tzu, Mencius,* The Rig Veda, *and* The Upanishads.

Renaissance Women Poets

Edited with an Introduction by
Danielle Clark

Presenting three powerful female voices from the Golden Age of English literature —Isabella Whitney, Mary Sidney, and Aemilia Lanyer—this volume repositions women writers of the Renaissance by presenting their poems in their historical and social context.

448 pp.   0-14-042409-1 $15.00

Romantic Fairy Tales

*Translated and Edited with an
Introduction by Carol Tully*

This enchanting and disturbing collection
vividly illustrates the development of German Romanticism through four key "literary fairy tales": Goethe's *The Fairy Tale* (1795),
Tieck's *Eckbert the Fair* (1797), Fouqué's
Undine (1811), and Brentano's *The Tale of
Honest Casper and Fair Annie* (1817).

192 pp.   0-14-044732-6 $11.00

See Johann Wolfgang von Goethe.

Seven Viking Romances

*Translated with an Introduction by
Hermann Pálsson and Paul Edwards*

Incorporating local myths and legends, as
well as sources from Homer to French
romances, these medieval stories feature
famous kings, difficult gods, and great
adventures.

304 pp.   0-14-044474-2 $13.95

Six Yüan Plays

*Translated with an Introduction by
Liu Jung-En*

Six vibrant plays from the thirteenth cen-
tury represent the first real Chinese theater
to develop free from conservative Confu-
cianism: *The Orphan of Chao, The Soul of
Ch'ien-Nü Leaves Her Body, The Injustice
Done to Tou Ngo, Chang Boils the Sea,
Autumn in Han Palace*, and *A Stratagem of
Interlocking Rings*.

288 pp.   0-14-044262-6 $17.00

Speaking of Śiva

*Translated with an Introduction by
A. K. Ramanujan*

This volume contains a collection of
vacanas (free-verse lyrics) centering
on the Hindu god Śiva, written by
four saints of the great bhakti protest
movement of the tenth century A.D.:
Basvanna, Devara Dasimayya,
Mahaadeviyakka, and Allama Prabhu.

208 pp.   0-14-044270-7 $13.00

Three Gothic Novels

*Edited by Peter Fairclough with an
Introduction by Mario Praz*

Horace Walpole's *The Castle of Otranto*,
published in 1765, is the prototype of
all Gothic novels; William Beckford's
Vathek combines Gothic romanticism
with Oriental exoticism; and Mary Shelley's
Frankenstein is a masterpiece of Gothic
horror.

512 pp.   0-14-043036-9 $11.95

See Mary Shelley and Horace Walpole.

Women's Indian Captivity Narratives

*Edited with an Introduction and Notes by
Kathryn Zabelle Derounian-Stodola*

Enthralling generations of readers, the
narrative of capture by Native Americans is
an archetype of American literature. Most
such narratives were fact-based, but the
stories themselves were often transformed
into spiritual autobiographies, spellbinding
adventure stories, sentimental tales, or
anti-Indian propaganda. The ten complete
narratives here span two hundred years
(1682–1892), and depict the experiences
of women such as Mary Rowlandson,
Hannah Dunstan, Sarah Wakefield, and
Mary Jemison.

224 pp.   0-14-043671-5 $13.95

SUBJECT CATEGORIES

ART/ARCHITECTURE

Henry Adams
Mont-Saint-Michel and Chartres

Leon Battista Alberti
On Painting

Benvenuto Cellini
Autobiography

Vincent van Gogh
The Letters of Vincent van Gogh

Georg Wilhelm Friedrich Hegel
Introductory Lectures on Aesthetics

William Morris
News from Nowhere and Other Writings

Leo Tolstoy
What Is Art?

Giorgio Vasari
Lives of the Artists, Volumes 1 and 2

AUTOBIOGRAPHY/BIOGRAPHY

Abélard and Héloïse
The Letters of Abélard and Héloïse

Henry Adams
The Education of Henry Adams

Jane Addams
Twenty Years at Hull-House

Adomnán of Iona
Life of St. Columba

Mary Antin
The Promised Land

John Aubrey
Brief Lives

Saint Augustine
Confessions

James Boswell
The Life of Samuel Johnson

Vera Brittain
Testament of Youth

John Bunyan
Grace Abounding to the Chief of Sinners

Frances Burney
Journals and Letters

Giovanni Giacomo Casanova
The Story of My Life

Benvenuto Cellini
Autobiography

Quentin Crisp
The Naked Civil Servant

Charles Darwin
Autobiographies

Frederick Douglass
My Bondage and My Freedom
Narrative of the Life of Frederick Douglass,
    an American Slave

Olaudah Equiano
The Interesting Narrative and
    Other Writings

Geoge Fox
The Journal

Benjamin Franklin
The Autobiography and Other Writings

Elizabeth Gaskell
The Life of Charlotte Brontë

Maxim Gorky
My Childhood

Ulysses S. Grant
Personal Memoirs

Thomas Wentworth Higginson
Army Life in a Black Regiment
    and Other Writings

Elspeth Huxley
The Flame Trees of Thika

Harriet Jacobs
Incidents in the Life of a Slave Girl

Henry James
A Life in Letters

Margery Kempe
The Book of Margery Kempe

Primo Levi
Moments of Reprieve

W. Somerset Maugham
The Summing Up

John Stuart Mill
Autobiography

Lady Mary Wortley Montagu
Selected Letters

Marianne Moore
Selected Letters

Murasaki Shikibu
The Diary of Lady Murasaki

Gérard de Nerval
Selected Writings

John Henry Newman
Apologia pro Vita Sua

Friedrich Nietzsche
Ecce Homo

Mary Prince
The History of Mary Prince

Jean-Jacques Rousseau
The Confessions

Lady Sarashina
As I Crossed a Bridge of Dreams:
    Recollections of a Woman in
    Eleventh-Century Japan

Madame de Sévigné
Selected Letters

William Tecumseh Sherman
Memoirs

Charles A. Siringo
A Texas Cowboy

Joshua Slocum
Sailing Alone around the World

Wallace Stegner
Wolf Willow

Lytton Strachey
Eminent Victorians

Teresa of Ávila
The Life of St. Teresa of Ávila by Herself

Sojourner Truth
Narrative of Sojourner Truth

Giorgio Vasari
Lives of the Artists, Volumes 1 and 2

Booker T. Washington
Up from Slavery

Women's Indian Captivity Narratives

DRAMA

Aeschylus
The Oresteia: Agamemnon/
    The Libation Bearers/The Eumenides
The Oresteian Trilogy
Prometheus Bound and Other Plays

Aristophanes
The Frogs and Other Plays
The Knights/The Peace/The Birds/
    The Assembly Women/Wealth
Lysistrata and Other Plays

**Pierre-Augustin Caron de
Beaumarchais**
The Barber of Seville and
    The Marriage of Figaro

Georg Büchner
Complete Plays, Lenz, and Other Writings

Anton Chekhov
Plays

Pierre Corneille
The Cid/Cinna/The Theatrical Illusion

Euripides
The Bacchae and Other Plays
Electra and Other Plays
Heracles and Other Plays
Medea and Other Plays
Orestes and Other Plays

John Gay
The Beggar's Opera

Johann Wolfgang von Goethe
Faust, Part 1 and Part 2

Henrik Ibsen
Brand
A Doll's House and Other Plays
Ghosts and Other Plays
Hedda Gabler and Other Plays
The Master Builder and Other Plays
Peer Gynt

Ben Jonson
Three Comedies

Christopher Marlowe
The Complete Plays

Menander
Plays and Fragments

Thomas Middleton
Five Plays

Arthur Miller
All My Sons
The Crucible
Death of a Salesman: Certain Private
    Conversations in Two Acts and a
    Requiem
The Portable Arthur Miller

Molière
The Misanthrope and Other Plays
The Miser and Other Plays

Eugene O'Neill
Early Plays

Luigi Pirandello
Six Characters in Search of an Author and
    Other Plays

Plautus
The Pot of Gold and Other Plays
The Rope and Other Plays

Jean Racine
Iphigenia/Phaedra/Athaliah,
Phèdre

Friedrich Schiller
Mary Stuart
The Robbers and Wallenstein

Lucius Annaeus Seneca
Four Tragedies and Octavia

William Shakespeare
The Pelican Shakespeare Series
    All's Well That Ends Well
    Antony and Cleopatra
    As You Like It
    The Comedy of Errors
    Coriolanus
    Cymbeline
    Hamlet
    Henry IV, Part 1
    Henry IV, Part 2
    Henry V
    Henry VI, Part 1
    Henry VI, Part 2
    Henry VI, Part 3
    Henry VIII
    Julius Caesar
    King John
    King Lear
        (The Quarto and the Folio Texts)
    King Lear
    Love's Labor's Lost
    Macbeth
    Measure for Measure
    The Merchant of Venice
    The Merry Wives of Windsor
    A Midsummer Night's Dream
    Much Ado about Nothing
    Othello
    Pericles
    Richard II
    Richard III
    Romeo and Juliet
    The Taming of the Shrew
    The Tempest
    Timon of Athens
    Titus Andronicus
    Troilus and Cressida
    Twelfth Night
    The Two Gentlemen of Verona
    The Winter's Tale

Four Comedies
Four Histories
Four Tragedies
The Portable Shakespeare
Three Roman Plays

George Bernard Shaw
Heartbreak House
Major Barbara
Man and Superman
Plays Unpleasant
Pygmalion

Saint Joan
Three Plays for Puritans

Richard Brinsley Sheridan
The School for Scandal and Other Plays

Sophocles
Electra and Other Plays
The Theban Plays
The Three Theban Plays: Antigone/ Oedipus
the King/Oedipus at Colonus

August Strindberg
Three Plays

J. M. Synge, W. B. Yeats, and Sean O'Casey
The Playboy of the Western World and Two
Other Irish Plays

Terence
The Comedies

Oscar Wilde
The Importance of Being Earnest and Other
Plays
The Portable Oscar Wilde

Early American Drama
Japanese Nō Dramas
Six Yüan Plays

John Maynard Keynes
The Economic Consequences of the Peace

Thomas Robert Malthus
An Essay on the Principle of Population

Karl Marx
Capital, Volumes 1, 2, and 3
Grundrisse: Foundations of the Critique of
Political Economy

Adam Smith
The Wealth of Nations, Books I–III
The Wealth of Nations, Books IV-V

Thorstein Veblen
The Theory of the Leisure Class

Max Weber
The Protestant Ethic and the "Spirit" of
Capitalism and Other Writings

Jean-Anthelme Brillat-Savarin
The Physiology of Taste

Elizabeth David
French Provincial Cooking
Italian Food

Henry Adams
The Education of Henry Adams

Alfred the Great and Assar
Alfred the Great

Ammianus Marcellinus
The Later Roman Empire (A.D. 354–378)

Anna Comnena
The Alexiad of Anna Comnena

Appian
The Civil Wars

Hannah Arendt
Eichmann in Jerusalem: A Report on the
Banality of Evil
On Revolution
The Portable Hannah Arendt

Arrian
The Campaigns of Alexander

Bede
The Age of Bede
Ecclesiastical History of the English People

William Bligh and Edward Christian
The Bounty Mutiny

Jacob Burckhardt
The Civilization of the Renaissance
in Italy

Edmund Burke
Reflections on the Revolution in France
The Portable Edmund Burke

Alvar Núñez Cabeza de Vaca
Chronicle of the Narváez Expedition

Julius Caesar
The Civil War
The Conquest of Gaul

Charles W. Chesnutt
The Marrow of Tradition

Marcus Tullius Cicero
Murder Trials
On Government
Selected Political Speeches
Selected Works

Carl von Clausewitz
On War

Christopher Columbus
The Four Voyages

J. Hector St. John de Crèvecoeur
Letters from an American Farmer and
Sketches of Eighteenth-Century America

Quintus Curtius Rufus
The History of Alexander

Bernal Díaz del Castillo
The Conquest of New Spain

Cassius Dio
The Roman History: The Reign of Augustus

W. E. B. Du Bois
The Souls of Black Folk

Einhard and Notker the Stammerer
Two Lives of Charlemagne

Friedrich Engels
The Condition of the Working Class in
England

Jean Froissart
Chronicles

S. M. Celeste Galilei
Letters to Father: Suor Maria Celeste to
Galileo, 1623–1633

Geoffrey of Monmouth
The History of the Kings of Britain

Gerald of Wales
The History and Topography of Ireland
The Journey Through Wales/The Description
of Wales

Edward Gibbon
The History of the Decline and Fall of the
Roman Empire, An Abridged Version
The History of the Decline and Fall of the
Roman Empire, Volumes I, II, and III

Gregory of Tours
A History of the Franks

Richard Hakluyt
Voyages and Discoveries

Herodotus
The Histories

Thomas Wentworth Higginson
Army Life in a Black Regiment
and Other Writings

Thomas Hobbes
Leviathan

Thomas Jefferson
Notes on the State of Virginia
The Portable Thomas Jefferson

**Jean de Joinville and Geoffroi de
Villehardouin**
Chronicles of the Crusades

Flavius Josephus
The Jewish War, Revised Edition

Justinian I
The Digest of Roman Law: Theft, Rapine,
Damage, and Insult

Bartolomé de Las Casas
A Short Account of the Destruction of the
Indies

Vladimir Ilich Lenin
The State and Revolution

Primo Levi
Moments of Reprieve

Abraham Lincoln
The Portable Abraham Lincoln

Titus Livy
The Early History of Rome
Rome and Italy
Rome and the Mediterranean
The War with Hannibal

Lord Thomas Babington Macaulay
The History of England

Niccolò Machiavelli
The Discourses
The Portable Machiavelli
The Prince

James Madison, Alexander Hamilton, and John Jay
The Federalist Papers

José Martí
Selected Writings

Karl Marx
Capital, Volumes 1, 2, and 3
Early Writings
Grundrisse: Foundations of the
    Critique of Political Economy
The Portable Karl Marx

Karl Marx and Friedrich Engels
The Communist Manifesto

Michael Psellus
Fourteen Byzantine Rulers

John Stuart Mill
On Liberty

Sir Thomas More
Utopia

Thomas Nickerson and Owen Chase
The Loss of the Ship *Essex*,
    Sunk by a Whale

Thomas Paine
Common Sense
Rights of Man
The Thomas Paine Reader

Francis Parkman, Jr.
The Oregon Trail

Pausanias
Guide to Greece, Volumes 1 and 2

Christine de Pisan
The Treasure of the City of the Ladies: Or,
    The Book of Three Virtues

Pliny the Elder
Natural History: A Selection

Pliny the Younger
The Letters of the Younger Pliny

Plutarch
The Age of Alexander
The Fall of the Roman Republic
Makers of Rome
Plutarch on Sparta
The Rise and Fall of Athens:
    Nine Greek Lives

Polybius
The Rise of the Roman Empire

Procopius
The Secret History

John Reed
Ten Days That Shook the World

Jacob A. Riis
How the Other Half Lives

Nicola Sacco and Bartolomeo Vanzetti
The Letters of Sacco and Vanzetti

Sallust
The Jugurthine War and
    The Conspiracy of Catiline

Domingo F. Sarmiento
Facundo

Suetonius
The Twelve Caesars

Cornelius Tacitus
The Agricola and The Germania
The Annals of Imperial Rome
The Histories

Thucydides
The History of the Peloponnesian War,
    Revised Edition

Voltaire
Letters on England

Max Weber
The Protestant Ethic and the "Spirit" of
    Capitalism and Other Writings

Rebecca West
Black Lamb and Grey Falcon: A Journey
    through Yugoslavia

Oscar Wilde
The Soul of Man under Socialism and
    Selected Critical Prose

Xenophon
A History of My Times
The Persian Expedition

Colonial American Travel Narratives
Early American Writing
Hippocratic Writings
Lives of the Later Caesars
The Portable Enlightenment Reader
The Portable Greek Historians
The Portable Sixties Reader
Women's Indian Captivity Narratives

LITERARY CRITICISM

Aristotle
Poetics

Malcolm Cowley
Exile's Return: A Literary Odyssey of
    the 1920s

Søren Kierkegaard
A Literary Review

D. H. Lawrence
Studies in Classic American Literature

John Ruskin
Unto This Last and Other Writings

Oscar Wilde
The Soul of Man under Socialism and
    Selected Critical Prose

W. B. Yeats
Writings on Irish Folklore, Legend, and Myth

Augustan Critical Writing
Classical Literary Criticism

LITERATURE

Edwin A. Abbott
Flatland

Henry Adams
Esther

Aesop
The Complete Fables

Henri Alain-Fournier
Le Grand Meaulnes

Louisa May Alcott
The Inheritance
Little Women
The Portable Louisa May Alcott
Work: A Story of Experience

Horatio Alger, Jr.
Ragged Dick and Struggling Upward

Kingsley Amis
Lucky Jim

Mulk Raj Anand
Untouchable

Sherwood Anderson
The Egg and Other Stories
Winesburg, Ohio

Mary Antin
The Promised Land

Apollonius of Rhodes
The Voyage of the Argo: The Argonautica

Apuleius
The Golden Ass

Aristotle
Poetics

Jane Austen
Emma
Lady Susan/The Watsons/Sanditon
Mansfield Park
Northanger Abbey
Persuasion
Pride and Prejudice
Sense and Sensibility

Jane Austen and Charlotte Brontë
The Juvenilia of Jane Austen and Charlotte
    Brontë

Isaac Babel
Collected Stories

Honoré de Balzac
The Black Sheep
Cousin Bette
Cousin Pons
Eugénie Grandet
A Harlot High and Low
History of the Thirteen
Lost Illusion
Old Goriot
Selected Short Stories
The Wild Ass's Skin

Charles Baudelaire
Baudelaire in English

L. Frank Baum
The Wonderful World of Oz:
  The Wizard of Oz/The Emerald City
  of Oz/Glinda of Oz

Aphra Behn
Oroonoko, The Rover, and Other Works

Edward Bellamy
Looking Backward, 2000–1887

Saul Bellow
The Adventures of Augie March
Dangling Man
The Dean's December
Henderson the Rain King
Herzog
Him with His Foot in His Mouth
Humboldt's Gift
Mosby's Memoirs and Other Stories
Mr. Sammler's Planet
Seize the Day
To Jerusalem and Back:
  A Personal Account
The Victim

Andrei Bely
Petersburg

Stephen Vincent Benét
The Devil and Daniel Webster

Arnold Bennett
The Old Wives' Tale

Béroul
The Romance of Tristan

Ambrose Bierce
Tales of Soldiers and Civilians

Algernon Blackwood
Ancient Sorceries and other Weird Stories

William Blake
The Portable Blake

Giovanni Boccaccio
The Decameron

Heinrich T. Böll
Billiards at Half-Past Nine
The Clown
The Lost Honor of Katherina Blum

Tadeusz Borowski
This Way for the Gas, Ladies and Gentlemen

Mary Elizabeth Braddon
Lady Audley's Secret

Anne Brontë
Agnes Grey
The Tenant of Wildfell Hall

Charlotte Brontë
Jane Eyre
The Professor
Shirley
Villette

Emily Brontë
Wuthering Heights

Charles Brockden Brown
Edgar Huntly: Or, Memoirs of a
  Sleep-Walker
Wieland and Memoirs of Carwin the
  Biloquist

**William Hill Brown and
Hannah Webster Foster**
The Power of Sympathy and
  The Coquette

Mikhail Bulgakov
The Master and Margarita

Ivan A. Bunin
The Gentleman from San Francisco
  and Other Stories

John Bunyan
The Pilgrim's Progress

Frances Hodgson Burnett
A Little Princess
The Secret Garden

Frances Burney
Evelina

Edgar Rice Burroughs
Tarzan of the Apes

Samuel Butler
Erewhon
The Way of All Flesh

George Washington Cable
The Grandissimes

Abraham Cahan
The Rise of David Levinsky

Cao Xueqin
The Story of the Stone, Volume 1: The
    Golden Days (Chapters 1–26)
The Story of the Stone, Volume 2: The Crab-
    Flower Club (Chapters 27–53)
The Story of the Stone, Volume 3: The
    Warning Voice (Chapters 54–80)
The Story of the Stone, Volume 4: The Debt
    of Tears (Chapters 81–98)
The Story of the Stone, Volume 5: The
    Dreamer Awakes (Chapters 99–120)

Lewis Carroll
Alice's Adventures in Wonderland and
    Through the Looking-Glass

Rosario Castellanos
The Book of Lamentations

Baldesar Castiglione
The Book of the Courtier

Willa Cather
Coming, Aphrodite!
My Ántonia
O Pioneers!
The Song of the Lark

Margaret Cavendish
The Blazing World and Other Writings

Benvenuto Cellini
Autobiography

Miguel de Cervantes Saavedra
Don Quixote
Exemplary Stories
The Portable Cervantes

Bruce Chatwin
In Patagonia

Geoffrey Chaucer
The Canterbury Tales
The Canterbury Tales: The First Fragment
Love Visions
The Portable Chaucer
Troilus and Criseyde

Anton Chekhov
The Lady with the Little Dog and Other
    Stories, 1896–1904
The Portable Chekhov
The Steppe and Other Stories, 1887–1891

Ward No. 6 and Other Stories, 1892–1895

Charles W. Chesnutt
Conjure Tales and Stories of the
    Color Line
The House Behind the Cedars
The Marrow of Tradition

G. K. Chesterton
The Man Who Was Thursday:
    A Nightmare

Erskine Childers
The Riddle of the Sands

Kate Chopin
At Fault
The Awakening and Selected Stories
Bayou Folk and A Night in Acadie
A Vocation and a Voice: Stories

Chrétien de Troyes
Arthurian Romances

John Cleland
Fanny Hill: Or, Memoirs of a Woman of
    Pleasure

Wilkie Collins
Armadale
The Law and the Lady
The Moonstone
No Name
The Woman in White

Carlo Collodi
Pinocchio

Arthur Conan Doyle
The Adventures and The Memoirs of
    Sherlock Holmes
The Hound of the Baskervilles
The Lost World and Other Thrilling Tales
The Sign of Four
A Study in Scarlet
The Valley of Fear and Selected Cases

Joseph Conrad
Chance
Heart of Darkness
Lord Jim
The Nigger of the "Narcissus"
Nostromo
The Portable Conrad
The Secret Agent
The Shadow-Line
Tales of Unrest

Typhoon and Other Stories
Under Western Eyes
Victory
Youth/Heart of Darkness/
 The End of the Tether

Benjamin Constant
Adolphe

Captain James Cook
The Journals of Captain Cook

James Fenimore Cooper
The Deerslayer
The Last of the Mohicans
The Pathfinder
The Pioneers
The Prairie
The Spy

Stephen Crane
Maggie, A Girl of the Streets
The Portable Stephen Crane
The Red Badge of Courage and
 Other Stories

Sor Juana Inés de la Cruz
Poems, Protests, and a Dream

Auobna Ottobah Cugoano
Thoughts and Sentiments on the Evil of
 Slavery

E. E. Cummings
The Enormous Room

Richard Henry Dana, Jr.
Two Years Before the Mast: A Personal
 Narrative of Life at Sea

Dante
The Divine Comedy, Volume 1:
 Inferno (Hell)
The Divine Comedy, Volume 2: Purgatory
The Divine Comedy, Volume 3: Paradise
The Portable Dante

Robertson Davies
Fifth Business

Daniel Defoe
A Journal of the Plague Year
Moll Flanders
Robinson Crusoe
Roxana

John W. De Forest
Miss Ravenel's Conversion from Secession
 to Loyalty

Thomas De Quincey
Confessions of an English Opium Eater

Charles Dickens
Barnaby Rudge
Bleak House
The Christmas Books, Volume 1: A
 Christmas Carol/The Chimes
David Copperfield
Dombey and Son
Geat Expectations
Hard Times
Little Dorrit
Martin Chuzzlewit
The Mystery of Edwin Drood
Nicholas Nickleby
The Old Curiosity Shop
Oliver Twist
Our Mutual Friend
The Pickwick Papers
Selected Journalism, 1850–1870
Selected Short Fiction
Sketches by Boz
A Tale of Two Cities

Denis Diderot
Jacques the Fatalist and His Master
The Nun
Rameau's Nephew and
 D'Alembert's Dream

John Dos Passos
Three Soldiers

Fyodor Dostoyevsky
The Brothers Karamazov
Crime and Punishment
The Devils
The Gambler/Bobok/A Nasty Story
The House of the Dead
The Idiot
Netochka Nezvanova
Notes from the Underground/The Double
Poor Folk and Other Stories
The Village of Stepanchikovo

Theodore Dreiser
Jennie Gerhardt
Sister Carrie

Alexandre Dumas
The Count of Monte Cristo
The Man in the Iron Mask
The Three Musketeers

Maria Edgeworth
The Absentee
Castle Rackrent and Ennui
Ormond

George Eliot
Adam Bede
Daniel Deronda
Felix Holt: The Radical
The Lifted Veil and Brother Jacob
Middlemarch
The Mill on the Floss
Romola
Scenes of Clerical Life
Silas Marner

Ralph Waldo Emerson
The Portable Emerson

Erasmus
Praise of Folly

Wolfram von Eschenbach
Parzival
Willehalm

Richard Fariña
Been Down So Long It Looks Like
    Up to Me

James T. Farrell
Studs Lonigan

William Faulkner
The Portable Faulkner

Fanny Fern
Ruth Hall: A Domestic Tale of the Present
    Time

Henry Fielding
Joseph Andrews/Shamela
Tom Jones

Sarah Fielding
The Adventures of David Simple

F. Scott Fitzgerald
The Beautiful and Damned
Jazz Age Stories
This Side of Paradise

Gustave Flaubert
Bouvard and Pécuchet
Madame Bovary
Salammbô
Sentimental Education
Three Tales

Theodor Fontane
Effi Briest

Ford Madox Ford
The Fifth Queen
The Good Soldier
Parade's End

E. M. Forster
Howard's End
A Room with a View
Selected Stories

Anatole France
The Gods Will Have Blood

Sir James Frazer
The Golden Bough, Abridged Edition

Harold Frederic
The Damnation of Theron Ware

Mary E. Wilkins Freeman
A New England Nun

William Gaddis
Carpenter's Gothic
JR
The Recognitions

Elizabeth Gaskell
Cranford/Cousin Phillis
Gothic Tales
Mary Barton
North and South
Ruth
Wives and Daughters

William H. Gass
Omensetter's Luck

Stella Gibbons
Cold Comfort Farm

André Gide
The Immoralist

Charlotte Perkins Gilman
Herland, The Yellow Wallpaper, and Selected
    Writings

George Gissing
New Grub Street
The Odd Women

William Godwin
Caleb Williams

Johann Wolfgang von Goethe
Elective Affinities
Maxims and Reflections
The Sorrows of Young Werther

Nikolai Gogol
Dead Souls
Diary of a Madman and Other Stories

Oliver Goldsmith
The Vicar of Wakefield

Ivan Goncharov
Oblomov

Sir Edmund Gosse
Father and Son

Gottfried von Strassburg
Tristan

Henry Green
Loving/Living/Party Going

Graham Greene
Brighton Rock
A Burnt-Out Case
The Captain and the Enemy
Collected Short Stories
The Comedians
The End of the Affair
England Made Me
A Gun for Sale
The Heart of the Matter
The Last Word and Other Stories
Loser Takes All
The Man Within
The Ministry of Fear
Our Man in Havana
The Portable Graham Greene
The Power and the Glory
The Quiet American
Stamboul Train
The Third Man and The Fallen Idol
Travels with My Aunt
Twenty-one Stories

Zane Grey
Riders of the Purple Sage

Jacob and Wilhelm Grimm
Selected Tales

H. Rider Haggard
She

Knut Hamsun
Hunger
Mysteries
Pan

Thomas Hardy
Desperate Remedies
The Distracted Preacher and Other Tales
Far from the Madding Crowd
The Hand of Ethelberta
Jude the Obscure
A Laodicean
The Mayor of Casterbridge
A Pair of Blue Eyes
The Pursuit of the Well-Beloved
    and The Well-Beloved
The Return of the Native
Tess of the D'Urbervilles
Two on a Tower
The Withered Arm and Other Stories
The Woodlanders

Joel Chandler Harris
Uncle Remus: His Songs and His Sayings

Bret Harte
The Luck of Roaring Camp and Other
    Writings

Jaroslav Hašek
The Good Soldier Švejk

Nathaniel Hawthorne
The Blithedale Romance
The House of the Seven Gables
The Marble Faun
The Portable Hawthorne
The Scarlet Letter
Selected Tales and Sketches

O. Henry
Selected Stories

Herman Hesse
Siddhartha

Ernst Theodor Hoffmann
The Life and Opinions of the
    Tomcat Murr
The Tales of Hoffmann

Homer
The Iliad
The Odyssey

Anthony Hope
The Prisoner of Zenda and
    Rupert of Hentzau

Gerard Manley Hopkins
Poems and Prose

William Dean Howells
A Hazard of New Fortunes
A Modern Instance
The Rise of Silas Lapham

Victor Hugo
Les Misérables
Notre-Dame of Paris

Elspeth Huxley
Red Strangers

J.-K. Huysmans
Against Nature
The Damned (Là-Bas)

Saint Ignatius of Loyola
Personal Writings

Gilbert Imlay
The Emigrants

Elizabeth Inchbald
A Simple Story

Washington Irving
The Legend of Sleepy Hollow
    and Other Stories

Henry James
The Ambassadors
The American
The Aspern Papers and
    The Turn of the Screw
The Awkward Age
The Bostonians
Daisy Miller
The Europeans
The Figure in the Carpet and Other Stories
The Golden Bowl
The Portable Henry James
The Portrait of a Lady
The Princess Casamassima
Roderick Hudson
Selected Tales
The Spoils of Poynton

The Tragic Muse
Washington Square
What Maisie Knew
The Wings of the Dove

Jerome K. Jerome
Three Men in a Boat and Three Men on the
    Bummell

Sarah Orne Jewett
The Country of the Pointed Firs and Other
    Stories

James Weldon Johnson
The Autobiography of an Ex-Colored Man

Samuel Johnson
The History of Rasselas, Prince of Abissinia
Selected Writings

James Joyce
Dubliners
Finnegans Wake
The Portable James Joyce
A Portrait of the Artist as a Young Man

Juvenal
Sixteen Satires

Franz Kafka
The Transformation ("Metamorphosis") and
    Other Stories

Jack Kerouac
On the Road
The Portable Jack Kerouac

Ken Kesey
One Flew Over the Cuckoo's Nest

Rudyard Kipling
The Jungle Books
Just So Stories
Kim
Plain Tales from the Hills
The Portable Kipling

Heinrich von Kleist
The Marquise of O— and Other Stories

Choderlos de Laclos
Les Liaisons Dangereuses

Madame de Lafayette
The Princesse de Clèves

William Langland
Piers the Ploughman

Ring Lardner
Selected Stories

Nella Larsen
Passing
Quicksand

Mary Lavin
In a Café

D. H. Lawrence
Apocalypse
The Fox/The Captain's Doll/The Ladybird
Lady Chatterley's Lover
Mr. Noon
The Prussian Officer and Other Stories
The Rainbow
Sons and Lovers
Twilight in Italy and Other Essays
Women in Love

Joseph Sheridan Le Fanu
Uncle Silas

Mikhail Lermontov
A Hero of Our Time

Primo Levi
If Not Now, When?
The Monkey's Wrench

Matthew Lewis
The Monk

Sinclair Lewis
Babbit
Main Street

Jack London
The Assassination Bureau, Ltd.
The Call of the Wild, White Fang, and Other
    Stories
Martin Eden
Northland Stories
The Portable Jack London
The Sea-Wolf and Other Stories
Tales of the Pacific

Longus
Daphnis and Chloe

Anita Loos
Gentlemen Prefer Blondes and But
    Gentlemen Marry Brunettes

H. P. Lovecraft
The Call of Cthulhu and Other Weird Stories
The Thing on the Doorstep and Other Weird
    Stories

George MacDonald
The Complete Fairytales

Bernard Malamud
The Fixer

Sir Thomas Malory
Le Morte D'Arthur

Klaus Mann
Mephisto

Thomas Mann
Death in Venice and Other Tales

Katherine Mansfield
The Garden Party and Other Stories

Alessandro Manzoni
The Betrothed (I promessi sposi)

José Martí
Selected Writings

Marguerite de Navarre
The Heptameron

Marie de France
The Lais of Marie de France

A. E. W. Mason
The Four Feathers

Charles W. Maturin
Melmoth the Wanderer

W. Somerset Maugham
Collected Short Stories,
    Volumes 1, 2, 3, and 4
Liza of Lambeth
The Magician
The Moon and Sixpence
Mrs. Craddock
The Narrow Corner
Of Human Bondage
The Painted Veil
The Razor's Edge
The Summing Up

Guy de Maupassant
Bel-Ami
Pierre and Jean
Selected Short Stories

François Mauriac
Thérèse

Herman Melville
Billy Budd and Other Stories
The Confidence-Man
Moby-Dick: Or, The Whale
Pierre: Or, The Ambiguities
Redburn
Typee

George Meredith
The Ordeal of Richard Feverel

Charles de Montesquieu
Persian Letters

William Morris
News from Nowhere and Other Writings

Multatuli
Max Havelaar: Or, The Coffee Auctions of
    the Dutch Trading Company

Murasaki Shikibu
The Tale of Genji

Iris Murdoch
The Bell
The Black Prince
A Fairly Honourable Defeat
The Good Apprentice
Nuns and Soldiers
The Sea, the Sea

Robert Musil
The Confusions of Young Törless

R. K. Narayan
The Guide
Malgudi Days
The Man-Eater of Malgudi
The Painter of Signs
The Ramayana
A Tiger for Malgudi

Thomas Nashe
The Unfortunate Traveller and
    Other Works

Gérard de Nerval
Selected Writings

Frank Norris
McTeague: A Story of San Francisco
The Octopus: A Story of California
The Pit: A Story of Chicago

Margaret Oliphant
Miss Marjoribanks

Dorothy Parker
Complete Stories
The Portable Dorothy Parker

Thomas Love Peacock
Nightmare Abbey/Crotchet Castle

Fernando Pessoa
The Book of Disquiet

Petronius and Seneca
The Satyricon/The Apocolocyntosis

Plutarch
Essays

Edgar Allan Poe
The Fall of the House of Usher and Other
    Writings
The Narrative of Arthur Gordon Pym
    of Nantucket
The Portable Poe
The Science Fiction of Edgar Allan Poe

Jan Potocki
The Manuscript Found in Saragossa

Abbé Prévost
Manon Lescaut

Mary Prince
The History of Mary Prince

Marcel Proust
Swann's Way

Alexander Pushkin
The Queen of Spades and Other Stories
Tales of Belkin and Other Prose Writings

Thomas Pynchon
Gravity's Rainbow
Vineland

Eça de Queirós
The Maias

Raymond Queneau
Zazie in the Metro

Francisco de Quevedo
Two Spanish Picaresque Novels

François Rabelais
Gargantua and Pantagruel

Ann Radcliffe
The Italian
The Mysteries of Udolpho

Samuel Richardson
Clarissa
Pamela

Susanna Rowson
Charlotte Temple and Lucy Temple

Rafael Sabatini
Captain Blood

Leopold von Sacher-Masoch
Venus in Furs

Saki
The Complete Saki

Ignatius Sancho
Letters of the Late Ignatius Sancho, an
    African

Friedrich Schiller
Mary Stuart

Olive Schreiner
The Story of an African Farm

Bruno Schulz
The Street of Crocodiles

Sir Walter Scott
The Antiquary
The Bride of Lammermoor
The Heart of Midlothian
Ivanhoe
Kenilworth
Redgauntlet
Rob Roy
The Tale of Old Mortality
Waverley

Catharine Maria Sedgwick
Hope Leslie

Lucius Annaeus Seneca
Dialogues and Letters

Varlam Shalamov
Kolyma Tales

Mary Shelley
Frankenstein

Shen Fu
Six Records of a Floating Life

Sir Philip Sidney
The Countess of Pembroke's Arcadia

Upton Sinclair
The Jungle

Isaac Bashevis Singer
The Death of Methuselah and Other Stories

I. J. Singer
The Brothers Ashkenazi

Charles A. Siringo
A Texas Cowboy

Tobias Smollett
The Expedition of Humphry Clinker

Wallace Stegner
Angle of Repose
Wolf Willow

Gertrude Stein
Three Lives

John Steinbeck
Burning Bright
Cannery Row
Cup of Gold
East of Eden
The Grapes of Wrath
In Dubious Battle
The Long Valley
The Moon Is Down
Of Mice and Men
Once There Was a War
The Pastures of Heaven
The Pearl
The Portable Steinbeck
The Red Pony
A Russian Journal
The Short Reign of Pippin IV
Sweet Thursday
To a God Unknown
Tortilla Flat
The Wayward Bus
The Winter of Our Discontent

Stendhal
The Charterhouse of Parma
Love
The Red and Black

Laurence Sterne
The Life and Opinions of Tristram Shandy
A Sentimental Journey

Robert Louis Stevenson
In the South Seas
Kidnapped
The Master of Ballantrae
The Strange Case of Dr. Jekyll and Mr. Hyde
    and Other Tales of Terror
Treasure Island

Elizabeth Stoddard
The Morgesons

Bram Stoker
Dracula

Harriet Beecher Stowe
Dred
The Minister's Wooing
Uncle Tom's Cabin: Or, Life Among the
    Lowly

Bamba Suso and Banna Kanute
Sunjata

Jonathan Swift
Gulliver's Travels

Sir Rabindranath Tagore
The Home and the World
Selected Short Stories

William Makepeace Thackeray
Vanity Fair

Henry David Thoreau
The Portable Thoreau
A Year in Thoreau's Journal: 1851

Leo Tolstoy
Anna Karenin
Anna Karenina
Childhood/Boyhood/Youth
The Death of Ivan Ilyich and Other Stories
How Much Land Does a Man Need?
    and Other Stories
The Kreutzer Sonata and Other Stories
Master and Man and Other Stories
The Portable Tolstoy
Resurrection
The Sebastopol Sketches
War and Peace

Anthony Trollope
Barchester Towers
Can You Forgive Her?
Dr. Wortle's School
The Eustace Diamonds
Framley Parsonage

He Knew He Was Right
The Last Chronicle of Barset
The Prime Minister
The Small House at Allington
The Warden
The Way We Live Now

Fanny Trollope
Domestic Manners of the Americans

Ivan Turgenev
Fathers and Sons
First Love
Home of the Gentry
Rudin
Sketches from a Hunter's Album
Spring Torrents

Mark Twain
The Adventures of Huckleberry Finn
The Adventures of Tom Sawyer
A Connecticut Yankee in King Arthur's Court
The Innocents Abroad
Life on the Mississippi
The Portable Mark Twain
The Prince and the Pauper
Pudd'nhead Wilson
Roughing It
Tales, Speeches, Essays, and Sketches
A Tramp Abroad

**Mark Twain and Charles Dudley
Warner**
The Gilded Age

Sigrid Undset
Gunnar's Daughter
Kristin Lavransdatter I: The Wreath
Kristin Lavransdatter II: The Wife
Kristin Lavransdatter III: The Cross

Giovanni Verga
Cavalleria Rusticana and Other Stories

Giambattista Vico
New Science

Gore Vidal
Duluth
Kalki
The Messiah
Myra Breckinridge/Myron

Virgil
The Aeneid

Voltaire
Candide
Micromégas and Other Short Fictions
The Portable Voltaire
Zadig/L'Ingénu

Jacobus de Voragine
The Golden Legend

Horace Walpole
The Castle of Otranto

Roboooa Woot
The Return of the Soldier

Edith Wharton
The Age of Innocence
The Custom of the Country
Ethan Frome
The House of Mirth
Summer

Phillis Wheatley
Complete Writings

Oscar Wilde
Complete Short Fiction
De Profundis and Other Writings
The Picture of Dorian Gray
The Portable Oscar Wilde
The Soul of Man under Socialism and
    Selected Critical Prose

Owen Wister
The Virginian

**Mary Wollstonecraft and
Mary Shelley**
Mary/Maria/Matilda

Virginia Woolf
Jacob's Room
Night and Day
The Voyage Out

Anzia Yezierska
Hungry Hearts

Yevgeny Zamyatin
We

Zitkala-Ša
American Indian Stories, Legends, and
    Other Writings

Émile Zola
L'Assommoir (The Dram Shop)

Au Bonheur Des Dames (The Ladies'
    Delight)
La Bête Humaine
The Debacle
The Earth
Germinal
Nana
Thérèse Raquin

Against Slavery
American Local Color Writing, 1880–1920
Beowulf
A Celtic Miscellany
The Classic of Mountains and Seas
The Death of King Arthur
Early American Writing
Four Stories by American Women
The Greek Alexander Romance
The Portable American Realism Reader
The Portable Beat Reader
The Portable Enlightenment Reader
The Portable Greek Reader
The Portable Harlem Renaissance Reader
The Portable Medieval Reader
The Portable Nineteenth-Century Russian
    Reader
The Portable North American Indian Reader
The Portable Renaissance Reader
The Portable Roman Reader
The Portable Twentieth-Century Russian
    Reader
The Portable Western Reader
The Quest of the Holy Grail
Romantic Fairy Tales
The Song of Roland
Tales from the Thousand and One Nights
Three Gothic Novels

NATURE CLASSICS

Mary Austin
The Land of Little Rain

Rachel L. Carson
Under the Sea Wind

George Catlin
North American Indians

Gerald Durrell
My Family and Other Animals

Meriwether Lewis and William Clark
The Journals of Lewis and Clark

Peter Matthiessen
Blue Meridian
The Cloud Forest
The Snow Leopard
The Tree Where Man Was Born
Under the Mountain Wall

Gavin Maxwell
Ring of Bright Water

John Muir
The Mountains of California
My First Summer in the Sierra
Travels in Alaska

Sigurd Olson
Songs of the North

John Wesley Powell
The Exploration of the Colorado River and Its Canyons

John Tanner
The Falcon

Henry David Thoreau
Cape Cod
The Maine Woods
The Portable Thoreau

PHILOSOPHY

Thomas Aquinas
Selected Writings

Hannah Arendt
Between Past and Future

Aristotle
The Art of Rhetoric
The Athenian Constitution
De Anima (On the Soul)
Ethics
The Metaphysics
Poetics
The Politics

Francis Bacon
The Essays

George Berkeley
Principles of Human Knowledge and Three Dialogues Between Hylas and Philonius

Ancius Boethius
The Consolation of Philosophy

Jean-Anthelme Brillat-Savarin
The Physiology of Taste

Edmund Burke
A Philosophical Enquiry into the Origin of Our Ideas of the Sublime and Beautiful
The Portable Edmund Burke

Marcus Tullius Cicero
The Nature of the Gods
On the Good Life

Confucius
The Analects

René Descartes
Discourse on Method and Related Writings
Meditations and Other Metaphysical Writings

Ralph Waldo Emerson
Selected Essays

David Hume
Dialogues Concerning Natural Religion
A Treatise of Human Nature

William James
Pragmatism and Other Writings

Søren Kierkegaard
Either/Or: A Fragment of Life
Fear and Trembling
A Literary Review
Papers and Journals: A Selection
Sickness unto Death

Lao Tzu
Tao Te Ching

François de La Rochefoucauld
Maxims

John Locke
An Essay Concerning Human Understanding

Lucretius
On the Nature of the Universe

Sir Charles Lyell
Principles of Geology

Marcus Aurelius
Meditations

Mencius
Mencius

John Stuart Mill and Jeremy Bentham
Utilitarianism and Other Essays

Michel de Montaigne
The Complete Essays
Essays: A Selection

Friedrich Nietzsche
Beyond Good and Evil
The Birth of Tragedy
A Nietzsche Reader
The Portable Nietzsche
Thus Spake Zarathustra
Twilight of the Idols and The Anti-Christ

Blaise Pascal
Pensées

Georges Perec
Species of Spaces and Other Pieces

Plato
Early Socratic Dialogues
Gorgias
The Last Days of Socrates: Euthyphro/The
    Apology/Crito/Phaedo
The Laws
Phaedrus and Letters VII and VIII
The Portable Plato
Protagoras and Meno
The Republic
The Symposium
Theaetetus
Timaeus and Critias

Plotinus
The Enneads

Jean-Jacques Rousseau
A Discourse on Inequality
Reveries of the Solitary Walker
The Social Contract

Arthur Schopenhauer
Essays and Aphorisms

Lucius Annaeus Seneca
Letters from a Stoic

Henry David Thoreau
Walden and Civil Disobedience
A Year in Thoreau's Journal: 1851

Voltaire
Philosophical Dictionary
The Portable Voltaire

Mary Wollstonecraft
A Vindication of the Rights of Woman

Xenophon
Conversations of Socrates

Early Greek Philosophy
German Idealist Philosophy
The Laws of Manu
The Portable Greek Reader

POETRY

Anna Akhmatova
Selected Poems

Ludovico Ariosto
Orlando Furioso, Part I and Part II

Farid ud-Din Attar
The Conference of the Birds

Matsuo Bashō
The Narrow Road to the Deep North and
    Other Travel Sketches
On Love and Barley: Haiku of Bashō

Charles Baudelaire
Baudelaire in English
Selected Poems

William Blake
The Complete Poems
The Portable Blake

Elizabeth Barrett Browning
Aurora Leigh and Other Poems

Robert Browning
Selected Poems

Robert Burns
Selected Poems

George Gordon, Lord Byron
Don Juan
Selected Poems

Lewis Carroll
The Hunting of the Snark

Catullus
The Poems of Catullus

Samuel Coleridge
The Complete Poems
The Portable Coleridge
Selected Poems

Sor Juana Inés de la Cruz
Poems, Protest, and a Dream

Dante
The Divine Comedy, Volumes 1, 2, and 3
La Vita Nuova
The Portable Dante

John Donne
The Complete English Poems

John Dryden
Selected Poems

T. S. Eliot
The Waste Land and Other Poems

Wolfram von Eschenbach
Willehalm

Robert Frost
Early Poems: The Boy's Will, North of
    Boston, Mountain Interval, and Other
    Poems

Johann Wolfgang von Goethe
Selected Verse

Thomas Hardy
Selected Poems

George Herbert
The Complete English Poems

Hesiod and Theognis
Hesiod and Theognis

Friedrich Hölderlin
Selected Poems and Fragments

Homer
The Iliad
The Iliad and The Odyssey Boxed Set
The Odyssey

Gerard Manley Hopkins
Poems and Prose

Horace
The Complete Odes and Epodes

Horace and Persius
The Satires of Horace and Persius

Victor Hugo
Selected Poems

James Weldon Johnson
Complete Poems
God's Trombones: Seven Negro Sermons in
    Verse
Lift Every Voice and Sing

Ben Jonson
The Complete Poems

Juvenal
The Sixteen Satires

John Keats
The Complete Poems: Second Edition
Selected Poems

Jules Laforgue
Selected Poems

Le Comte de Lautréamont
Maldoror and Poems

D. H. Lawrence
Complete Poems

Li Po and Tu Fu
Poems

Henry Wadsworth Longfellow
Selected Poems

Osip Mandelstam
Selected Poems

Andrew Marvell
The Complete Poems

Edna St. Vincent Millay
Early Poems

John Milton
The Complete Poems
Paradise Lost

Marianne Moore
Complete Poems

Pablo Neruda
Twenty Love Poems and a Song of Despair

Gérard de Nerval
Selected Writings

Omar Khayyám
The Ruba'iyat of Omar Khayyám

Ovid
The Erotic Poems
Fasti
Heroides
Metamorphoses

Dorothy Parker
Complete Poems
The Portable Dorothy Parker

Pindar
The Odes

Alexander Pushkin
Eugene Onegin

Arthur Rimbaud
Collected Poems

Edwin Arlington Robinson
Selected Poems

Pierre de Ronsard
Selected Poems

Christina Rossetti
The Complete Poems

William Shakespeare
The Narrative Poems (Pelican Shakespeare)
The Sonnets (Pelican Shakespeare)
The Sonnets and A Lover's Complaint

Edmund Spenser
The Faerie Queene
The Shorter Poems

Robert Louis Stevenson
Selected Poems

Algernon Charles Swinburne
Poems and Ballads and Atalanta in Calydon

Sir Rabindranath Tagore
Selected Poems

Alfred, Lord Tennyson
Idylls of the King
Selected Poems

Marina Tsvetayeva
Selected Poems

Virgil
Aeneid
The Eclogues
The Georgics

Phillis Wheatley
Complete Writings

Walt Whitman
The Complete Poems
Leaves of Grass
The Portable Walt Whitman

William Wordsworth
The Poems, Volumes 1 and 2
The Prelude: The Four Texts
Selected Poems

Beowulf: A Verse Translation
A Celtic Miscellany
The Earliest English Poems,
    Third Revised Edition
The Epic of Gilgamesh
English Romantic Verse
Medieval English Verse
The Metaphysical Poets
The Nibelungenlied
Nineteenth-Century American Poetry
The Penguin Book of First World War Poetry
The Penguin Book of French Poetry,
    1820–1950
The Penguin Book of Modern African Poetry
The Penguin Book of Renaissance Verse
    1509–1659
The Penguin Book of Victorian Verse
The Poem of the Cid
Poems of Heaven and Hell from
    Ancient Mesopotamia
Poems of the Late T'ang
The Portable Romantic Poets
The Psalms in English
Renaissance Women Poets
Sir Gawain and the Green Knight

PSYCHOLOGY

Carl Jung
The Portable Jung

RELIGION

Adomnán of Iona
Life of St. Columba

Anselm of Aosta
The Prayers and Meditations of St. Anselm

Farid ud-Din Attar
The Conference of the Birds

Saint Augustine
City of God
Confessions

Bede
The Ecclesiastical History of the English
    People

Bede, Brendan, and Eddius Stephanus
The Age of Bede

John Bunyan
Grace Abounding to the Chief of Sinners
The Pilgrim's Progress

Meister Eckhart
Selected Writings

Wolfram von Eschenbach
Parzival

Eusebius
The History of the Church

Hildegard of Bingen
Selected Writings

Saint Ignatius of Loyola
Personal Writings

William James
The Varieties of Religious Experience:
    A Study in Human Nature

Julian of Norwich
Revelations of Divine Love

Lao Tzu
Tao Te Ching

Michel de Montaigne
An Apology for Raymond Sebond

R. K. Narayan
The Ramayana

John Henry Newman
Apologia pro Vita Sua

Blaise Pascal
Pensées

Teresa of Ávila
The Life of St. Teresa of Ávila by Herself

Thomas à Kempis
The Imitation of Christ

Leo Tolstoy
A Confession and
    Other Religious Writings

William Tyndale
The Obedience of a Christian Man

Jacobus de Voragine
The Golden Legend

The Bhagavad Gita
Buddhist Scriptures
The Cistercian World: Monastic Writings of
    the Twelfth Century
The Cloud of Unknowing and Other Works
The Dhammapada
Early Christian Lives
Early Christian Writings: The Apostolic
    Fathers
Hindu Myths
The Koran
The Laws of Manu
Medieval Writings on Female Spirituality
Poems of Heaven and Hell from Ancient
    Mesopotamia
The Portable World Bible
The Rig Veda
Speaking of Siva
The Upanishads

SAGAS

Snorri Sturluson
King Harald's Saga

Beowulf
Early Irish Myths and Sagas
Egil's Saga
Eyrbyggja Saga
Hrafnkel's Saga
Laxdaela Saga
The Mabinogion
Njal's Saga
Orkneyinga Saga: The History of the Earls of
    Orkney
The Saga of King Hrolf Kraki
The Saga of Volsungs
The Sagas of Icelanders: A Selection

Sagas of Warrior-Poets
Seven Viking Romances
The Vinland Sagas and The Norse Discovery
of America

SCIENCE

Charles Darwin
The Origin of Species
The Portable Darwin
The Voyage of the *Beagle*: Charles Darwin's
Journal of Researches

Sir Charles Lyell
Principles of Geology

TRAVEL

Bruce Chatwin
In Patagonia

Christopher Columbus
The Four Voyages

Charles Dickens
American Notes for General Circulation
Pictures from Italy, 1850–1870

Gustave Flaubert
Flaubert in Egypt

Gerald of Wales
The Journey Through Wales/The Description
of Wales

Johann Wolfgang von Goethe
Italian Journey

Graham Greene
Journey Without Maps
The Lawless Roads

Alexander von Humboldt
Personal Narrative of a Journey to the
Equinoctial Regions of the New Continent

Henry James
Italian Hours

**Samuel Johnson and
James Boswell**
A Journey to the Western Islands of
Scotland and The Journal of a Tour to the
Hebrides

D. H. Lawrence
D. H. Lawrence and Italy:
Twilight in Italy/Sea and
Sardinia/Etruscan Places
Sea and Sardinia
Sketches of Etruscan Places
Twilight in Italy and Other Essays

Sir John Mandeville
The Travels of Sir John Mandeville

Shiva Naipaul
North of South: An African Journey

Marco Polo
The Travels

John Steinbeck
The Log from the *Sea of Cortez*
A Russian Journal
Travels with Charley in Search of America

Robert Louis Stevenson
In the South Seas

J. M. Synge
The Aran Islands

Henry David Thoreau
A Week on the Concord and Merrimack
Rivers

Mark Twain
The Innocents Abroad

Rebecca West
Black Lamb and Grey Falcon:
A Journey through Yugoslavia

Colonial American Travel Narratives

PENGUIN CLASSICS PRINTED GUIDES

(available as printed guides—free of charge in packs of 10—
and online at www.penguinclassics.com/guides)

The Adventures of Augie March by Saul Bellow

The Age of Innocence by Edith Wharton

Anna Karenin by Leo Tolstoy

Cousin Bette by Honoré de Balzac

David Copperfield by Charles Dickens

Fifth Business by Robertson Davies

Howards End by E. M. Forster

The Inheritance by Louisa May Alcott

Jude the Obscure by Thomas Hardy

Kristin Lavransdatter trilogy by Sigrid Undset

Les Misérables by Victor Hugo

My Ántonia by Willa Cather

The Portrait of a Lady by Henry James

A Room with a View by E. M. Forster

The Sea, The Sea by Iris Murdoch

The Secret Garden by Frances Hodgson Burnett

The Story of My Life by Giacomo Casanova

The Woman in White/The Moonstone by Wilkie Collins

PENGUIN CLASSICS ONLINE-ONLY GUIDES

(only available online at www.penguinclassics.com/guides)

Alice's Adventures in Wonderland by Lewis Carroll

The Awakening by Kate Chopin

Candide by Voltaire

Crime and Punishment by Fyodor Dostoyevksy

The Fifth Queen by Ford Madox Ford

Great Expectations by Charles Dickens

Herzog by Saul Bellow

The House of Mirth by Edith Wharton

Moby-Dick by Herman Melville

On the Road by Jack Kerouac

Sense and Sensibility and *Pride and Prejudice* by Jane Austen

The Song of the Lark by Willa Cather

The Tale of Genji by Murasaki Shikibu

Wuthering Heights by Emily Brontë

GREAT BOOKS FOUNDATION DISCUSSION GUIDES
FOR PENGUIN CLASSICS TITLES
(available online at www.penguinclassics.com/guides and www.greatbooks.org)

The Age of Innocence by Edith Wharton (April 2003)

Anna Karenina by Leo Tolstoy

Carpenter's Gothic by William Gaddis

The Communist Manifesto by Karl Marx and Friedrich Engels

Dubliners by James Joyce

Eichmann in Jerusalem by Hannah Arendt

Emma by Jane Austen (July 2003)

Frankenstein by Mary Shelley (March 2003)

The Grapes of Wrath, Of Mice and Men, and *The Pearl* by John Steinbeck
(also available as a printed guide)

Jane Eyre by Charlotte Brontë

The Last Days of Socrates by Plato

The Master and Margarita by Mikhail Bulgakov (June 2003)

Moby-Dick by Herman Melville (February 2003)

Narrative of the Life of Frederick Douglass, an American Slave by Frederick Douglass

The Odyssey by Homer

The Oresteia by Aeschylus (May 2003)

The Prince by Niccolò Machiavelli

The Red and the Black by Stendhal

Seize the Day by Saul Bellow

To request printed guides, call the Penguin Marketing Department at (800) 778-6425
or reading@penguinputnam.com

YEAR	WINNER	LIFE DATES	NATIONALITY
1907	Rudyard Kipling	1865–1936	British
1913	Sir Rabindranath Tagore	1861–1941	Indian
1920	Knut Hamsun	1859–1952	Norwegian
1921	Anatole France	1844–1924	French
1923	William Butler Yeats	1865–1939	Irish
1925	George Bernard Shaw	1856–1950	Irish
1928	Sigrid Undset	1882–1949	Norwegian
1929	Thomas Mann	1875–1955	German
1930	Sinclair Lewis	1885–1951	American
1933	Ivan A. Bunin	1870–1953	Russian
1934	Luigi Pirandello	1867–1936	Italian
1936	Eugene O'Neill	1888–1953	American
1946	Hermann Hesse	1877–1962	Swiss
1947	André Gide	1869–1951	French
1948	T. S. Eliot	1888–1965	British
1949	William Faulkner	1897–1962	American
1952	François Mauriac	1885–1970	French
1962	John Steinbeck	1902–1968	American
1971	Pablo Neruda	1904–1973	Chilean
1972	Heinrich T. Böll	1917–1985	German
1976	Saul Bellow	1915–	American
1978	Isaac Bashevis Singer	1904–1991	American

John Adams and Abigail Adams
The Letters of John and Abigail Adams

Aristophanes
*Lysistrata and Other Plays

Donald Barthelme
Sixty Stories

Karel Capek
R.U.R.

Thomas De Quincey
*Confessions of an English
Opium Eater

Charles Dickens
*Bleak House

Alexandre Dumas
The Black Tulip

Olaudah Equiano
*The Interesting Narrative and
    Other Writings

James T. Farrell
Young Lonigan

Sigmund Freud
The Joke and Its Relation to the
    Unconscious
The Psychology of Love
The Psychopathology of Everyday Life
The Schreber Case
The Uncanny
The Wolfman and Other Cases

Joel Chandler Harris
Nights with Uncle Remus

Heraclitus
Fragments

Homer
*The Iliad

E.W. Hornung
Raffles: The Amateur Cracksman

Samuel Johnson
*Selected Essays

Immanuel Kant
Critique of Pure Reason

Thomas More
*Utopia

Ezra Pound
Early Writings

Catherine Maria Sedgwick
A New-England Tale

George Bernard Shaw
Plays Pleasant

Mary Shelley
*Frankenstein

John Steinbeck
America and Americans and
    Selected Nonfiction

Bram Stoker
*Dracula

Sun-tzu
The Art of War

Alexis de Tocqueville
Democracy in America

Mark Twain
*The Portable Twain

H.G. Wells
Tono-Bungay

Edith Wharton
The Portable Edith Wharton

Walt Whitman
*The Portable Whitman

The Desert Fathers: Sayings of the
    Early Christian Monks
Homeric Hymns
The Roots of Ayurveda
Women's Early American Historical
    Narratives

ALSO AVAILABLE FROM PENGUIN

Jesse Fernandez

Jorge Luis Borges

COLLECTED FICTIONS
Translated by Andrew Hurley

"An unparalleled treasury of marvels."
— *Chicago Tribune*

Literature   5 ¹/₂ x 8 ⁷/₁₆   French Flaps
0-14-028680-2   576 pp. $16.95

SELECTED POEMS
Edited by Alexander Coleman

"A surfeit of riches." — *San Francisco Chronicle*

Literature/Poetry   5 ¹/₂ x 8 ⁷/₁₆   French Flaps
0-14-058721-7   496 pp. $17.95

*Winner of the
National Book
Critics Circle
Award in Criticism*

SELECTED NON-FICTIONS
Edited by Eliot Weinberger

"Superb . . . indispensable to both the longtime Borges
reader and the newcomer." — *The Wall Street Journal*

Literature/Essays   5 ¹/₂ x 8 ⁷/₁₆   French Flaps
0-14-029011-7   576 pp. $17.00

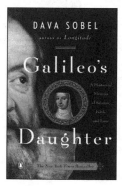

GALILEO'S DAUGHTER*
A Historical Memoir of Science, Faith, and Love
Dava Sobel

"Sobel is a master storyteller. . . . Reading *Galileo's
Daughter*, we hear Galileo's voice, we sense his pain and
share his excitement, and once again we marvel at how
the human mind, and heart, can lift so much."
—*The New York Times*

Winner of a *Los Angeles Times* Book Prize

Science/History 5 ¹/₂ x 8 ⁷/₁₆ b/w illustrations throughout
432 pp. 0-14-028055-3 $14.00

For the letters that inspired Galileo's Daughter, *see* Letters to
Father: Suor Maria Celeste to Galileo *by S. M. Celeste Galilei, p. 73*

PENGUIN
www.penguinputnam.com

Two works by "the presiding genius of postwar American fiction"

(The New York Times)

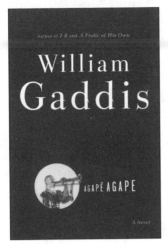

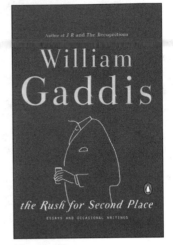

Literature
5 ⅝ x 8 ¼ hardcover
0-670-03131-3
128 pp. $23.95

Agapē Agape
With an afterword
by Joseph Tabbi

Literature/Essays
5¹/₁₆ x 7¾
0-14-200238-0
208 pp. $14.00

The Rush for Second Place
Essays and Occasional Writings
Edited with an Introduction
by Joseph Tabbi

"William Gaddis confronted our modern world without flinching. He mapped and delved. His reach was enormous, Pynchonian, and his tonal register was supple enough to allow him lyricism and straight-on portraiture as well as myriad strains of satire." —from Sven Birkerts's review of *Agapē Agape* in *The New York Times Book Review*

VIKING PENGUIN
www.penguinputnam.com

For additional titles by William Gaddis, see p. 73

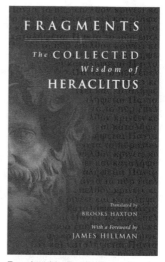

THE COMPLETE PELICAN SHAKESPEARE

General Editors: Stephen Orgel and A.R. Braunmuller

"*Here is an elegant text for either study or the rehearsal room.*" —Patrick Stewart

Literature/Drama   7¹/₈ x 9¹/₄
hardcover b/w illustrations throughout
0-14-100058-9   1,728 pp. $65.00

The classic one volume Shakespeare, including all the plays and poems, now completely revised and updated

The Complete Pelican Shakespeare features:

- Authoritative and meticulously researched texts

- Illuminating new introductions and notes by distinguished scholars

- Essays on Shakespeare's life, the theatrical world of his time, and the selection of texts

- A handsome new design inside and out

- Deluxe packaging, including a full-linen case, ribbon marker, Smyth-sewn binding, printed endpapers, acid-free paper, and illustrations throughout

For individual titles in the Pelican Shakespeare series, see pp. 165–166

PENGUIN
www.penguinputnam.com/pelican

CLICK ON A CLASSIC
www.penguinclassics.com

With a new look and feel, the award-winning
Penguin Classics Web site includes:

- New features such as samplers from forthcoming publications, audio and video downloads, and hundreds of contextual essays from renowned authors

- New monthly newletters for consumers and booksellers, with details on current and upcoming publications

- Academic Services, with Penguin's unique interactive College Faculty Information Service, convention schedules, desk copy ordering, and Teachers Guides, offers professors and students the definitive classics experience

Other site features include:

- Information on all Penguin Classics titles and authors

- Downloadable and printable catalogs

- Ongoing contests and giveaways of posters, books, and mousepads

- The definitive history of Penguin Classics

- Discussion Guides from the Great Books Foundation, Readers Guides, and Teachers Guides

- New and improved version of the popular global discussion board

- Powerful advanced search and browse functions by author, subject, and era

- Interactive quizzes, games, and crossword puzzles

A

Absentee, The 62
Adam Bede 62
Adolphe 45
Adventures and The Memoirs of
    Sherlock Holmes, The 42
Adventures of Augie March, The 18
Adventures of David Simple, The 68
*Adventures of Huckleberry Finn, The ...191
Adventures of Tom Sawyer, The 191
Aeneid 196
Against Nature 96
Against Slavery 211
Age of Alexander, The 152
Age of Bede, The 17
Age of Innocence, The 199
Agnes Grey 23
Agricola and The Germania, The 181
Alcestis and Other Plays 65
Alexiad of Anna Comnena, The 7
Alfred the Great 6
Alice's Adventures in Wonderland
    and Through the Looking-Glass 31
All My Sons 134
All's Well That Ends Well 165
Ambassadors, The 99
American, The 99
American Indian Stories, Legends,
    and Other Writings 205
American Local Color Writing,
    1880–1920 212
*American Notes for General Circulation ..53
An Apology for Raymond Sebond 136
An Essay Concerning Human
    Understanding 119
An Essay on the Principle of Population ...124
Analects, The 43
Annals of Imperial Rome, The 181
Ancient Sorceries and Other Weird Stories .21
Angle of Repose 172
Anna Karenin 185
Anna Karenina 185
Antiquary, The 162
Antony and Cleopatra 165
Apocalypse 114

Apologia pro Vita Sua 142
Aquinas: Selected Writings 8
Aran Islands, The 181
Armadale 40
Army Life in a Black Regiment
    and Other Writings 91
Art of Rhetoric, The 10
Arthurian Romances 39
As I Crossed a Bridge of Dreams 161
As You Like It 165
Aspern Papers and
    The Turn of the Screw, The 100
Assassination Bureau, Ltd, The 119
At Fault 38
Athenian Constitution, The 10
Au Bonheur Des Dames
    (The Ladies' Delight) 206
Aurora Leigh and Other Poems 25
Autobiographies (Darwin) 50
Autobiography (Cellini) 34
Autobiography (Mill) 133
Autobiography and Other Writings, The
    (Franklin) 71
Autobiography of an
    Ex-Colored Man, The 104
Awakening and Selected Stories, The 38
Awkward Age, The 100

B

Babbitt 118
Bacchae and Other Plays, The 65
Barchester Towers 187
Barnaby Rudge 53
Barber of Seville and
    The Marriage of Figaro, The 17
Baudelaire in English 16
Bayou Folk and A Night in Acadie 38
Beautiful and Damned, The 68
Been Down So Long
    It Looks Like Up to Me 66
Beggar's Opera, The 75
Bel-Ami 130
Bell, The 139
Beowulf 206
*Beowulf : A Verse Translation 207
Beowulf: A Prose Translation 207

Bernard Shaw Library, The 168
Betrothed, The 125
Between Past and Future 9
Beyond Good and Evil 142
*Bhagavad Gita, The 207
Billiards at Half-Past Nine 22
Billy Budd and Other Stories 131
Birth of Tragedy, The 143
Black Lamb and Grey Falcon 198
Black Prince, The 139
Black Sheep, The 14
Blazing World and Other Writings, The ...33
Bleak House 53
Blithedale Romance, The 88
Blue Meridian 128
Book of Disquiet, The 147
Book of Lamentations, The 32
Book of the Courtier, The 32
Bostonians, The 100
Bounty Mutiny, The 21
Bouvard and Pécuchet 68
Brand 96
Bride of Lammermoor, The 162
Brief Lives 12
Brighton Rock 81
Brothers Ashkenazi, The 170
Brothers Karamazov, The 57
Buddhist Scriptures 212
Burning Bright 173
Burnt-Out Case, A 81

C

Caleb Williams 78
Call of Cthulhu and
    Other Weird Stories, The 121
Call of the Wild, White Fang,
    and Other Stories, The 120
Campaigns of Alexander, The 11
Can You Forgive Her? 187
Candide 197
Cannery Row 173
Canterbury Tales, The 35
Canterbury Tales: The First
    Fragment, The 36
Cape Cod 184

Capital, Vols. 1-3 127
Captain and the Enemy, The 81
Captain Blood 159
Carpenter's Gothic 73
Castle of Otranto, The 198
Castle Rackrent and Ennui 62
Cavalleria Rusticana and
    Other Stories 195
Celtic Miscellany, A 212
Chance 43
Charlotte Temple and Lucy Temple 159
Charterhouse of Parma, The 176
Childhood/Boyhood/Youth 186
Christmas Books, The 54
Chronicle of the Narváez Expedition 29
Chronicles 72
Chronicles of the Crusades 105
Cid/Cinna/The Theatrical Illusion, The ...46
Cistercian World, The 212
City of God 12
Civil War, The 29
Civil Wars, The 8
Civilization of the
    Renaissance in Italy, The 27
Clarissa 157
Classic of Mountains and Seas, The 207
*Classical Literary Criticism 212
Cloud Forest, The 128
*Cloud of Unknowing
    and Other Writings, The 207
Cold Comfort Farm 77
Collected Poems (Rimbaud) 158
Collected Short Stories (Greene) 81
Collected Short Stories, Vols. 1-4
    (Maugam) 129
Collected Stories (Babel) 13
Colonial American Travel Narratives 213
Comedians, The 81
Comedies, The 182
Comedy of Errors, The 165
Coming, Aphrodite! and Other Stories 32
Common Sense 145
*Communist Manifesto, The 128
Complete English Poems, The (Donne) ...57
Complete English Poems, The (Herbert) ...89
Complete Essays, The (Montaigne) 136

Complete Fables, The (Aesop) 4

Complete Fairy Tales,
The (MacDonald) 123

Complete Odes and Epodes,
The (Horace) 93

*Complete Pelican Shakespeare, The 165

Complete Plays, The (Marlowe) 126

Complete Plays, Lenz, and
Other Writings (Büchner) 26

Complete Poems, The (Blake) 21

Complete Poems, The (Coleridge) 40

Complete Poems (Johnson) 104

Complete Poems, The (Jonson) 105

Complete Poems, The (Keats) 108

Complete Poems (Lawrence) 114

Complete Poems, The (Marvell) 127

Complete Poems, The (Milton) 135

Complete Poems (Moore) 137

Complete Poems (Parker) 146

Complete Poems, The (Rossetti) 158

Complete Poems, The (Whitman) 200

Complete Saki, The 160

Complete Short Fiction (Wilde) 200

Complete Stories (Parker) 146

Complete Writings (Wheatley) 200

Condition of the Working Class
in England, The 64

Conference of the Birds, The 11

Confessions 12

Confessions, The 158

Confession and Other
Religious Writings, A 186

Confessions of an English Opium Eater 52

Confidence-Man, The 131

Confusions of Young Törless, The 140

Conjure Tales and Stories
of the Color Line 37

Connecticut Yankee in
King Arthur's Court, A 191

Conquest of Gaul, The 30

Conquest of New Spain, The 53

Consolation of Philosophy, The 22

Conversations of Socrates 203

Coriolanus 165

Count of Monte Cristo, The 60

Countess of Pembroke's Arcadia, The 170

Country of the Pointed Firs
and Other Stories, The 103

Cousin Bette 14

Cousin Pons 14

Clown, The 22

Cranford/Cousin Phillis 74

Crime and Punishment 58

Crucible, The 135

Cup of Gold 174

Custom of the Country, The 199

Cymbeline 165

D

D. H. Lawrence and Italy 115

Daisy Miller 100

Damnation of Theron Ware, The 72

Damned (Là-Bas), The 96

Dangling Man 18

Daniel Deronda 62

Daphnis and Chloe 121

David Copperfield 54

De Anima (On the Soul) 11

De Profundis and Other Writings 201

Dead Souls 79

Dean's December, The 18

Death in Venice and Other Tales 125

Death of a Salesman 135

Death of Ivan Ilyich and
Other Stories, The 186

Death of King Arthur, The 207

Death of Methuselah
and Other Stories, The 170

Debacle, The 206

Decameron, The 22

Deerslayer, The 46

Desperate Remedies 85

Devil and Daniel Webster
and Other Writings, The 20

Devils, The 58

Dhammapada, The 207

Dialogues and Letters 164

Dialogues Concerning
Natural Religion 95

Diary of a Madman and Other Stories 79

Diary of Lady Murasaki, The 138

Digest of Roman Law, The 107

Discourse on Inequality, A 159

Discourse on Method
  and Related Writings 52

Discourses, The 123

Distracted Preacher and Other Tales, The . .85

Divine Comedy, The, Vols. 1-3 50

Doll's House and Other Plays, A 97

*Dombey and Son 54

Domestic Manners of the Americans 189

Don Juan 29

*Don Quixote 34

Dr. Wortle's School .188

Dracula 178

Dred 179

Dubliners 106

Duluth 195

E

Early American Drama 213

Early American Writing 213

Early Christian Lives 213

Early Christian Writings 214

Earliest English Poems, The 213

*Early Greek Philosophy 214

*Early History of Rome, The 119

Early Irish Myths and Sagas 214

Early Plays (O'Neill) 145

Early Poems (Frost) .72

Early Poems (Millay) 134

Early Writings (Marx) 127

Earth, The 206

East of Eden 174

Ecce Homo 143

Ecclesiastical History of the English People .17

Eclogues, The 196

Edgar Huntly 25

Education of Henry Adams, The 3

*Effi Briest 70

Egil's Saga 208

Eichmann in Jerusalem 9

Either/Or 109

Elective Affinities 78

Electra and Other Plays (Euripides) 65

Electra and Other Plays (Sophocles) 172

Emigrants, The 98

Eminent Victorians 180

Emma 12

End of the Affair, The 82

England Made Me 82

English Romantic Verse 214

Enneads, The 152

Enormous Room, The 49

Epic of Gilgamesh, The 208

Erewhon 29

Erotic Poems, The .145

Essays and Aphorisms (Schopenhauer) . . .161

Essays, The (Bacon) 14

Essays (Montaigne) 136

Essays (Plutarch) 152

Esther 3

Ethan Frome 199

Ethics 11

Eugene Onegin 155

Eugénie Grandet 15

Europeans, The 100

Eustace Diamonds, The 188

Evelina 28

Exemplary Stories 35

Exile's Return 47

Expedition of Humphry Clinker, The 171

Exploration of the
  Colorado River and Its Canyons, The . .154

F

Facundo 161

Faerie Queene, The 172

Fairly Honourable Defeat, A 139

Falcon, The 182

Fall of the House of Usher
  and Other Writings, The 153

Fall of the Roman Republic, The 152

Fanny Hill 40

Far from the Madding Crowd 85

Fasti 145

Father and Son 80

Fathers and Sons 190

Faust, Parts 1 and 2 .78

Fear and Trembling 110

Federalist Papers, The 124

Felix Holt: The Radical 63

Fifth Business 51
Fifth Queen, The 70
Figure in the Carpet
 and Other Stories, The 100
Finnegans Wake 106
First Love 190
Five Plays 133
Fixer, The 124
Flame Trees of Thika, The 96
Flatland 3
Flaubert in Egypt 69
Four Comedies 167
Four Feathers, The 128
Four Histories 167
Four Stories by American Women 214
Four Tragedies 167
Four Tragedies and Octavia 164
Four Voyages, The 41
Fourteen Byzantine Rulers 133
Fox/The Captain's Doll/
 The Ladybird, The 115
Framley Parsonage 188
Frankenstein 169
French Provincial Cooking 51
Frogs and Other Plays, The 10

G

Garden Party and Other Stories, The 125
Gargantua and Pantagruel 156
Gentleman from San Francisco
 and Other Stories, The 26
Gentlemen Prefer Blondes and
 But Gentlemen Marry Brunettes 121
Georgics, The 196
German Idealist Philosophy 214
Germinal 206
Ghosts and Other Plays 97
Gilded Age, The 192
God's Trombones 104
Gods Will Have Blood, The 71
Golden Ass, The 8
Golden Bough, The 72
Golden Bowl, The 100
Golden Legend, The 198
Good Apprentice , The 139

Good Soldier, The 70
Good Soldier Švejk, The 88
Gothic Tales 74
Grace Abounding to the
 Chief of Sinners 27
Grandissimes, The 29
Grapes of Wrath, The 174
Gravity's Rainbow 155
Great Expectations 54
Grundrisse 127
Guide to Greece 146
Guide, The 140
*Gulliver's Travels 180
Gun for Sale, A 82
Gunnar's Daughter 193

H

Hamlet 165
Hand of Ethelberta, The 86
Hard Times 55
Harlot High and Low, A 15
Hazard of New Fortunes, A 94
He Knew He Was Right 188
Heart of Darkness 44
Heart of Midlothian, The 163
Heart of the Matter, The 82
Heartbreak House 168
Hedda Gabler and Other Plays 97
Henderson the Rain King 18
Henry IV, Part 1 165
Henry IV, Part 2 165
Henry V 165
Henry VI, Part 1 165
Henry VI, Part 2 165
Henry VI, Part 3 165
Henry VIII 165
Heptameron, The 126
Heracles and Other Plays 66
Herland, The Yellow Wall-Paper,
 and Selected Writings 77
*Hero of Our Time, A 117
Heroides 145
Herzog 18
Hesiod and Theognis 90
Him with His Foot in His Mouth 19

Hindu Myths 215
Hippocratic Writings 215
Histories, The (Herodotus) 90
Histories, The (Tacitus) 181
History and Topography
    of Ireland, The 75
History of Alexander, The 49
History of England, The 122
History of Mary Prince, The 154
History of My Times, A 203
History of Rasselas,
    Prince of Abissinia, The 104
History of the Church, The 66
History of the Decline and Fall of the Roman
    Empire, The, abridged 76
History of the Decline and Fall of the Roman
    Empire, The, Vols. 1-3 76
History of the Franks, A 83
History of the Kings of Britain, The 75
History of the Peloponnesian War, The ..184
History of the Thirteen 15
Home and the World, The 182
Home of the Gentry 190
Hope Leslie 164
Hound of the Baskervilles, The 42
House Behind the Cedars, The 37
House of Mirth, The 200
House of the Dead, The 58
House of the Seven Gables, The 88
How Much Land Does a Man Need?
    and Other Stories 186
How the Other Half Lives 157
Howards End 70
Hrafnkel's Saga 208
Humboldt's Gift 19
Hunger 85
Hungry Hearts 204
Hunting of the Snark, The 31

I

Idylls of the King 182
Idiot, The 58
If Not Now, When? 117
Iliad, The 92, 93
Iliad and The Odyssey Boxed Set, The ...92
Imitation of Christ, The 183

Immoralist, The 77
Importance of Being Earnest
    and Other Plays, The 201
In a Café 114
In Dubious Battle 174
In Patagonia 35
In the South Seas 177
Incidents in the Life of a Slave Girl 99
Inheritance, The 6
Innocents Abroad, The 191
Interesting Narrative
    and Other Writings, The 64
Introductory Lectures on Aesthetics 89
Iphigenia/Phaedra/Athaliah 156
Italian, The 157
Italian Food 51
Italian Hours 101
Italian Journey 78
Ivanhoe 163

J

Jacob's Room 202
Jacques the Fatalist and His Master 57
Jane Eyre 24
Japanese Nō Dramas 215
Jazz Age Stories 68
Jennie Gerhardt 60
Jewish War, The 105
Joseph Andrews/Shamela 67
Journal, The 71
Journal of the Plague Year, A 51
Journals and Letters (Burney) 28
Journals of Captain Cook, The 45
Journals of Lewis and Clark, The 118
Journey Through Wales/
    The Description of Wales, The 75
Journey to the Western Islands
    of Scotland/The Journal of
    a Tour to the Hebrides, A 105
Journey Without Maps 82
JR 73
Jude the Obscure 86
Jugurthine War and
    The Conspiracy of Catiline, The 160
Julius Caesar 165
Jungle, The 170

Jungle Books, The 111
Just So Stories 111

K

Kalki 195
Kenilworth 163
Kidnapped 178
Kim 111
King Harald's Saga 171
King John 165
King Lear 166
King Lear (The Quarto
  and the Folio Texts) 166
Knights/The Peace/The Birds/
  The Assembly Women/Wealth, The 10
Kolyma Tales 168
Koran, The 208
Kreutzer Sonata and Other
  Stories, The 186
Kristin Lavransdatter, Vol. 1 193
Kristin Lavransdatter, Vols. 2 and 3 194

L

L'Assommoir (The Dram Shop) 205
La Bête Humaine 206
La Vita Nuova 50
Lady Audley's Secret 23
Lady Chatterley's Lover 115
Lady Susan/The Watsons/Sanditon 12
Lady with the Little Dog
  and Other Stories, 1896–1904, The 36
Laforgue: Selected Poems 112
Lais of Marie de France, The 126
Land of Little Rain, The 13
Laodicean, A 86
Last Chronicle of Barset, The 188
Last of the Mohicans, The 46
Last Word and Other Stories, The 82
Later Roman Empire, The 6
Law and the Lady, The 41
Lawless Roads, The 82
Laws of Manu, The 209
Laxdaela Saga 209
Le Grand Meaulnes 5
Le Morte D'Arthur 124

Leaves of Grass 200
Les Liaisons Dangereuses 111
Les Misérables 94
Legend of Sleepy Hollow
  and Other Stories, The 98
Letters from a Stoic 164
Letters from an American Farmer and Sketches
  of Eighteenth-Century America 47
Letters of Abélard and Héloïse, The 3
Letters of Sacco and Vanzetti, The 160
Letters of the Late Ignatius Sancho,
  an African 160
Letters of the Younger Pliny, The 151
Letters of Vincent van Gogh, The 79
Letters on England 197
Letters to Father 73
Leviathan 91
Life and Opinions of the
  Tomcat Murr, The 91
Life and Opinions of Tristram Shandy 177
Life in Letters, A 101
Life of Charlotte Brontë, The 74
Life of Samuel Johnson, The 22
Life of St. Columba 4
Life of St. Teresa of Ávila
  by Herself, The 183
Life on the Mississippi 191
Lift Every Voice and Sing 104
Lifted Veil and Brother Jacob, The 63
Literary Review, A 110
Little Dorrit 55
Little Princess, A 28
Little Women 6
Lives of the Artists, Vols. 1 and 2 194
Lives of the Later Caesars 209
Liza of Lambeth 129
Log from the Sea of Cortez, The 174
Long Valley, The 174
Looking Backward 17
Lord Jim 44
Loser Takes All 82
Loss of the Ship Essex,
  Sunk by a Whale, The 142
Lost Honor of Katherina Blum, The 22
Lost Illusion 15

Lost World and Other
Thrilling Tales, The 42
Love 176
Love Visions 36
Love's Labor's Lost 166
Loving/Living/Party Going 80
Luck of Roaring Camp
and Other Writings, The 88
Lucky Jim 6
Lysistrata and Other Plays 10

M

Mabinogion, The 209
Macbeth 166
*Madame Bovary 69
Maggie: A Girl of the Streets 47
Magician, The 129
Maias, The 156
Main Street 118
Maine Woods, The 184
Major Barbara 168
Makers of Rome 152
Maldoror and Poems 113
Malgudi Days 140
Man and Superman 168
Man in the Iron Mask, The 61
Man Who Was Thursday, The 38
Man Within, The 82
Man-Eater of Malgudi, The 141
Manon Lescaut 154
Mansfield Park 12
Manuscript Found in Saragossa, The ...154
Marble Faun, The 89
Marquise of O— and Other Stories, The ...111
Marrow of Tradition, The 37
Master and Margarita, The 26
Master Builder and Other Plays, The ...97
Master of Ballantrae, The 178
Martin Chuzzlewit 55
Martin Eden 120
Mary Barton 74
Mary Stuart 161
Mary/Maria/Matilda 202
Master and Man and Other Stories 186
Max Havelaar 138

Maxims (La Rochefoucauld) 113
Maxims and Reflections (Goethe) 78
Mayor of Casterbridge, The 86
McTeague 143
Measure for Measure 166
Medea and Other Plays 66
Medieval English Verse 215
Medieval Writings on Female
Spirituality 215
Meditations 126
Meditations and Other
Metaphysical Writings 53
Melmoth the Wanderer 129
Memoirs (Sherman) 170
Mencius 133
Mephisto 125
Merchant of Venice, The 166
Merry Wives of Windsor, The 166
Messiah, The 195
Metamorphoses 145
Metaphysical Poets, The 215
Metaphysics, The 11
Micromégas and Other Short Fictions ...197
Middlemarch 63
Midsummer Night's Dream, A 166
Mill on the Floss, The 63
Minister's Wooing, The 179
Ministry of Fear, The 82
Misanthrope and Other Plays, The 136
Miser and Other Plays, The 136
Miss Marjoribanks 144
Miss Ravenel's Conversion from
Secession to Loyalty 52
Moby-Dick 132
Modern Instance, A 94
Moll Flanders 52
Moments of Reprieve 117
Monk, The 118
Monkey's Wrench, The 117
Mont-Saint-Michel and Chartres 3
The Moon and Sixpence, The 130
The Moon Is Down, The 174
The Moonstone, The 41
The Morgesons, The 178
Mosby's Memoirs and Other Stories 19

Mountains of California, The 137
Mr. Noon 115
Mr. Sammler's Planet 19
Mrs. Craddock 130
Much Ado about Nothing 166
Murder Trials 39
My Ántonia 32
My Bondage and My Freedom 59
My Childhood 80
My Family and Other Animals 61
My First Summer in the Sierra 137
Myra Breckinridge/Myron 195
Mysteries 85
Mysteries of Udolpho, The 157
*Mystery of Edwin Drood, The 55

N

Naked Civil Servant, The 48
Nana 206
Narrative of Arthur Gordon Pym
   of Nantucket, The 153
Narrative of Sojourner Truth 189
Narrative of the Life of Frederick
   Douglass, an American Slave 59
Narrative Poems, The (Shakespeare) 166
Narrow Corner, The 130
Narrow Road to the Deep North
   and Other Travel Sketches, The 16
Natural History 151
Nature of the Gods, The 39
Netochka Nezvanova 58
New England Nun and Other Stories, A 72
New Grub Street 77
New Science 195
News from Nowhere
   and Other Writings 137
Nibelungenlied, The 209
Nicholas Nickleby 55
Nietzsche Reader, A 143
Night and Day 203
Nigger of the "Narcissus", The 44
Nightmare Abbey/Crotchet Castle 147
Nineteenth-Century American Poetry 215
*Njal's Saga 209
No Name 41

North American Indians 33
North and South 74
North of South 140
Northanger Abbey 12
Northland Stories 120
Nostromo 44
Notes from the Underground/The Double .58
Notes on the State of Virginia 103
Notre-Dame of Paris 95
Nun, The 57
Nuns and Soldiers 139

O

O Pioneers! 33
Obedience of a Christian Man, The 193
Oblomov 79
Octopus, The 143
Odd Women, The 77
Odes, The (Pindar) 148
Odyssey, The 92, 93
Of Human Bondage 130
Of Mice and Men 174
*Old Curiosity Shop, The 55
Old Goriot 15
Old Wives' Tale, The 20
*Oliver Twist 55
Omensetter's Luck 75
On Government 39
On Liberty 133
On Love and Barley 16
On Painting 5
On Revolution 9
On the Good Life 39
On the Nature of the Universe 122
On War 40
Once There Was a War 175
One Flew Over the Cuckoo's Nest 109
Ordeal of Richard Feverel, The 133
Oregon Trail, The 146
Oresteia, The 4
Oresteian Trilogy, The 4
Orestes and Other Plays 66
Origin of Species, The 51
Orkneyinga Saga 209

Orlando Furioso 10
Ormond 62
Oroonoko, The Rover, and
    Other Works 17
Othello 166
Our Man in Havana 83
Our Mutual Friend 56

P

Painted Veil, The 130
Painter of Signs, The 141
Pair of Blue Eyes, A 86
Pamela 157
Pan 85
Papers and Journals (Kierkegaard) 110
Parade's End 70
Paradise Lost 135
Parzival 65
Passing 113
Pastures of Heaven, The 175
Pathfinder, The 46
Pearl, The 175
Peer Gynt 97
Penguin Book of
    First World War Poetry, The 216
Penguin Book of French Poetry, The 216
Penguin Book of Modern
    African Poetry, The 216
Penguin Book of Renaissance
    Verse 1509–1659, The 216
Penguin Book of Victorian Verse, The ...216
Pensées 146
Pericles 166
Persian Expedition, The 203
Persian Letters 137
Personal Memoirs (Grant) 80
Personal Narrative of a Journey
    to the Equinoctial Regions of the
    New Continent 95
Personal Writings (Ignatius) 98
Persuasion 13
Phèdre 156
Philosophical Dictionary 197
Philosophical Enquiry into
    the Origin of Our Ideas of
    the Sublime and Beautiful, A 27

Physiology of Taste, The 23
Pickwick Papers, The 56
*Picture of Dorian Gray, The 201
Pictures from Italy 56
Pierre 132
Pierre and Jean 130
Piers the Ploughman 112
Pilgrim's Progress, The 27
Pinocchio 41
Pioneers, The 46
Pit, The 144
Plain Tales from the Hills 111
Playboy of the Western World
    and Two Other Irish Plays, The 181
Plays (Chekhov) 37
Plays and Fragments (Menander) 132
Plays Unpleasant 168
Plutarch on Sparta 152
Poem of the Cid, The 209
Poems (Li Po and Tu Fu) 118
Poems and Ballads and Atalanta
    in Calydon 181
Poems and Prose (Hopkins) 93
Poems of Catullus, The 33
Poems of Heaven and Hell from
    Ancient Mesopotamia 216
Poems, Protest, and a Dream 48
Poetics 11
Politics, The 11
Poor Folk and Other Stories 58
Portable Abraham Lincoln, The 119
Portable American
    Realism Reader, The 217
Portable Arthur Miller, The 134
Portable Beat Reader, The 217
Portable Blake, The 21
Portable Cervantes, The 34
Portable Chaucer, The 35
Portable Chekhov, The 36
Portable Coleridge, The 40
Portable Conrad, The 43
Portable Dante, The 49
Portable Darwin, The 50
Portable Dorothy Parker, The 146
Portable Edmund Burke, The 27

Portable Emerson, The 64
Portable Enlightenment Reader, The 217
Portable Faulkner, The 67
Portable Graham Greene, The 81
Portable Greek Historians, The 217
Portable Greek Reader, The 217
Portable Hannah Arendt, The 9
Portable Harlem Renaissance
   Reader, The 218
Portable Hawthorne, The 88
Portable Henry James, The 99
Portable Jack Kerouac, The 108
Portable Jack London, The 119
Portable James Joyce, The 106
Portable Jung, The 107
Portable Karl Marx, The 127
Portable Kipling, The 110
Portrait of the Artist as a Young Man, A ...106
Portable Louisa May Alcott, The 5
Portable Machiavelli, The 123
Portable Mark Twain, The 190
Portable Medieval Reader, The 218
Portable Nietzsche, The 142
Portable Nineteenth-Century
   Russian Reader, The 218
Portable North American
   Indian Reader, The 218
Portable Oscar Wilde, The 200
Portable Plato, The 149
Portable Poe, The 153
Portable Renaissance Reader, The 218
Portable Roman Reader, The 218
Portable Romantic Poets, The 219
Portable Shakespeare, The 164
Portable Sixties Reader, The 219
Portable Steinbeck, The 173
Portable Stephen Crane, The 47
Portable Thomas Jefferson, The 103
Portable Thoreau, The 183
Portable Tolstoy, The 185
Portable Twentieth-Century
   Russian Reader, The 219
Portable Voltaire, The 197
Portable Walt Whitman, The 200
Portable Western Reader, The 219
Portable World Bible, The 219

Portrait of a Lady, The 101
Pot of Gold and Other Plays, The 151
Power and the Glory, The 83
Power of Sympathy/The Coquette, The ...25
Pragmatism and Other Writings 102
Prairie, The 46
Praise of Folly 65
Prayers and Meditations of St. Anselm, The .7
Prelude, The 203
Pride and Prejudice 13
Prime Minister, The 188
Prince, The 123
Prince and the Pauper, The 191
Princess Casamassima, The 101
Princesse de Clèves, The 112
Principles of Geology 122
Principles of Human Knowledge
   and Three Dialogues Between
   Hylas and Philonius 20
Prisoner of Zenda and Rupert
   of Hentzau, The 93
Professor, The 24
Prometheus Bound and Other Plays 4
Promised Land, The 8
Protagoras and Meno 150
Protestant Ethic and the "Spirit"
   of Capitalism and Other
   Writings, The 198
Prussian Officer and Other Stories, The ...115
Pudd'nhead Wilson 192
Pursuit of the Well-Beloved and The Well-
   Beloved, The 86
Pygmalion 169

Q

Queen of Spades
   and Other Stories, The 155
Quest of the Holy Grail, The 210
Quicksand 113
Quiet American, The 83

R

Ragged Dick and Struggling Upward 6
Rainbow, The 115
Ramayana, The 141
Rameau's Nephew and

D'Alembert's Dream 57
Razor's Edge, The 130
Recognitions, The 73
*Red and the Black, The 176
Red Badge of Courage
    and Other Stories, The 47
Red Pony, The 175
Red Strangers 96
Redburn 132
Redgauntlet 163
Reflections on the Revolution
    in France 27
Renaissance Women Poets 219
Republic, The 150
Resurrection 187
Return of the Native, The 87
Return of the Soldier, The 199
Revelations of Divine Love 107
Reveries of the Solitary Walker 159
Richard II 166
Richard III 166
Riddle of the Sands, The 38
Riders of the Purple Sage 84
Rig Veda, The, The 210
Rights of Man 145
Ring of Bright Water 131
Rise and Fall of Athens 153
Rise of David Levinsky, The, The 30
Rise of Silas Lapham 94
Rise of the Roman Empire, The 153
Rob Roy 163
Robbers and Wallenstein, The 161
Robert Fagles's Translations of Homer
    with Introductions and
    Notes by Bernard Knox 92
*Robinson Crusoe 52
Roderick Hudson 101
Roman History, The 57
Romance of Many Dimensions, A 3
Romance of Tristan, The 20
Romantic Fairy Tales 220
Rome and Italy 119
Rome and the Mediterranean 119
Romeo and Juliet 166
Romola 63
Room with a View, A 71

Rope and Other Plays, The 151
Roughing It 192
Roxana 52
Rubaiyat of Omar Khayyám, The 144
Rudin 190
Russian Journal, A 175
Ruth 74
Ruth Hall 67

S

Saga of King Hrolf Kraki, The 210
Saga of the Volsungs, The 210
Sagas of Icelanders, The 210
Sagas of Warrior-Poets 210
Sailing Alone around the World 171
Saint Joan 169
Salammbô 69
Satires of Horace and Persius, The 94
Satyricon/The Apocolocyntosis, The 148
Scarlet Letter, The 89
Scenes of Clerical Life 63
School for Scandal and Other Plays, The ..170
Science Fiction of Edgar Allan Poe, The ...153
Sea and Sardinia 115
Sea, the Sea, The 139
Sea-Wolf and Other Stories, The 120
Sebastopol Sketches, The 187
Secret Agent, The 44
Secret Garden, The 28
Secret History, The 155
Seize the Day 19
Selected Essays (Emerson) 64
Selected Journalism (Dickens) 56
Selected Letters (Montagu) 136
Selected Letters (Moore) 137
Selected Letters (Sévigné) 164
Selected Poems (Akhmatova) 5
Selected Poems (Baudelaire) 16
Selected Poems (Browning) 25
Selected Poems (Burns) 28
Selected Poems (Byron) 29
Selected Poems (Coleridge) 40
Selected Poems (Dryden) 60
Selected Poems (Hardy) 87
Selected Poems (Hugo) 95

Selected Poems (Keats) 108
Selected Poems (Longfellow) 120
Selected Poems (Mandelstam) 124
Selected Poems (Robinson) 158
Selected Poems (Ronsard) 158
Selected Poems (Stevenson) 178
Selected Poems (Tagore) 182
Selected Poems (Tennyson) 182
Selected Poems (Tsvetayeva) 189
Selected Poems (Wordsworth) 203
Selected Poems and Fragments (Hölderlin) 91
Selected Political Speeches (Cicero) 39
Selected Short Fiction (Dickens) 56
Selected Short Stories (Balzac) 15
Selected Short Stories (Maupassant) 131
Selected Short Stories (Tagore) 182
Selected Stories (Forster) 71
Selected Stories (Henry) 89
Selected Stories (Lardner) 112
Selected Tales (Grimm) 84
Selected Tales (James) 101
Selected Tales and Sketches (Hawthorne) ..89
Selected Verse (Goethe) 78
Selected Works (Cicero) 39
Selected Writings (Eckhart) 61
Selected Writings (Hildegard) 91
Selected Writings (Johnson) 104
Selected Writings (Martí) 126
Selected Writings (Nerval) 141
Sense and Sensibility 13
Sentimental Education 69
*Sentimental Journey, A 177
Seven Viking Romances 220
Shadow-Line, The 44
She 84
Shirley 24
Short Account of the
    Destruction of the Indies, A 113
Short Reign of Pippin IV, The 175
Shorter Poems, The 172
Sickness unto Death, The 110
Siddhartha 90
Sign of Four, The 42
Silas Marner 63
Simple Story, A 98

Sir Gawain and the Green Knight 211
Sister Carrie 60
Six Records of a Floating Life 169
Six Yüan Plays 220
Sixteen Satires (Juvenal) 107
Sketches by Boz 56
Sketches from a Hunter's Album 190
Sketches of Etruscan Places 116
Small House at Allington, The 188
Snow Leopard, The 128
Social Contract, The 159
Song of Roland, The 211
Song of the Lark, The 33
Songs of the North 144
Sonnets (Shakespeare) 166
Sonnets and A Lover's Complaint, The 167
Sons and Lovers 116
Sorrows of Young Werther, The 78
Soul of Man under Socialism
    and Selected Critical Prose, The 202
Souls of Black Folk, The 60
Speaking of Śiva 220
Species of Spaces and Other Pieces 147
Spoils of Poynton, The 102
Spring Torrents 190
Spy, The 46
Stamboul Train 83
State and Revolution, The 117
Steppe and Other Stories,
    1887–1891, The 37
Story of an African Farm, The 162
Story of My Life, The 31
Story of the Stone, The , Vols. 1-5 ......30, 31
Strange Case of Dr. Jekyll and Mr. Hyde and
    Other Tales of Terror, The 177
Street of Crocodiles, The 162
Studies in Classic American Literature 116
Studs Lonigan 66
Study in Scarlet, A 43
Summer 200
Summing Up, The 130
Sunjata 180
Swann's Way 155
Sweet Thursday 175
Symposium, The 150

T

Tale of Genji, The 138
Tale of Old Mortality, The 163
Tales of Hoffmann, The 91
Tale of Two Cities, A 56
Tales from the Thousand and One Nights .211
Tales of Belkin and Other Prose Writings ..155
Tales of Soldiers and Civilians
    and Other Stories 20
Tales of the Pacific 120
Tales of Unrest 44
Tales, Speeches, Essays, and Sketches 192
Taming of the Shrew, The 166
Tao Te Ching 112
Tarzan of the Apes 28
Tempest, The 166
Ten Days That Shook the World 157
Tenant of Wildfell Hall, The 23
Tess of the D'Urbervilles 87
Texas Cowboy, A 171
Testament of Youth 23
Theaetetus 150
Theban Plays, The 172
Theory of the Leisure Class, The 194
Thérèse 131
Thérèse Raquin 206
Thing on the Doorstep and
    Other Weird Stories, The 122
Third Man and The Fallen Idol, The 83
This Side of Paradise 68
This Way for the Gas,
    Ladies and Gentlemen 22
Thoughts and Sentiments
    on the Evil of Slavery 48
Thomas Paine Reader, The 145
Three Comedies (Jonson) 105
Three Gothic Novels 220
Three Lives 173
Three Men in a Boat and
    Three Men on the Bummel 103
Three Musketeers, The 61
Three Plays (Strindberg) 180
Three Plays for Puritans 169
Three Roman Plays (Shakespeare) 167

Three Soldiers 57
Three Tales (Flaubert) 69
Three Theban Plays, The 172
Thus Spake Zarathustra 143
Tiger for Malgudi, A 141
Timaeus and Critias 151
Timon of Athens 166
Titus Andronicus 166
To a God Unknown 175
To Jerusalem and Back 19
Tom Jones 68
Tortilla Flat 176
Tragic Muse, The 102
Tramp Abroad, A 192
Transformation ("Metamorphosis") and Other
    Stories, The 107
Travels, The 153
Travels in Alaska 137
Travels of Sir John Mandeville, The 125
Travels with Charley in Search
    of America 176
Travels with My Aunt 83
Treatise of Human Nature, A 96
Treasure Island 178
Tree Where Man Was Born, The 128
Tristan 80
Troilus and Cressida 166
Troilus and Criseyde 36
Twelfth Night 166
Twelve Caesars, The 180
Twenty Love Poems and
    a Song of Despair 141
Twenty Years at Hull-House 4
Twenty-One Stories 83
Twilight in Italy and Other Essays 116
Twilight of the Idols and The Anti-Christ .143
Two Gentlemen of Verona, The 166
Two Lives of Charlemagne 62
Two on a Tower 87
Two Spanish Picaresque Novels 156
Two Years Before the Mast 49
Typee 132
Typhoon and Other Stories 45

U

Uncle Remus 88
Uncle Silas 116
Uncle Tom's Cabin 179
Under the Mountain Wall 129
Under the Sea Wind 31
Under Western Eyes 45
Unfortunate Traveller
 and Other Works, The 141
Unto This Last and Other Writings 159
Untouchable 7
Up from Slavery 198
Upanishads, The 211
Utilitarianism and Other Essays 134
Utopia 137

V

Valley of Fear and Selected Cases, The 43
*Vanity Fair 183
Varieties of Religious Experience, The 102
Venus in Furs 160
Vicar of Wakefield, The 79
Victim, The 19
Victory 45
Village of Stepanchikovo, The 58
Villette 24
Vindication of the Rights of Woman, A ...202
Vineland 156
Vinland Sagas and The Norse
 Discovery of America, The 211
Virginian, The 202
Vocation and a Voice, A 38
Voyage of the Argo, The 8
Voyage of the Beagle, The 51
Voyage Out, The 203
Voyages and Discoveries 84

W

Walden and Civil Disobedience 184
War and Peace 187
War with Hannibal, The 119
Ward No. 6 and Other Stories, 1892–1895 ..37

Warden, The 188
Washington Square 102
Waste Land and Other Poems, The 64
Waverley 163
Way of All Flesh, The 29
Way We Live Now, The 189
Wayward Bus, The 176
We 204
Wealth of Nations, The 171
Week on the Concord
 and Merrimack Rivers, A 184
What Is Art? 187
What Maisie Knew 102
Wieland and Memoirs of
 Carwin the Biloquist 25
Wild Ass's Skin, The 15
Willehalm 65
Winesburg, Ohio 7
Wings of the Dove, The 102
Winter of Our Discontent, The 176
Winter's Tale, The 166
Withered Arm and Other Stories, The   87
Wives and Daughters 74
Wolf Willow 173
Women in Love 116
Woman in White, The 41
Women's Indian Captivity Narratives 220
Wonderful World of Oz, The 16
Woodlanders, The 87
Work 6
Writings on Irish Folklore, Legend,
 and Myth 204
*Wuthering Heights 24

Y

Year in Thoreau's Journal: 1851, A 184
Youth/Heart of Darkness/
 The End of the Tether 45

Z

Zadig/L'Ingénu 197
Zazie in the Metro 156